Python for Business Analytics

Mahadi Hasan Miraz · Narishah Mohamed Salleh · Hwang Ha Jin

Python for Business Analytics

Unlocking Data Insights for Strategic Decision-Making

Mahadi Hasan Miraz
School of Creative Industries
Astana IT University
Astana, Kazakhstan

Narishah Mohamed Salleh
Department of Business Analytics
Sunway University
Sunway, Malaysia

Hwang Ha Jin
School of Creative Industries
Astana IT University
Astana, Kazakhstan

ISBN 978-981-96-8290-4   ISBN 978-981-96-8291-1 (eBook)
https://doi.org/10.1007/978-981-96-8291-1

© The Editor(s) (if applicable) and The Author(s), under exclusive license to Springer Nature Singapore Pte Ltd. 2025

This work is subject to copyright. All rights are solely and exclusively licensed by the Publisher, whether the whole or part of the material is concerned, specifically the rights of translation, reprinting, reuse of illustrations, recitation, broadcasting, reproduction on microfilms or in any other physical way, and transmission or information storage and retrieval, electronic adaptation, computer software, or by similar or dissimilar methodology now known or hereafter developed.

The use of general descriptive names, registered names, trademarks, service marks, etc. in this publication does not imply, even in the absence of a specific statement, that such names are exempt from the relevant protective laws and regulations and therefore free for general use.

The publisher, the authors and the editors are safe to assume that the advice and information in this book are believed to be true and accurate at the date of publication. Neither the publisher nor the authors or the editors give a warranty, expressed or implied, with respect to the material contained herein or for any errors or omissions that may have been made. The publisher remains neutral with regard to jurisdictional claims in published maps and institutional affiliations.

This Springer imprint is published by the registered company Springer Nature Singapore Pte Ltd.
The registered company address is: 152 Beach Road, #21-01/04 Gateway East, Singapore 189721, Singapore

If disposing of this product, please recycle the paper.

Competing Interests The authors have no competing interests to declare that are relevant to the content of this manuscript.

User Guide: Python for Business Analysis Book Purpose

This book helps businesspeople, analysts, and students use Python to make data-driven choices. Whether you're new to Python or trying to improve your analytics abilities, the book gives a step-by-step introduction to solving business challenges using Python.

For whom is this book?

- Business analysts and decision makers seeking data analytics strategy integration
- Business, data science, and analytics students and faculty
- Python novices seeking business-oriented examples
- Professionals seeking analytics or data science skills enhancement

Rambling through the Book

- Python novices
- Beginning with Chapters 1 and 2. Use Jupyter Notebooks or Google Colab to code. Learn fundamental syntax before getting into analytics.
- Business Analysts and Programmers
- Complete Chapters 3-6 to concentrate on data processing, analysis, and case-based learning. You may revisit crucial chapters if needed.

Performance-focused students

- Try case studies as mini-projects. Try the exercises and practice questions at the conclusion of each chapter before reading the handbook.

Teachers and Trainers

- Unitise each chapter. Assignments and seminars might include examples and exercises. Add your own data for variation.

Tips for maximising it

- While reading, try: Run each sample code in an IDE or Jupyter notebook.
- Use your data: Use industry or personal datasets to mimic the book's methods.

- Review summary and major points: The chapters finish with nice insights—no more.
- Download companion files or GitHub links from the book for study.

Things You Might Need

- Python 3.7+ Jupyter notebook or Google Colab. Pandas, NumPy, Matplotlib, Seaborn, Scikit-learn, Statsmodels

Final statement

- This book uses data to address business challenges, not only programming. Focus on "What purpose can this review serve?" as you go. Your Python abilities will benefit from this mentality.

Contents

1 Python for Business Analytics: Unlocking Data Insights for Strategic Decision-Making 1
   1.1 Importance of Business Analytics 1
   1.2 Why Python? 1
   1.3 Overview of Python's Ecosystem for Data Analysis 1
   1.4 Installing Python and Essential Packages 2
   1.5 Setting Up Your Environment 2
   1.6 Exercises 3
   References 4

2 Basics of Python Programming 5
   2.1 Python Syntax and Basic Constructs 5
   2.2 Data Types and Variables 6
   2.3 Control Flow (If Statements, Loops) 6
   2.4 Functions and Modules 7
   2.5 Basic Input/Output Operations 7
   2.6 Exercises 8
   References 8

3 Data Manipulation with Pandas 9
   3.1 Introduction to Pandas 9
   3.2 DataFrames and Series 9
   3.3 Importing and Exporting Data 10
   3.4 Data Cleaning and Preprocessing 11
   3.5 Handling Missing Values 11
   3.6 Data Transformation and Aggregation 11
   3.7 Exercises 12
   References 13

4	**Data Visualisation with Matplotlib and Seaborn**		15
	4.1	Importance of Data Visualisation	15
	4.2	Basic Plots with Matplotlib	15
	4.3	Advanced Visualisation with Seaborn	17
	4.4	Customizing Plots	18
	4.5	Interactive Visualisations with Plotly	19
	4.6	Exercises	19
	References		20
5	**Descriptive Analytics**		21
	5.1	Descriptive Statistics in Python	21
	5.2	Measures of Central Tendency and Variability	21
	5.3	Data Summarisation Techniques	22
	5.4	Exercises	23
6	**Predictive Analytics with Scikit-Learn**		25
	6.1	Introduction to Predictive Analytics	25
	6.2	Overview of Scikit-Learn	25
	6.3	Data Preparation for Modelling	25
	6.4	Building and Evaluating Regression Models	26
	6.5	Classification Models and Their Applications	27
	6.6	Model Validation Techniques	28
	6.7	Exercises	28
7	**Advanced Analytics and Machine Learning**		31
	7.1	Introduction to Advanced Machine Learning	31
	7.2	Clustering Algorithms	31
	7.3	Principal Component Analysis (PCA)	32
	7.4	Time Series Forecasting	32
	7.5	Exercises	33
	Reference		34
8	**Case Studies and Real-World Applications**		35
	8.1	Case Study: Sales Forecasting	35
	8.2	Case Study: Customer Segmentation	36
	8.3	Case Study: Financial Risk Analysis	37
	8.4	Case Study: Marketing Campaign Analysis	37
	8.5	Exercises	38
9	**Automating Data Analysis with Python**		41
	9.1	Automating Repetitive Tasks	41
	9.2	Scheduling and Running Automated Scripts	42
	9.3	Introduction to Airflow for Workflow Automation	42
	9.4	Exercises	44

10	**Best Practices and Future Trends**		47
	10.1	Best Practices in Data Analytics	47
	10.2	Ethical Considerations in Data Analysis	47
	10.3	The Future of Business Analytics and Python's Role	47
	10.4	Continuing Your Learning Journey	49
	References		50
11	**Outline of the Study**		51
	11.1	Keeping Up Your Education: What Is a Research Proposal?	51
	11.2	What Is a Problem Statement and Why?	51
	11.3	What Are the Different Kinds of Literature Reviews?	51
	11.4	What Constitutes Contemporary Theory and Practice?	52
	11.5	What Are the Study's Structure and Design?	52
	11.6	What Is Methodology?	52
	11.7	Qualitative Method?	53
	11.8	Interviews and the Varieties of Them	53
	11.9	Method of Quantitative	53
	11.10	What Are Surveys and Questionnaires?	53
	11.11	Mixed?	53
	11.12	What Are Structure Semi-Structure and Self-Administrative Questionnaires?	54
	11.13	Why Need Result and Discussion?	54
	11.14	Future Research	54
	11.15	Keeping Up Your Education	55
	Reference		55
12	**Python's Impact on AI and Medicine**		57
	12.1	Introduction	57
		12.1.1 Medical AI Uses Python	57
		12.1.2 AI in Medicine: A Paradigm Shift	58
		12.1.3 AI-Based Medical Discovery	58
		12.1.4 Ethical Implications and Challenges of AI in Medicine	59
		12.1.5 The Future of Python in AI/Medicine	59
		12.1.6 Problem Statement: The Need to Study Python's Impact on AI and Medicine	59
		12.1.7 Increasing Medical Data Complexity	60
		12.1.8 Correct Diagnosis and Tailored Treatment	60
		12.1.9 AI Medicine Ethics and Practice	60
		12.1.10 Affordable, Efficient Healthcare Is Essential	61
	12.2	Bridging the Gap Between AI Research and Clinical Application	61
		12.2.1 Python Is Ideal for Medical AI	61
	12.3	Applications of Python and AI in Medicine	62
		12.3.1 Imaging, Diagnosis	62

		12.3.2	Predictive Analytics, Personalised Medicine	62
		12.3.3	Healthcare NLP	62
		12.3.4	AI-Driven Drug Discovery	63
		12.3.5	Robotics and Python in Medicine	63
	12.4	Ethics and Issues		63
	12.5	Python's AI/Health Future		63
	12.6	Conclusion		64
		12.6.1	Importance	65
	References			66
13	**Web-Based Food Recommendation**			69
	13.1	Introduction		69
	13.2	Problem Statement		70
	13.3	Research Question		70
	13.4	Research Objective		71
	13.5	Domain (Introduction)		71
		13.5.1	Mood	71
		13.5.2	Food Category Choice	71
		13.5.3	Price	72
	13.6	Predictive Model		73
	13.7	Tools and Techniques		73
		13.7.1	Python	73
		13.7.2	Python Libraries	74
		13.7.3	Tableau	74
		13.7.4	HyperText Markup Language HTML	75
		13.7.5	PHP HyperText Pre-Processor (PHP)	75
	13.8	BALC Framework		76
		13.8.1	Identify Domain	76
		13.8.2	Data Extraction	76
		13.8.3	Data Cleaning/Preparation	78
		13.8.4	Predictive Model	80
		13.8.5	Visualisation/EDA	82
	13.9	SDLC Framework		84
		13.9.1	Planning and Requirement Analysis	84
		13.9.2	Design	84
		13.9.3	Development	86
		13.9.4	Integration and Testing	88

		13.9.5	Deployment and Maintenance	91
	13.10		Results from the Prediction Model	91
	13.11		Results from the Web-User Interface	93
	13.12		Instruction Manuals	93
	13.13		Discussion of Contribution from the Results	93
	13.14		Future Work	96

Appendix 1: Main Dataset 96
Appendix 2: Supportive Dataset 97
Appendix 3: Full Python Codes 97
Appendix 4: Google Survey Responses for Validation Purposes 97
Appendix 5: Tableau Link 97
Appendix 6: Dashboard 98
Appendix 7: Gantt Chart 98
Appendix 8: Capstone Showcase Poster 99
References 100

14 RateMyStay 103

	14.1	Introduction	103
	14.2	Problem Statement and Summary of Solution	104
	14.3	Research Questions	104
	14.4	Significance of Research	105
	14.5	Literature Review Introduction	105
	14.6	Domain of Study	106
		14.6.1 Hotel Review Websites	106
		14.6.2 Challenges Faced in the World Due to Issues with Hotel Review Systems	106
	14.7	Software Development Framework and Methodology	106
		14.7.1 System Development Life Cycle (SDLC): Iterative Process	106
		14.7.2 Sentiment Analysis	115
	14.8	Summary of Sentiment Analysis	115
	14.9	TextBlob	115
		14.9.1 Introduction of TextBlob	115
		14.9.2 Workflow of TextBlob	118
		14.9.3 How TextBlob Enhances Sentiment Analysis for Hotel Reviews	120
	14.10	PHP (Hypertext Preprocessor)	121
		14.10.1 Introduction of PHP	121
		14.10.2 Features of PHP	121
		14.10.3 How PHP Enhances Dynamic Web Development and Data Processing in Our System	125
	14.11	Summary for PHP	126

	14.12	Power BI	126
		14.12.1 Introduction of Power BI	126
		14.12.2 How Power BI Empowers Data Visualisation and Decision-Making	126
	14.13	Web Scraper	128
		14.13.1 Introduction of Web Scraper	128
		14.13.2 The Challenges and Ethical Concerns in Web Scraping	128
		14.13.3 How Web Scraper Enables Data Extraction and Analysis	128
		14.13.4 Summary for Web Scrapper	131
	14.14	Visual Studio	131
		14.14.1 Introduction of Visual Studio	131
		14.14.2 Incorporating Bootstrap: Mobile-First, Responsive Design	133
	14.15	Methodology	135
		14.15.1 Introduction of Methodology	135
	14.16	Framework	135
		14.16.1 Information Gathering	135
		14.16.2 Data Storage	137
	14.17	Dataset Page	138
	14.18	Future Work	139
	References		140
15	**Integration of AI and Machine Learning**		145
	15.1	Introduction	145
		15.1.1 Problem Statement	145
	15.2	Literature Review	145
		15.2.1 Theoretical Framework	147
	15.3	Methodology	147
	15.4	Discussion	148
	15.5	Conclusion	148
	References		148
16	**Automotive Prices Analytics**		151
	16.1	Introduction	151
		16.1.1 Problem Statement	151
		16.1.2 Research Objectives	152
	16.2	Literature Review	153
	16.3	Research Methodology	154
		16.3.1 Data Visualisation	155
		16.3.2 Pre-Development Preparations	156
		16.3.3 Design	156
		16.3.4 Function Workflows	157
		16.3.5 Development	158
		16.3.6 Model Deployment	184

	16.4	Results and Analysis	186
		16.4.1 Overview	186
		16.4.2 Results of the XGBoost Model	188
	16.5	Conclusion	191
	References		192
17	**Analytics for Tour Package and Recommendation System**		**195**
	17.1	Introduction	195
	17.2	Significance of Research	195
	17.3	Problem Statements	196
	17.4	Research Questions and Objectives	196
	17.5	Literature Review	196
	17.6	Methodology	197
		17.6.1 Create and Train Model	202
	17.7	Running the KNN Model—Python Terminal	208
		17.7.1 Interpretation of Training Dataset Results	211
		17.7.2 Test Model	212
	17.8	SDLC Framework	213
		17.8.1 Overview of SDLC	213
		17.8.2 Requirement Planning and Analysis	214
		17.8.3 Defining	214
		17.8.4 Designing	215
		17.8.5 Coding and Development	216
		17.8.6 Testing	246
	17.9	Result and Analysis	249
		17.9.1 EDA in Tour Package Dashboard	251
		17.9.2 Power BI User Visualisation Dashboard	253
	17.10	Tour Package Model Recommendation Performance Analysis	253
		17.10.1 Cosine Similarity	255
		17.10.2 Reliability Benchmark for Recommendations	255
		17.10.3 Comparison with Airbnb Model	257
	17.11	Summary	259
	17.12	RoamRadar Website	259
		17.12.1 Login Page	263
		17.12.2 Navigation Bar	267
		17.12.3 Homepage	268
	17.13	About Us Page	269
		17.13.1 Tour Package Recommendation Page	274
	17.14	Validation—Adoption of USE Questionnaires	274
		17.14.1 Usability Test	275
	17.15	Conclusion	278
		17.15.1 Limitation and Future Work	279
	References		279

About the Authors

Dr. Mahadi Hasan Miraz is an Associate Professor in the school of creative industries, Astana IT University, Kazakhstan. Before that, he was a lecturer at Curtin University Malaysia's Department of Digital Marketing. He also was a lecturer at Business School (Department of Business Analytics), Sunway University, Malaysia. Additionally, he was an assistant principal at the University of Utara Malaysia (UUM), Malaysia.

Furthermore, he was involved in the FRGS government project of his outstanding performance. He is actively involved with national and international research grant projects. As a researcher, he published about *60+ research papers (1400 citations)*, including Journal articles and book chapters/books. He serves as the Editor/Lead Guest Editor/Editor/Editorial Board Member/Reviewer, particularly in Elsevier (Scopus), ABDC, CABS and Web of Science Indexed Journals.

His core research areas are Fintech, Blockchain, supply chain management, production & operations management, operations research, research methodology, engineering management, technology management, and educational management.

Ts. Dr. Narishah Mohamed Salleh is a Lecturer in Business Analytics, ERP Transformation Specialist, IR4.0 Innovation Architect and Data Scientist Bridging Industry and Research, leading expert in enterprise systems, digital transformation, and data analytics, blending over 20 years of industry leadership with impactful academic contributions. A PhD holder in Software Engineering from *UKM*, she specializes in Requirements Engineering with Lean Six Sigma precision.

At Sunway University, she develops and delivers industry-aligned modules in ERP, AI, Machine Learning, RPA, and analytics tools, preparing graduates to thrive in the digital economy. Her award-winning projects include intelligent automation, integrated financial supply chains, and warehouse intelligence platforms that have redefined operational excellence in global enterprises.

Driven by a mission to equip future-ready leaders, Dr. Narishah bridges the gap between innovation, technology, and real-world business impact.

Prof. Dr. Hwang, Ha Jin is currently Professor and Director of School of Creative Industries, Astana IT University (AITU), Kazakhstan. Before joining AITU in January 2024, He served as Head and Professor of Information Systems at Department of Business Analytics, Sunway Business School, Sunway University (SU), Malaysia (2016-2023). Dr. Hwang worked at KIMEP University, Kazakhstan for six years (2010-2016), where he served as Dean of Bang College of Business (Feb. 2014-June 2016). He also served as Vice President of External Relations and Cooperation (2005-2009) and worked as Professor of Management Information Systems (1991-2010) for Catholic University of Daegu, Korea. Professor Ha Jin Hwang received MBA (1986) and DBA (1990) from Mississippi State University, U.S.A. He taught at Minnesota State University (Associate Professor of MIS, 1989-1991), Mankato, Minnesota, U.S.A.

He served as President of Korea Association of Information Systems (2005) and President of Korea Internet Electronic Commerce Association (2008). His research interest includes AI in Education, Social Media Analytics, Logistics and Supply Chain Management, Internet of Things and its Applications, Emerging Technologies in Digital Transformation, etc.

Chapter 1
Python for Business Analytics: Unlocking Data Insights for Strategic Decision-Making

1.1 Importance of Business Analytics

Social media and consumer feedback transactions generate vast amounts of data for businesses. This data helps business analytics make strategic decisions, get sights, and improve performance. Effective analytics boosts efficiency, competitiveness, and decision-making. Businesses today rely on business analytics (Ibeh et al., 2024). Companies may increase profitability and sustainability by using multiple forms of data to make better decisions, streamline processes, and personalise consumer interactions. This article highlights the importance of business analytics in many organisational elements.

1.2 Why Python?

Python's enormous library, ease of use and customizability have made it the dominant business analytics technology. Staying ahead in a changing sector requires business analytics tools and strategies (Ayele et al., 2024). Python dominates business analytics due to its flexibility, usability, and power. This chapter will explore Python's many benefits for firms utilising data to make strategic decisions and why it is the ideal business analytics tool.

1.3 Overview of Python's Ecosystem for Data Analysis

Python modules and utilities cover all data analysis pipeline steps. Key elements:

- Pandas: Data manipulation matters.
- NumPy supports massive multidimensional arrays and matrices.

- Matplotlib and Seaborn enable static animated and interactive visualisations.
- Scikit-Learn: A powerful machine learning and predictive analytics library.
- Online Jupyter Notebooks: Write and share live code equations visualisations, and narrative text.

1.4 Installing Python and Essential Packages

To install Python and essential packages, follow these steps:

1. **Download and Install Python**: Visit the Python official website and download the latest version suitable for your operating system. Follow the installation instructions provided on the website.
2. **Install Packages Using pip**: Python comes with a package manager called pip. You can use pip to install essential packages like pandas, NumPy, matplotlib, Seaborn, and scikit-learn. Open your terminal or command prompt and run the following commands:

```
pip install pandas numpy matplotlib seaborn
↪ scikit-learn
```

3. **Verify Installation**: To verify the installation of Python and the packages, you can run a simple script in your Python environment:

```
import pandas as pd
import numpy as np
import matplotlib.pyplot as plt
import seaborn as sns
from sklearn import datasets

print("All packages installed successfully!")
```

1.5 Setting Up Your Environment

Setting up your environment involves configuring your development tools and workspace to streamline your workflow. Here are the steps to set up your environment:

1. **Choose an Integrated Development Environment (IDE)**: Popular IDEs for Python include PyCharm, Visual Studio Code, and Jupyter Notebook. Download and install the IDE of your choice.
2. **Create a Virtual Environment**: Virtual environments help isolate dependencies for different projects. To create a virtual environment, run the following command in your terminal or command prompt:

```
python -m venv myenv
```

Activate the virtual environment:

```
# On Windows
myenv\Scripts\activate

# On macOS and Linux
source myenv/bin/activate
```

3. **Install Essential Packages in the Virtual Environment**: With the virtual environment activated, install the required packages:

```
pip install pandas numpy matplotlib seaborn
    scikit-learn
```

4. **Set Up Jupyter Notebook**: If you prefer using Jupyter Notebook, install it using pip:

```
pip install notebook
```

Start Jupyter Notebook:

```
jupyter notebook
```

This will open a web interface where you can create and run Jupyter notebooks.

1.6 Exercises

Question 1: Explain the difference between a list and a dictionary in Python. Provide an example of each.

Question 2: What is the purpose of the Pandas library in Python, and why is it useful for business analytics?

Question 3: Write a Python command to:

1. Filter rows where the 'Product' is 'A'.
2. Group the data by 'Region' and calculate the total 'Sales' for each region.

Question 4: Why is data visualisation important in business analytics? Mention two popular Python libraries used for visualisation.

Question 5: Using the DataFrame from Question 3, create a bar chart that shows total sales for each product.

Question 6: What function would you use in Pandas to read data from a CSV file into a DataFrame? Provide an example.

Question 7: What is the purpose of a linear regression model in business analytics? Describe a scenario where it could be used.

Question 8: You are tasked with analysing sales data to determine which region generates the most revenue. Using Python, write a step-by-step approach to achieve this analysis.

References

Ayele, E. D., Gavriel, S., Gonzalez, J. F., Teeuw, W. B., Philimis, P., & Gillani, G. (2024, May). Emerging industrial internet of things open-source platforms and applications in diverse sectors. *In Telecom, 5*(02), 369–399.

Ibeh, C. V., Elufioye, O. A., Olorunsogo, T., Asuzu, O. F., Nduubuisi, N. L., & Daraojimba, A. I. (2024). Data analytics in healthcare: A review of patient-centric approaches and healthcare delivery. *World Journal of Advanced Research and Reviews, 21*(02), 1750–1760.

Chapter 2
Basics of Python Programming

2.1 Python Syntax and Basic Constructs

Clear syntax makes Python ideal for beginners and specialists. Basic Python is needed for advanced data analysis (Abdul Kadhar et al., 2021).

Here are some basic constructs in Python:

```python
# Variables
x = 5
y = "Hello, World!"

# Printing
print(x)
print(y)

# Lists
my_list = [1, 2, 3, 4, 5]
print(my_list)

# Conditional Statements
if x > 2:
    print("x is greater than 2")
else:
    print("x is not greater than 2")

# Loops
for i in my_list:
    print(i)
```

2.2 Data Types and Variables

Python supports various data types including integers, floats, strings, lists, tuples, and dictionaries. Variables in Python are dynamically typed, meaning you don't need to declare their type explicitly.

Examples:

```python
# Integer
a = 10

# Float
b = 20.5

# String
c = "Python"

# List
d = [1, 2, 3]

# Tuple
e = (4, 5, 6)

# Dictionary
f = {"name": "John", "age": 30}
```

2.3 Control Flow (If Statements, Loops)

Control flow in Python is managed using if statements, for loops, and while loops.

Examples:

```
# If statement num =
10
if num > 0:
     print("Positive number") elif num
== 0:
     print("Zero")
else:
     print("Negative number")

# For loop
for i in range(5): print(i)

#  While   loop
count = 0
while count < 5: print(
     count ) count +=
     1
```

2.4 Functions and Modules

Functions are defined using the 'def' keyword. Modules are Python files containing functions and variables.

Examples:

```
# Function
def greet(name):
     return "Hello, " + name print(
greet("Alice"))

# Importing a module
import    math print(
math.sqrt(16))
```

2.5 Basic Input/Output Operations

Input and output operations in Python can be performed using built-in functions like 'input()' and 'print()'.

Examples:

```
# Input
name = input("Enter your name: ") print("
Hello, " + name)

# Output
print("This is a sample output.")
```

2.6 Exercises

Exercise 1: Define two variables: name (a string) and age (an integer). Print a sentence that says 'My name is [name] and I am [age] years old'.

Exercise 2: Write a Python programme to swap the values of two variables a and b without using a third variable.

Exercise 3: Write a Python programme that takes a number as input and checks whether it is even or odd. If the number is even, print 'Even', otherwise print 'Odd'.

Exercise 4: Write a Python programme that takes a temperature as input (in Celsius) and prints:

> 'It's cold' if the temperature is below 10,
> 'It's warm' if the temperature is between 10 and 25,
> 'It's hot' if the temperature is above 25.

Exercise 5: Write a Python programme to print the numbers from 1 to 10 using a for loop.

Exercise 6: Write a Python programme that takes an integer as input and prints the multiplication table for that number up to 10.

Exercise 7: Using a while loop, write a Python programme that keeps asking the user for input until they enter the word 'stop'.

References

Abdul Kadhar, K. M., & Anand, G. (2021). *Visualizing the Data. In Data Science with Raspberry Pi: Real-Time Applications Using a Localized Cloud* (pp. 121-134). Berkeley, CA: Apress.

Chapter 3
Data Manipulation with Pandas

3.1 Introduction to Pandas

Pandas is a flexible Python data manipulation and analysis program. It provides rapid easy data formats and analysis (Gupta Bagchi, 2024). Pandas a crucial data scientist tool effectively analyses structured data and facilitates data analysis with many capabilities.

History and development Wes McKinney designed Pandas in 8 to provide a powerful and versatile Python data analysis tool (Sarkar et al., 2018). Pandas is a prominent data science and business analytics tool named after panel data an econometric term for multidimensional datasets. It offers more powerful data manipulation features based on NumPy another Python numerical computing framework.

Key features of Pandas:

- Provides DataFrame and Series objects for handling data.
- It supports data alignment and the integrated handling of missing data.
- Offers robust group-by functionality for aggregation and transformation.
- Allows for flexible reshaping and pivoting of data sets.
- Facilitates time-series functionality.

3.2 DataFrames and Series

A Series is a one-dimensional array-like object containing an array of data and an associated array of data labels called its index. It is similar to a column in a table.

```
import pandas as pd

# Creating a Series data = [1,
2, 3, 4, 5]
series = pd.Series(data) print(series)

# Output
# 0    1
# 1    2
# 2    3
# 3    4
# 4    5
# dtype : int64
```

A DataFrame is a two-dimensional size-mutable and potentially heterogeneous tabular data structure with labelled axes (rows and columns). It is similar to a table in a database or an Excel spreadsheet.

```
# Creating a DataFrame from a dictionary data = {
    'Name': ['Mahadi', 'Anee', 'Hasib', 'Aleay'], 'Age': [25, 30, 35
    , 40],
    'City': ['New York', 'Los Angeles', 'Chicago', '
        ↪ Houston']
}
df = pd.DataFrame(data) print(df)
#   Outpu t          Age      City
#          Name
# 0        Mahadi    25   New York
# 1        Anee      30   Los Angeles
# 2        Hasib     35   Chicago
# 3        Aleay     40   Houston
```

3.3 Importing and Exporting Data

You can import and export data using pandas' built-in functions. Pandas supports various file formats like CSV, Excel, SQL, and JSON.

Examples:

```
# Importing data from a CSV file df = pd.
read_csv('data.csv') print(df.head())

# Exporting data to a CSV file df.to_csv('
output.csv', index=False)
```

3.4 Data Cleaning and Preprocessing

Data cleaning and preprocessing involve handling missing values, removing duplicates, and transforming data.

Examples:

```
# Handling missing values
df.fillna(0, inplace=True)        # Replace missing values with
    ↪ 0

# Removing duplicates df.drop_duplicates(inplace=True)

# Data transformation df['New_Column'] = df['Age'] * 2
```

3.5 Handling Missing Values

Handling missing values is crucial for accurate data analysis. Pandas provides several methods for handling missing values.

Examples:

```
# Checking for missing values print(df.isnull().sum())

# Filling missing values with the mean
df.fillna(df.mean(), inplace=True)

# Dropping rows with missing values df.dropna(inplace=True)
```

3.6 Data Transformation and Aggregation

Transforming Data: Transformation involves changing data format structure or values to meet specific needs.

Applying a Function to Columns:

```
# Convert all strings to lowercase in 'City' column df['City'] = df['City'].apply(lambda x: x.lower())
```

Using 'applymap' for Element-wise Operations:

```
# Apply a function to every element in the DataFrame
df = df.applymap(lambda x: x * 2 if isinstance(x, (int,
    ↪ float)) else x)
```

Aggregation is the process of combining multiple values to produce a summary statistic. Group By:

```
# Group by 'City' and calculate the mean age grouped_df = df.
groupby('City')['Age'].mean() print(grouped_df)
```

Pivot Tables:

```
# Create a pivot table
pivot_table = df.pivot_table(values='Age', index='City',
    ↪ aggfunc='mean')
print(pivot_table)
```

Aggregation Functions:

```
# Apply multiple aggregation functions
agg_df = df.agg({'Age': ['mean', 'max', 'min']}) print(agg_df)
```

3.7 Exercises

Exercise 1: Using Pandas, load a CSV file called sales_data.csv into a DataFrame and display the first five rows of the DataFrame.

Exercise 2: Using the same DataFrame, write Python code to:

> Display the column names of the DataFrame.
> Get the total number of rows and columns.

Exercise 3: Filter the DataFrame to show only rows where the Sales column is greater than 500. Display the filtered DataFrame.

Exercise 4: Using a DataFrame that contains columns Region, Product, and Sales, group the data by Region and calculate the total Sales for each region.

Exercise 5: Sort the DataFrame by the Sales column in descending order and display the sorted DataFrame.

Exercise 6: Check if there are any missing values in the DataFrame. If any, fill the missing values in the Sales column with the mean of that column.

Exercise 7: Create a new column called Sales_Tax that contains 10% of the values in the Sales column.

Exercise 8: You have two DataFrames: df1 (containing customer data) and df2 (containing sales data). Both DataFrames have a column Customer_ID. Merge these two DataFrames on the Customer_ID column.

Exercise 9: Create a pivot table that shows the total Sales for each Product in each Region.

References

Gupta, P., & Bagchi, A. (2024). *Essentials of python for artificial intelligence and machine learning.* Springer.

Sarkar, D., Bali, R., & Sharma, T. (2018). Practical machine learning with Python. *Book Practical Machine Learning with Python*, 25-30.

Chapter 4
Data Visualisation with Matplotlib and Seaborn

4.1 Importance of Data Visualisation

Data visualisation helps analysts and decision-makers detect patterns trends and outliers (Nelli, 2023). Make simpler data explanation. Trends relationships and anomalies are identified. Speaks simply and quickly to diverse audiences. Data storytelling improved data analysis narrative and context.

4.2 Basic Plots with Matplotlib

Data visualisation is needed for business and data analytics. Analysts can explain and illustrate complex data findings. Power flexibility and usability distinguish Matplotlib from other Python data visualisation tools. Basic Matplotlib plots assist business analysts in analysing data and deciding.

Value of data visualisation simplifies difficult data. Charts and graphs clarify trends and deviations. Effective Communication: Visualisations convey ideas fast. They help non-technical stakeholders understand data outcomes. Finding Trends and Patterns: Charts assist analysts in finding unexpected data patterns. This skill is needed for strategic planning and prediction. Improve Data Quality: Visualisation can find missing numbers inaccuracies and inconsistencies. The analysis is exact with instant processing. Decision help: Clear concise data visualisations help organisational strategies and procedures.

Why Matplotlib? Flexibility and Customisation: Matplotlib is configurable. Users can customise static animated and interactive scenes. Matplotlib supports line scatter bar histogram and pie charts. Exploring and displaying raw data requires these basic visuals. Python library integration: Matplotlib works with Pandas NumPy and Seaborn. Integration simplifies data processing and visualisation. Usability: The library is easy for novices and specialists. Very simple syntax lets users create charts with minimal coding. Large Active Community and Support: Matplotlib has substantial documentation tutorials and examples. Installing Matplotlib If you haven't installed Matplotlib yet you can do so using pip:

```
pip install matplotlib
```

Creating Basic Plots Import Matplotlib and start with some basic plots:

```python
import matplotlib.pyplot as plt

# Line Plot
x = [1, 2, 3, 4, 5]
y = [10, 15, 13, 20, 25]

plt.plot(x, y) plt.title('
Line Plot') plt.xlabel('X Axis')
plt.ylabel('Y Axis') plt.show()
```

Bar Plot

```python
# Bar Plot
categories = ['A', 'B', 'C', 'D'] values = [4, 7, 1, 8]

plt.bar(categories, values) plt.title('
Bar Plot') plt.xlabel('Categories')
plt.ylabel('Values') plt.show()
```

Histogram

```python
# Histogram
data = [1, 2, 2, 3, 3, 3, 4, 4, 4, 4]

plt.hist(data, bins=4)
plt.title('Histogram')
plt.xlabel('Value') plt.ylabel('
Frequency') plt.show()
```

Scatter Plot

4.3 Advanced Visualisation with Seaborn

```
# Scatter Plot
x = [5, 7, 8, 7, 2, 17, 2, 9, 4, 11]
y = [99, 86, 87, 88, 100, 86, 103, 87, 94, 78]

plt.scatter(x, y) plt.title('
Scatter Plot') plt.xlabel('X Axis')
plt.ylabel('Y Axis') plt.show()
```

4.3 Advanced Visualisation with Seaborn

Seaborn is built on top of Matplotlib and provides a high-level interface for drawing attractive statistical graphics. It simplifies complex visualisations and enhances them with additional functionality.

Installing Seaborn If you haven't installed Seaborn yet you can do so using pip:

```
pip install seaborn
```

Creating Advanced Plots Import Seaborn and create advanced visualisations:

```
import seaborn as sns

# Line Plot
data = sns.load_dataset('tips') sns.lineplot(x='
total_bill', y='tip', data=data) plt.title('Line Plot with Seaborn')
plt.show()
```

Bar Plot

```
# Bar Plot
sns.barplot(x='day', y='total_bill', data=data)
plt.title('Bar Plot with Seaborn')
plt.show()
```

Histogram and KDE Plot

```
# Histogram and KDE Plot sns.histplot(data
['total_bill'], kde=True) plt.title('Histogram with KDE')
plt.show()
```

Scatter Plot with Regression Line

```python
# Scatter Plot with Regression Line
sns.lmplot(x='total_bill', y='tip', data=data)
plt.title('Scatter Plot with Regression Line')
plt.show()
```

Pair Plot Pair plots are useful for visualising pairwise relationships in a dataset:

```python
# Pair Plot
sns.pairplot(data)
plt.title('Pair Plot with Seaborn')
plt.show()
```

4.4 Customizing Plots

Customizing plots helps in tailoring the visualisations to better communicate the insights. Both Matplotlib and Seaborn offer extensive customization options.

Customizing Matplotlib Plots

```python
# Customizing Matplotlib Plot
plt.plot(x, y, color='green', linestyle='dashed',
        linewidth=2, marker='o', markerfacecolor='blue',
        markersize=12)
plt.title('Customized Line Plot')
plt.xlabel('X Axis')
plt.ylabel('Y Axis')
plt.grid(True)
plt.show()
```

Customizing Seaborn Plots

```python
# Customizing Seaborn Plot
sns.set(style="whitegrid")
sns.barplot(x='day', y='total_bill', data=data, palette='viridis')
plt.title('Customized Bar Plot')
plt.show()
```

4.5 Interactive Visualisations with Plotly

Plotly is a powerful library for creating interactive visualisations that can be easily shared and embedded in web applications. Installing Plotly if you haven't installed Plotly yet you can do so using pip:

```
pip install plotly
```

Creating Interactive Plots Import Plotly and create interactive visualisations:

```
import plotly.express as px
```

4.6 Exercises

Exercise 1: **Line Plot** Using Matplotlib, create a line plot of the following data where x = [1, 2, 3, 4, 5] and y = [2, 3, 5, 7, 11]. Label the axes as 'X-axis' and 'Y-axis', and give the plot a title 'Line Plot Example'.

Exercise 2: **Bar Plot** Create a bar plot using Matplotlib to display the sales of four products: Products = ['A', 'B', 'C', 'D'] and Sales = [350, 250, 400, 300]. Label the bars appropriately.

Exercise 3: **Histogram** Generate a histogram using random data. Create a dataset of 1000 random numbers drawn from a normal distribution using np.random.randn(1000) and plot the histogram with 30 bins.

Exercise 4: **Customizing Line Plot** Create a line plot with the following specifications:

> x = [1, 2, 3, 4, 5]
> y1 = [10, 20, 15, 25, 30] (Plot in red colour with dashed lines)
> y2 = [5, 15, 10, 20, 25] (Plot in blue colour with a solid line) Add a legend, labels for both axes, and a title.

Exercise 5: **Seaborn Bar Plot** Using Seaborn, create a bar plot of the titanic dataset to show the average fare (fare) paid by passengers in each passenger class (class). Add appropriate axis labels and a title.

Exercise 6: Check if there are any missing values in the DataFrame. If any, fill the missing values in the Sales column with the mean of that column.

Exercise 7: Seaborn Scatter Plot with Regression Line Using the tips dataset, create a scatter plot with a regression line to show the relationship between total_bill and tip.

References

Nelli, F. (2023). Machine learning with scikit-learn. In *Python data analytics: with pandas, numPy, and matplotlib* (pp. 259-287). Berkeley, CA: Apress.

Chapter 5
Descriptive Analytics

5.1 Descriptive Statistics in Python

Descriptive statistics summarise and organise characteristics of a data set. Python provides several libraries such as pandas and NumPy to perform descriptive statistics.

Examples:

```
import pandas as pd
# Load data
data = pd.read_csv('data.csv')

# Descriptive statistics print(data
.describe())
```

5.2 Measures of Central Tendency and Variability

Measures of central tendency include mean, median, and mode, while measures of variability include range, variance, and standard deviation.

Examples:

```python
# Mean
mean_value = data['column_name'].mean() print("
Mean:", mean_value)

# Median
median_value = data['column_name'].median()
print("Median:", median_value)

# Mode
mode_value = data['column_name'].mode()[0] print("
Mode:", mode_value)

# Standard Deviation
std_dev = data['column_name'].std() print("
Standard Deviation:", std_dev)
```

5.3 Data Summarisation Techniques

Data summarisation involves aggregating data to extract meaningful insights. Techniques include groupby, pivot tables, and cross-tabulation.

Examples:

```python
# Group By
grouped_data = data.groupby('category_column')['
    ↪ value_column'].sum()
print(grouped_data)

# Pivot Table
pivot_table = data.pivot_table(values='value_column',
    ↪ index='category_column', aggfunc='mean') print(
pivot_table)

# Cross-Tabulation
cross_tab = pd.crosstab(data['column1'], data['column2']) print(cross_tab)
```

5.4 Exercises

Exercise 1: **Calculating Summary Statistics** Using the dataset sales_data that contains columns: Product, Region, Sales, and Profit, calculate the following descriptive statistics for the Sales and Profit columns:

> Mean
> Median
> Standard deviation
> Minimum and maximum values

Exercise 2: **Frequency Distribution** Using the sales_data dataset, create a frequency distribution table showing how often each Region appears in the dataset.

Exercise 3: **Grouping Data** Using the sales_data dataset, calculate the total Sales and average Profit for each Region. Use groupby functionality to group the data by Region.

Exercise 6: **Boxplot for Distribution of Sales** Create a boxplot to visualise the distribution of Sales in the sales_data dataset.

Exercise 5: **Seaborn Bar Plot** Using Seaborn, create a bar plot of the titanic dataset to show the average fare (fare) paid by passengers in each passenger class (class). Add appropriate axis labels and a title.

Exercise 9: **Range, Variance, and Standard Deviation** For the Profit column in the sales_data dataset, calculate the range, variance, and standard deviation.

Exercise 10: **Pairplot** Use the Seaborn library to create a pairplot of the Sales and Profit columns to visualise relationships and distributions in the sales_data dataset.

Chapter 6
Predictive Analytics with Scikit-Learn

6.1 Introduction to Predictive Analytics

Predictive analytics uses historical data statistical methods and machine learning to forecast outcomes. Analysing current and historical data predictive analytics helps companies forecast trends risks and growth opportunities. This chapter emphasises predictive analytics' role in modern business decision-making with its ideas methodologies and applications.

6.2 Overview of Scikit-Learn

Python machine learning library Scikit-Learn is popular and powerful. It uses NumPy SciPy and Matplotlib to produce simple effective data mining and analysis tools. Installing Scikit-Learn: If you haven't installed Scikit-Learn yet, you can do so using pip:

Importing Scikit-Learn into your Python script:

```
pip install scikit-learn
    import sklearn
```

6.3 Data Preparation for Modelling

Before building predictive models, it is crucial to prepare the data. This includes cleaning the data handling missing values encoding categorical variables and splitting the data into training and testing sets.

Loading and Exploring Data

```
import pandas as pd
# Load data into a DataFrame data = pd.
read_csv('data.csv') print(data.head())
```

Handling Missing Values

```
# Fill missing values with the mean of the column data.fillna(data.
mean(), inplace=True)
```

Encoding Categorical Variables

```
from sklearn.preprocessing import LabelEncoder
# Encode categorical variables
label_encoder = LabelEncoder()
data['category'] = label_encoder.fit_transform(data['
    ↪ category'])
```

Splitting Data into Training and Testing Sets

```
from sklearn.model_selection import train_test_split
# Define features and target variable
X = data.drop('target', axis=1) y = data['
target']
# Split the data
X_train, X_test, y_train, y_test = train_test_split(X, y,
    ↪   test_size=0.2, random_state=42)
```

6.4 Building and Evaluating Regression Models

Regression models are used to predict continuous outcomes. Common regression algorithms include Linear Regression Decision Tree Regression and Random Forest Regression.

Linear Regression

```python
from sklearn.linear_model import LinearRegression
from sklearn.metrics import mean_squared_error, r2_score

# Initialize the model
model = LinearRegression()

# Train the model
model.fit(X_train, y_train)

# Make predictions
y_pred = model.predict(X_test)

# Evaluate the model
mse = mean_squared_error(y_test, y_pred)
r2 = r2_score(y_test, y_pred)

print(f"Mean Squared Error: {mse}")
print(f"R-squared: {r2}")
```

6.5 Classification Models and Their Applications

Classification models predict categorical outcomes. Common algorithms include Logistic Regression, Decision Trees, and Random Forests.

Logistic Regression

```python
from sklearn.linear_model import LogisticRegression
from sklearn.metrics import accuracy_score, confusion_matrix

# Initialize the model
model = LogisticRegression()

# Train the model
model.fit(X_train, y_train)

# Make predictions
y_pred = model.predict(X_test)
```

```
# Evaluate the model
accuracy = accuracy_score(y_test, y_pred) conf_matrix =
confusion_matrix(y_test, y_pred)

print (f" Accuracy :     { accuracy }") print(f"Confusion
Matrix:\n{conf_matrix}")
```

6.6 Model Validation Techniques

Model validation techniques ensure that the model generalises well to unseen data. Common techniques include cross-validation, train-test split, and validation curves.

Cross-Validation

```
from sklearn.model_selection import cross_val_score
# Perform 5-fold cross-validation
scores = cross_val_score(model, X, y, cv=5)

print(f"Cross-validation   scores: {scores}") print(f"Mean cross-
validation score: {scores.mean()}")
```

6.7 Exercises

Exercise 1: Calculating Summary Statistics Using the dataset sales_data that contains columns: Product, Region, Sales, and Profit, calculate the following descriptive statistics for the Sales and Profit columns:

- Mean
- Median
- Standard deviation
- Minimum and maximum values

Exercise 2: Frequency Distribution Using the sales_data dataset, create a frequency distribution table showing how often each Region appears in the dataset.

Exercise 3: Grouping Data Using the sales_data dataset, calculate the total Sales and average Profit for each Region. Use groupby functionality to group the data by Region.

6.7 Exercises

Exercise 6: **Boxplot for Distribution of Sales** Create a boxplot to visualise the distribution of Sales in the sales_data dataset.

Exercise 5: **Seaborn Bar Plot** Using Seaborn, create a bar plot of the titanic dataset to show the average fare (fare) paid by passengers in each passenger class (class). Add appropriate axis labels and a title.

Exercise 9: **Range, Variance, and Standard Deviation** For the Profit column in the sales_data dataset, calculate the range, variance, and standard deviation.

Exercise 10: **Pairplot** Use the seaborn library to create a pairplot of the Sales and Profit columns to visualise relationships and distributions in the sales_data dataset.

Chapter 7
Advanced Analytics and Machine Learning

7.1 Introduction to Advanced Machine Learning

Modern technology including machine learning (ML) has inspired healthcare finance marketing and other breakthroughs. Fundamental machine learning methods support predictive and prescriptive analytics whereas advanced methods offer more powerful accurate and sophisticated solutions (Troisi & Maione, 2024). The Python ecosystem of modules and frameworks allows researchers and practitioners to employ advanced machine learning.

7.2 Clustering Algorithms

Clustering algorithms group data points based on their similarities. Common algorithms include K-Means, DBSCAN, and Hierarchical Clustering.

K-Means Clustering

```python
from sklearn.cluster import KMeans import matplotlib.pyplot as plt

# Initialize the model
kmeans = KMeans(n_clusters=3)

# Fit the model
kmeans.fit(X)
```

```
# Predict clusters
clusters = kmeans.predict(X)

# Plot the clusters
plt.scatter(X[:, 0], X[:, 1], c=clusters, cmap='viridis') plt.title('K-Means Clustering')
plt.show()
```

7.3 Principal Component Analysis (PCA)

Principal Component Analysis (PCA) is a dimensionality reduction technique that transforms high-dimensional data into a lower-dimensional space.

PCA Example

```
from sklearn.decomposition import PCA

# Initialize the model pca = PCA(n_components=2)

# Fit and transform the data X_pca = pca.fit_transform(X)

# Plot the transformed data plt.scatter(X_pca[:, 0], X_pca[:, 1]) plt.title('Principal Component Analysis') plt.show()
```

7.4 Time Series Forecasting

Time series forecasting involves predicting future values based on historical data. Common algorithms include ARIMA, SARIMA, and LSTM.

ARIMA Example

```
import pandas as pd
import matplotlib.pyplot as plt
from statsmodels.tsa.arima.model import ARIMA

# Load the dataset
```

```
data = pd.read_csv('timeseries_data.csv', parse_dates=['
    ↪ Date'], index_col='Date')

# Initialize the model
model = ARIMA(data['Value'], order=(5, 1, 0))

# Fit the model model_fit =
model.fit()

# Make predictions
forecast = model_fit.forecast(steps=12)

# Plot the forecast
plt.plot(data['Value'], label='Historical') plt.plot(forecast, label
='Forecast', color='red') plt.title('ARIMA Time Series
Forecast') plt.show()
```

7.5 Exercises

Exercise 1: **Handling Missing Data** Given a dataset customer_data with columns Age, Income, Purchase_Frequency, and Spending_Score, identify and handle any missing values in the data. Use mean imputation for Age and Income.

Exercise 2: **Feature Scaling** Scale the Income and Spending_Score columns of the customer_data dataset using standardisation (z-score normalisation).

Exercise 3: **Train-Test Split** Using the customer_data dataset, split the data into training and testing sets with a ratio of 80:20, using Spending_Score as the target variable and the rest of the columns as features.

Exercise 4: **Building a Linear Regression Model** Using the training data from the previous exercise, build a linear regression model to predict the Spending_Score. Evaluate the model on the test set and print the mean squared error (MSE).

Exercise 5: **Logistic Regression for Classification** Given a dataset churn_data with a target column Churn (0 for no churn, 1 for churn) and features Customer_Tenure, Monthly_Spend, and Contract_Length, build a logistic regression model to predict whether a customer will churn.

Exercise 6: **K-Means Clustering** Using the customer_data dataset, apply K-means clustering to segment customers based on Income and Spending_Score. Set the number of clusters to 3 and visualise the results.

Exercise 7: **Principal Component Analysis (PCA)** Perform PCA on the customer_data dataset to reduce the dimensions of Income, Age, and Purchase_Frequency into two principal components.

Exercise 8: s Grid Search for Model Optimization Use grid search to optimise the hyperparameters of a decision tree classifier on the churn_data dataset. Focus on tuning the max_depth and min_samples_split parameters.

Reference

Troisi, O., & Maione, G. (2024). Data-driven decision making: Empowering businesses through advanced analytics and machine learning. *Journal Environmental Sciences and Technology, 3*(1), 515–525.

Chapter 8
Case Studies and Real-World Applications

8.1 Case Study: Sales Forecasting

```
import pandas as pd
data = pd.read_csv('DrMahadiStudent_data.csv',
    ↪ parse_dates=['Date'], index_col='Date')

monthly_sales = data['Sales'].resample('M').sum() # Modeling

with ARIMA
from statsmodels.tsa.arima.model import ARIMA import
matplotlib.pyplot as plt

# ARIMA design
model = ARIMA(monthly_sales, order=(5, 1, 0)) model_fit = model.
fit()
# Make predictions
forecast = model_fit.forecast(steps=12) #         Plot
the     results  plt.figure(figsize=(12, 6))
plt.plot(monthly_sales, label='Historical Sales') plt.plot(forecast,
label='Forecast', color='red') plt.title('Sales Forecasting with
ARIMA') plt.xlabel('Date')
plt.ylabel('Sales') plt .
legend () plt.show()
```

8.2 Case Study: Customer Segmentation

Companies that segment their customer base might target specific consumer groups with specialised marketing techniques. In this case, study we will use clustering techniques to divide the customers based on their purchasing patterns.

Dataset Description: The variable states as 'CustomerID' 'PurchaseAmount' and 'PurchaseFrequency'.

Data Preparation

```python
import pandas as pd

# Load the dataset
data = pd.read_csv('customer_data.csv')

# Extract features for clustering
X = data[['PurchaseAmount', 'PurchaseFrequency']]
```

K-Means Clustering

```python
from sklearn.cluster import KMeans import matplotlib.pyplot as plt

# Determine the optimal number of clusters using the
    ↪ elbow method sse
= []
for k in range(1, 11):
    kmeans = KMeans(n_clusters=k)
    kmeans . fit ( X) sse.append(
    kmeans.inertia_)

# Plot the elbow curve plt . figure (
figsize =(10 , 6)) plt.plot(range(1, 11), sse,
marker='o') plt.title('Elbow Method for Optimal K')
plt.xlabel('Number of clusters') plt.ylabel('SSE')
plt.show()
```

```python
# Fit the K-Means model kmeans =
KMeans(n_clusters=3)
data['Cluster'] = kmeans.fit_predict(X)
```

8.3 Case Study: Financial Risk Analysis

Financial risk analysis involves assessing the risk of financial loss using predictive models and historical data.

```python
import pandas as pd
from sklearn.model_selection import train_test_split from sklearn.ensemble import RandomForestClassifier from sklearn.metrics import accuracy_score,
    ↪ confusion_matrix

# Load the dataset
data = pd.read_csv('financial_data.csv')

# Prepare the features and target
X = data.drop('Risk', axis=1) y = data['Risk']

# Split the data
X_train, X_test, y_train, y_test = train_test_split(X, y,
    ↪ test_size=0.2, random_state=42)

# Initialize the model
model = RandomForestClassifier()

# Train the model model.fit(X_train, y_train)

# Make predictions
y_pred = model.predict(X_test)

# Evaluate the model
accuracy = accuracy_score(y_test, y_pred) conf_matrix = confusion_matrix(y_test, y_pred)
```

```python
print(f" Accuracy :    {accuracy}") print(f"Confusion Matrix:\n{conf_matrix}")
```

8.4 Case Study: Marketing Campaign Analysis

Marketing campaign analysis evaluates the effectiveness of marketing campaigns and optimises future strategies.

```
import pandas as pd

# Load the dataset
data = pd.read_csv('marketing_campaign.csv')

# Summarize campaign performance
campaign_summary = data.groupby('Campaign')['Response'].
    ↪ mean()

print(campaign_summary)
```

8.5 Exercises

Exercise 1: **Analysing Customer Segments** You are given a dataset retail_data.csv with columns: CustomerID, Age, Annual_Income, Spending_Score, and Gender. Use K-Means clustering to segment the customers into different groups based on their spending behaviour and income. Analyse the characteristics of each segment.

- Load the dataset and explore the data.
- Apply K-Means clustering with 3 clusters.
- Visualise the customer segments using a scatter plot (plot Annual_Income vs. Spending_Score and colour the points based on the clusters).
- Describe the key characteristics of each customer segment.

Exercise 2: **Employee Attrition Prediction** A company wants to predict employee attrition using data from its human resources department. The dataset employee_data.csv contains features such as Age, Monthly_Income, Job_Level, Satisfaction_Level, Years_At_Company, and a target variable Attrition (1 for attrition, 0 for retention).

- Load the dataset and preprocess the data (handle missing values, encode categorical variables, etc.).
- Split the data into training and test sets.
- Build a logistic regression model to predict employee attrition.
- Evaluate the model using accuracy, precision, and recall.
- Interpret the coefficients of the logistic regression model to explain which factors are most important in predicting attrition.

Exercise 3: **Sales Forecasting Using Time Series Analysis** You are working for a retail company that wants to forecast monthly sales for the next 12 months. You are provided with historical sales data in sales_data.csv, containing two columns: Date and Sales.

8.5 Exercises

- Load the dataset and convert the Date column to a datetime format.
- Plot the time series of sales data.
- Apply an ARIMA model to forecast the next 12 months of sales.
- Plot the forecasted sales against the actual sales for comparison.

Exercise 4: **Loan Default Prediction** A financial institution has provided you with data on past loans and whether the customer defaulted (Default = 1) or not (Default = 0). The dataset loan_data.csv contains features such as Loan_Amount, Interest_Rate, Credit_Score, and Employment_Status.

- Load and explore the dataset.
- Apply feature scaling to the numerical variables (Loan_Amount, Interest_Rate, and Credit_Score).
- Build a decision tree classifier to predict loan default.
- Visualise the decision tree and interpret the results.

Exercise 5: **Building a Recommendation System** An e-commerce platform wants to recommend products to its users based on their purchase history. You are provided with the transaction history of users in ecommerce_data.csv, which includes columns User_ID, Product_ID, and Purchase_Amount.

- Load and preprocess the dataset.
- Create a user-item matrix where each row represents a user, and each column represents a product.
- Apply a collaborative filtering technique (such as matrix factorization or nearest-neighbor) to build a recommendation system.
- Recommend products for a specific user based on the model.

Chapter 9
Automating Data Analysis with Python

9.1 Automating Repetitive Tasks

Python with its extensive libraries and frameworks is well-suited for automating data-related tasks.

Common Repetitive Tasks

- Data extraction and loading
- Data cleaning and preprocessing
- Regular report generation
- Data backups

Automating with Python Example: Automating Data Extraction and Loading:

```python
import pandas as pd

def extract_data(file_path): return pd.read_csv(file_path)

def load_data_to_database(df, database_connection): df.to_sql('table_name', con=database_connection,
    if_exists='replace', index=False)

# Define file path and database connection file_path = 'data.csv'
database_connection = 'your_database_connection_string'
```

```
# Extract and load data
data = extract_data(file_path) load_data_to_database(data, database_connection)
```

Example: Automating Data Cleaning

```
def         clean_data  ( df): df.fillna(method='
    ffill', inplace=True) df.drop_duplicates(inplace=
    True)
    return df

# Clean the extracted data cleaned_data
= clean_data(data)
```

9.2 Scheduling and Running Automated Scripts

Automated scripts can be scheduled to run at specific times or intervals using tools like cron jobs on Unix-based systems or Task Scheduler on Windows.

Using Cron Jobs (Unix-based Systems)

1. Open the cron table:

```
crontab -e
```

2. Add a cron job to run a Python script daily at midnight:

```
0 0 * * * /usr/bin/python3 /path/to/your_script.
    ↪ py
```

Using Task Scheduler (Windows)

3. Open Task Scheduler.
4. Create a new basic task.
5. Set the trigger to your preferred schedule (e.g. daily).
6. Set the action to run your Python script using the Python executable.

9.3 Introduction to Airflow for Workflow Automation

Apache Airflow is an open-source platform to programmatically author schedule and monitor workflows. It allows for complex data pipelines to be managed effectively.

Installing Airflow

```
pip install apache-airflow
```

9.3 Introduction to Airflow for Workflow Automation

Setting Up Airflow

1. Initialise the Airflow database:

   ```
   airflow db init
   ```

2. Start the Airflow web server:

   ```
   airflow webserver --port 8080
   ```

3. Start the Airflow scheduler:

   ```
   airflow scheduler
   ```

Creating an Airflow DAG (Directed Acyclic Graph) Example: Simple ETL Pipeline

```
from airflow import DAG
from airflow.operators.python_operator import
    ↪ PythonOperator
from datetime import datetime, timedelta import pandas
as pd

default_args = {'owner': 'airflow','depends_on_past':
    ↪ False,'start_date': datetime(2024, 1, 1), 'retries'
    ↪ : 1,'retry_delay': timedelta(minutes=5)}

dag = DAG('simple_etl',default_args=default_args, description='A
    simple ETL DAG',                          schedule_interval=
         ↪ timedelta(days=1))
```

```python
def extract():
    data = pd.read_csv('/path/to/data.csv') data.to_pickle('/
    path/to/temp_data.pkl')

def transform():
    data = pd.read_pickle('/path/to/temp_data.pkl') data.fillna(
    method='ffill', inplace=True) data.to_pickle('/path/to/
    clean_data.pkl')

def load():
    data = pd.read_pickle('/path/to/clean_data.pkl') data.to_sql('
    table_name', con='
        ↪ your_database_connection_string', if_exists='
        ↪ replace', index=False)

t1 = PythonOperator(task_id='extract',
    python_callable=extract,dag=dag)

t2 = PythonOperator(task_id='transform', python_callable=
    transform,dag=dag)

t3 = PythonOperator(task_id='load',
    python_callable=load,dag=dag )

t1 >> t2 >> t3
```

9.4 Exercises

Exercise 1: Automating Missing Data Handling: You are provided with a dataset sales_data.csv that has missing values in several columns, such as Product_ID, Sales, and Customer_Age. Write a Python script to automate the process of:

- Identifying missing values in the dataset.
- Automatically filling missing numeric values with the column mean.
- Automatically filling missing categorical values with the most frequent value.
- Saving the cleaned dataset to a new file cleaned_sales_data.csv.

Exercise 2: Generating Automated Summary Reports: You are given a dataset employee_performance.csv with columns such as Employee_ID, Department, Performance_Score, Salary, and Years_at_Company. Automate the process of generating a report that provides:

- The average performance score per department.
- The top 5 highest-paid employees.
- Summary statistics for Salary and Years_at_Company.
- Save the report to a text file performance_report.txt.

9.4 Exercises

Exercise 3: Automating Monthly Sales Analysis: You are working with a dataset monthly_sales.csv, which contains daily sales data for the past year with columns: Date and Sales_Amount. Write a Python script to automate the following tasks:

- Convert the Date column to a datetime format.
- Aggregate daily sales to calculate total sales for each month.
- Automatically generate a bar chart that shows total sales for each month.
- Save the chart as monthly_sales_chart.png.

Exercise 4: Automating Model Training and Evaluation: You have a dataset loan_data.csv containing customer data and whether they defaulted on a loan (Default). Your task is to automate the training and evaluation of multiple machine learning models (logistic regression, decision tree, and random forest). The script should:

- Load and preprocess the data.
- Split the data into training and testing sets.
- Train the models and compare their performance using accuracy and F1-score.
- Print a summary report of the model evaluation.

Exercise 5: Creating a Reusable Data Pipeline Function: Write a Python function data_pipeline() that automates the following tasks on any dataset:

- Loads the dataset from a CSV file.
- Handles missing data (fills missing numeric values with the median and categorical values with the mode).
- Scales numeric features using standard scaling.
- Saves the preprocessed data to a new file.

Test this function on a dataset of your choice.

Chapter 10
Best Practices and Future Trends

10.1 Best Practices in Data Analytics

Best practices must be followed if data analytics is to be as trustworthy and valuable as feasible (Müller et al., 2016). These standards aim to produce useful insights reproducibility of results and correctness and consistency of data.

10.2 Ethical Considerations in Data Analysis

With data analytics' growing sway ethical issues are critical. Analysts must ensure their work lessens bias advances equity and safeguards people's privacy. Data privacy aims to safeguard and manage personal information so that it is used only for authorised purposes and remains confidential.

- Have the individuals whose data is being utilised give their informed permission.
- Anonymization alters data in such a way that personal identities are not visible.
- Data Minimization: Get and use just the information that is strictly required for the research.

10.3 The Future of Business Analytics and Python's Role

Python's robust environment and versatility have made it a significant player in the ever-changing field of business analytics. Many variables are influencing the future direction of the field.

1. Integration of AI and Machine Learning: As AI and machine learning technologies evolve, their integration into business analytics will become even more critical. Future research should explore advanced algorithms and models that can provide more accurate predictions and insights.
2. Big Data Analytics: The volume of data generated by businesses is growing exponentially. Research should focus on developing efficient techniques for handling, processing, and analysing big data to extract valuable insights.
3. Real-time Analytics: Businesses increasingly require real-time data analysis to make immediate decisions. Future research should aim to enhance the capabilities of real-time analytics platforms, ensuring they can handle large volumes of data quickly and accurately.
4. Data Privacy and Security: With the increasing amount of data being collected, ensuring its privacy and security is paramount. Research should focus on developing robust encryption methods, secure data storage solutions, and frameworks for maintaining data privacy.
5. Visualisation Techniques: As the complexity of data increases, so does the need for advanced visualisation techniques that can present data in a clear and understandable manner. Research should explore new ways to visualise complex datasets and enhance the user experience.
6. Industry-specific Solutions: Different industries have unique data analytics needs. Future research should focus on developing tailored analytics solutions for various industries, such as healthcare, finance, retail, and manufacturing, to address their specific challenges.
7. Ethical AI and Fairness: As AI and machine learning become more integrated into business analytics, ensuring that these technologies are used ethically and fairly is crucial. Research should explore ways to mitigate biases in AI models and promote transparency and accountability.
8. Edge Computing and IoT: With the rise of the Internet of Things (IoT), edge computing is becoming more important for processing data closer to its source. Future research should investigate how edge computing can be leveraged to enhance business analytics capabilities.
9. Education and Training: As the field of business analytics evolves, so must the education and training programmes that prepare the next generation of data scientists and analysts. Research should focus on developing comprehensive curricula that cover the latest tools, techniques, and best practices.
10. Collaboration and Open Science: Encouraging collaboration between researchers, businesses, and academia can lead to significant advancements in business analytics. Future research should promote open science initiatives, data sharing, and collaborative projects to drive innovation.

10.4 Continuing Your Learning Journey

Continuous learning and education are essential in the rapidly evolving field of business analytics. To stay ahead of the curve and maintain your expertise, consider the following strategies:

1. Online Courses and Certifications: Enrol in online courses and certification programmes offered by reputable institutions. Platforms like Coursera, edX, and Udacity offer courses in data science, machine learning, and business analytics. These courses can help you acquire new skills and stay updated with the latest trends and technologies.
2. Reading Research Papers and Books: Regularly read research papers, books, and articles related to business analytics and data science. Journals like the Journal of Business Analytics, Harvard Business Review, and IEEE Transactions on Knowledge and Data Engineering publish cutting-edge research and case studies.
3. Attending Conferences and Workshops: Participate in conferences, workshops, and seminars to learn from industry experts and network with peers. Events like the Strata Data Conference, KDD (Knowledge Discovery and Data Mining), and the International Conference on Machine Learning (ICML) provide valuable insights into the latest advancements in the field.
4. Joining Professional Organisations: Become a member of professional organisations like the Institute for Operations Research and the Management Sciences (INFORMS), the Data Science Association, and the Association for Computing Machinery (ACM). These organisations offer resources, networking opportunities, and access to exclusive events and publications.
5. Practical Experience: Apply your knowledge through practical experience. Work on real-world projects, participate in hackathons, and collaborate with other professionals in the field. Practical experience helps solidify your understanding and provides valuable insights into real-world challenges.
6. Staying Updated with Technology: Keep abreast of the latest tools, software, and technologies used in business analytics. Follow tech blogs, watch tutorials, and experiment with new tools to enhance your skill set.
7. Mentorship and Networking: Seek mentorship from experienced professionals and build a strong network within the industry. Mentors can provide guidance, share their experiences, and help you navigate your career path. Networking with peers can lead to collaborative opportunities and knowledge sharing.
8. Continuous Skill Development: Focus on developing both technical and soft skills. Technical skills include programming, data analysis, and machine learning, while soft skills encompass communication, problem-solving, and critical thinking. A well-rounded skill set is crucial for success in business analytics.

By adopting these strategies, you can ensure that you stay current with the latest developments in business analytics and continue to grow your expertise in the field.

References

Kolasińska-Morawska, K., Sułkowski, Ł, Buła, P., Brzozowska, M., & Morawski, P. (2022). Smart logistics—Sustainable technological innovations in customer service at the last-mile stage: The polish perspective. *Energies, 15*(17), 6395.

Müller, R. D., Seton, M., Zahirovic, S., Williams, S. E., Matthews, K. J., Wright, N. M., Shephard, G. E., Maloney, K. T., Barnett-Moore, N., & Hosseinpour, M. (2016). Ocean basin evolution and global-scale plate reorganization events since Pangea breakup. *Annual Review of Earth and Planetary Sciences, 44*(1), 107–138.

Chapter 11
Outline of the Study

11.1 Keeping Up Your Education: What Is a Research Proposal?

An organised paper describing the intended study is called a research proposal (Teixeira & Picinin, 2024). It includes the planned study's research design methods timeframe significance literature review and research questions. A research proposal tries to persuade others—like funding agencies ethics committees or academic supervisors—that the study is desirable and doable.

11.2 What Is a Problem Statement and Why?

A problem statement is a synopsis of the issues that the team tackling the challenge has to address. It points up an issue or knowledge vacuum that the study seeks to close at this time. The reason the problem statement is so crucial is that it directs the research process and keeps it relevant and concentrated.

11.3 What Are the Different Kinds of Literature Reviews?

A thorough synopsis of earlier study on a subject is a literature review. Scholarly publications books and other materials linked to a certain research topic are scanned by it. The literature evaluation serves to point up gaps that will be filled in the planned study and to give a foundation for comprehending the state of the art.

Forms of reviews of the literature

- Narrative Review: Highlights the synthesis and interpretation of results in its summary of the literature on the subject.
- Systematic Review: High-quality evidence on a particular topic is provided by summarising and analysing several research using an organised technique.
- Meta-analysis: Gathers statistical information from many research to produce a stronger conclusion.
- Scoping Review: Often used to map major concepts it ascertains the breadth and depth of research on a subject.

11.4 What Constitutes Contemporary Theory and Practice?

Modern theory and practice describe the models procedures and approaches in use in a certain area at the moment. It comprises cutting-edge techniques and the most recent research results that tackle the possibilities and problems of the contemporary period. Ensuring that your research successfully tackles pertinent issues and placing it in a current context requires an awareness of modern theory and practice.

11.5 What Are the Study's Structure and Design?

Research design is the general approach you decide to use to logically and coherently combine the many parts of your research. It has an analysis measurement and data collecting chart. Effective solution of the research issue is guaranteed by a sound research design.

The framework of a research describes the organisation of the study and how the theoretical and conceptual elements will direct the research process. It defines the variables explains the connections between them and describes how to test these connections.

11.6 What Is Methodology?

Methodology is the methodical approach to carrying out research. It covers data collecting and analysis procedures methodologies and approaches.

11.7 Qualitative Method?

The purpose of qualitative approaches is to grasp things from a comprehensive viewpoint. Often this entails gathering non-numerical information to comprehend ideas viewpoints or experiences.

11.8 Interviews and the Varieties of Them

- A structured interview proceeds according to a predefined series of questions.
- Semi-structured interview: Replies are free to vary but a guideline is followed.
- Unstructured interviews are informal conversational interviews without a predefined question list.

11.9 Method of Quantitative

In quantitative approaches, patterns test hypotheses and forecasts are found by gathering and analysing numerical data.

11.10 What Are Surveys and Questionnaires?

Self-administered surveys with structural and semi-structural components:

- Predetermined answers to set questions make up structured questionnaires.
- Open-ended questions on semi-structured questionnaires provide more in-depth answers.
- Self-completed questionnaires: the responders fill them out on their own time apart from the researcher.

11.11 Mixed?

Mixing quantitative and qualitative approaches leverages the strengths of each and provides a more comprehensive view of the research question.

11.12 What Are Structure Semi-Structure and Self-Administrative Questionnaires?

Structured semi-structured and self-administered questionnaires each have unique attributes that influence their utility in data collection:

- Structured Questionnaires: These contain pre-determined questions and answers, ensuring consistency in responses and simplifying data analysis.
- Semi-Structured Questionnaires: While they include some structured questions, they also allow for open-ended responses, providing richer qualitative data.
- Self-Administered Questionnaires: Respondents complete these independently, reducing interviewer bias and allowing for a larger geographic reach.

11.13 Why Need Result and Discussion?

Results and discussion are crucial components of any research study. They provide a clear presentation of the findings and interpret their implications:

- Results: This section presents the data collected during the research in an organised manner, often using tables, graphs, and statistical analyses.
- Discussion: This section interprets the results, explaining their significance, implications, and how they fit into the broader context of the research field.

11.14 Future Research

Future research in business analytics and Python should focus on several key areas to ensure continued advancement and relevance. These areas include:

1. Integration of AI and Machine Learning
2. Big Data Analytics
3. Real-time Analytics
4. Data Privacy and Security
5. Visualisation Techniques
6. Industry-specific Solutions
7. Ethical AI and Fairness
8. Edge Computing and IoT
9. Education and Training
10. Collaboration and Open Science

11.15 Keeping Up Your Education

Continuous learning and education are essential in the rapidly evolving field of business analytics. To stay ahead of the curve and maintain your expertise, consider the following strategies:

- Online Courses and Certifications
- Reading Research Papers and Books
- Attending Conferences and Workshops
- Joining Professional Organisations
- Practical Experience
- Staying Updated with Technology
- Mentorship and Networking
- Continuous Skill Development

Reference

Teixeira, T., & Picinin, C. T. (2024). University rankings: Proposal for a future research agenda through a systematic literature review. *Sustainability*, *16*(7), 3043.

Chapter 12
Python's Impact on AI and Medicine

12.1 Introduction

AI and medicine mix as Python and AI improve diagnostics, medicinal research, and healthcare (Fouladvand et al., 2023). AI-driven medical apps need adaptability, usability, and a big library (Shi et al., 2023). This chapter discusses Python's impact on clinical decision support systems, medical imaging, personalised medicine, robotics, and more. Over the decades, medical AI has changed healthcare. AI has changed medical diagnosis, treatment, drug development, and patient care (Khadka et al., 2024). Python was crucial to the AI revolution due to its simplicity, versatility, and many specialist libraries. AI and health would have failed without Python's robust and accessible infrastructure (Qureshi et al., 2024). Healthcare's future depends on Python's machine learning, deep learning, natural language processing, and computer vision capabilities. Healthcare personnel face challenges as diagnostic imaging, clinical records, genetic sequencing, and real-time patient monitoring technology advance. Traditional data analysis and decision-making methods struggle with large, heterogeneous datasets (Yang et al., 2024). Python-based AI analyses these data sources quickly and accurately. They assist doctors in data-driven decision-making to enhance patient outcomes, eliminate medical errors, and streamline healthcare (Osuala et al., 2023).

12.1.1 Medical AI Uses Python

Python is popular in AI and healthcare due to its simplicity and integration (Zia et al., 2022). Python's simple syntax helps healthcare facilities innovate and iterate quickly. Open-source AI libraries like TensorFlow, PyTorch, Scikit-learn, Keras, Pandas, and others have arisen around the language (Lavrova et al., 2023). A little coding lets developers and data scientists build complex healthcare AI models. Medical image processing, predictive analytics, and personalised medicine use TensorFlow and PyTorch neural networks. Pandas and NumPy handle massive medical data. Python dominates NLP systems that analyse unstructured medical texts like clinical notes and research papers. Robotic surgery and rehabilitation show Python's AI-driven medical solutions' versatility (Harbi & George, 2024).

12.1.2 AI in Medicine: A Paradigm Shift

Medical AI overwhelms efficiency. Disease diagnosis, treatment, and care are evolving with Python-powered AI (Chanthati, 2024). Machine learning models can identify medical data patterns and linkages that clinicians cannot. AI systems can diagnose cancer from radiographs, predict disease progression, and suggest treatments based on genetic and clinical data for early detection (Williams et al., 2018). Medical imaging is one of the most exciting AI applications in medicine since deep learning models can accurately evaluate X-rays, MRIs, CT scans, and other diagnostic images. Python-based AI systems can spot tiny anomalies doctors miss, enhancing diagnostic confidence. These aid decision-making and reduce misdiagnosis, improving patient outcomes (Victoria et al., 2024). Python-based AI has advanced tailored medicine beyond imaging. Genetic profiles and other health data can help AI systems tailor cancer treatments (Nicholas et al., 2024). This personalised approach boosts treatment efficacy and decreases side effects, which is a major healthcare advancement (Kim et al., 2024).

12.1.3 AI-Based Medical Discovery

Python and AI in drug development are revolutionising pharma. Traditional drug discovery takes years and billions (Akhlaghi et al., 2024). Python-based AI algorithms mimic and anticipate new chemical compound-biological target interactions, speeding drug candidate identification. Artificial intelligence algorithms can predict medicine molecule efficacy in treating specific diseases by assessing massive chemical structures and biological data, reducing clinical trials, and speeding up patient treatment (Busch et al., 2024).

Biomedical researchers use Python to modify genetic and protein data, uncover new therapeutic targets, and model biological processes (Siino, 2024). Python-based AI models can analyse these enormous data sets to find unknown genetic variance-disease outcome correlations, improving treatments and possibly curing diseases.

12.1 Introduction

12.1.4 Ethical Implications and Challenges of AI in Medicine

Python-powered AI could transform medicine, but ethics remain a concern. Healthcare decision-making with AI issues accountability, openness, and impartiality. They test AI systems, especially diagnosis and treatment recommendation systems, for reliability and interpretability (Çubukçu et al., 2024). Medical AI models must be constructed on high-quality data and clinically tested to reduce mortality. High medical AI use creates data privacy and security risks (Li et al., 2024). AI healthcare systems pose concerns about collecting, keeping, and exploiting sensitive medical data. Healthcare Python developers must understand these issues, protect patient data, and build ethical AI models.

12.1.5 The Future of Python in AI/Medicine

Python medical AI is promising. Federated Learning and Forcement Learning should improve healthcare AI. Federated learning enables AI models to learn from decentralised data and could improve patient privacy (Li et al., 2024). Dynamics-based reinforcement learning aids real-time surgery and emergency care decisions. AI-driven healthcare needs Python's big library and community. After AI becomes more mainstream, Python will improve healthcare outcomes, clinical procedures, and health knowledge. Python shaped AI and medicine. Simple and powerful libraries and frameworks make it the healthcare AI language of choice. Python leads the AI revolution in medicine by improving diagnostics, drug discovery, and tailored treatment. Python will maximise AI's impact on patient care and outcomes as healthcare digitises.

12.1.6 Problem Statement: The Need to Study Python's Impact on AI and Medicine

AI could improve healthcare by transforming many sectors. AI improves diagnosis, therapy, drug development, and care (Allam et al., 2024). Despite its prominence in medicine, AI presents considerable barriers to widespread adoption and use. Understanding AI tools and technologies is essential for improving technical, ethical, and model (Rath et al., 2024). Python's simplicity, versatility, and machine learning, deep learning, and data analysis packages make it ideal for AI development.

12.1.7 Increasing Medical Data Complexity

Medical data is complex; therefore, studying Python's impact on AI and health is vital. Electronic health records, genetic sequencing, wearable health devices, and advanced imaging have inundated doctors with data (Javaid et al., 2024). Traditional big data analysis and insight methods are becoming harder. AI, especially deep learning models, can automate data processing and analysis to improve doctor decisions. Python is needed for big data management and AI machine learning. Despite its potential, healthcare has not adopted AI. They are lacking AI development tools and capabilities. Many healthcare organisations struggle to adopt AI-driven solutions due to the complexity of AI programming language. Python's easy syntax and frameworks like TensorFlow, Keras, and Scikit-learn help healthcare professionals and corporations build AI (Evans & Snead, 2024). Understanding how Python assists healthcare AI applications is essential to gaining acceptance and preparing healthcare personnel to exploit AI's full potential.

12.1.8 Correct Diagnosis and Tailored Treatment

In modern medicine, diagnostic and therapeutic errors delay care and reduce efficacy. Python-based AI models can identify diseases using medical imaging, predict outcomes, and customise therapies. Sometimes, AI algorithms can detect radiological cancers better than humans. For early intervention and customised treatment, predictive analytics can forecast illness (Silva et al., 2024). The report does not explain how Python enhances AI and medicine. Python has been used to build various AI tools, but understanding how to enhance and adapt them to medical domains is needed. Python's diagnosis accuracy and therapeutic customisation help healthcare organisations leverage AI.

12.1.9 AI Medicine Ethics and Practice

AI in healthcare presents transparency, accountability, and data privacy problems. AI systems, especially machine learning-based ones, are 'black boxes', making healthcare decisions difficult (Restrepo et al., 2024). AI systems can be untrustworthy for life-or-death healthcare decisions without openness. Training AI algorithms on biassed datasets may worsen healthcare disparities. Python packages for explainable AI (XAI), machine learning fairness, and safe data processing can address these ethical and practical challenges (Visan & Negut, 2024). These Python tools have not been proven to lessen medical AI's ethical hazards. Python can help solve ethical programming and model generation concerns in healthcare AI development, ensuring dependable and successful systems.

12.1.10 Affordable, Efficient Healthcare Is Essential

Healthcare systems worldwide must improve patient outcomes and minimise costs. Python-powered AI can automate tedious tasks, remove diagnostic errors, and enable personalised treatment plans that enhance healthcare at lower costs (Pacheco et al., 2024). AI-automated massive data set processing may save healthcare professionals time. AI models improve patient scheduling and resource distribution, improving hospital efficiency. Despite their potential benefits, the economic influence of Python-based AI solutions on healthcare systems has not been studied. The literature on how AI might enhance clinical outcomes is expanding, but Python's role in making AI models more efficient, cost-effective, and scalable is understudied. Python's impact on AI and medicine can improve healthcare firms' AI ROI and patient care.

12.2 Bridging the Gap Between AI Research and Clinical Application

Medical AI research and use are far off. Many academic and experimental AI models struggle to enter clinical practice due to scalability, healthcare system integration, and regulatory approval issues.

1. Python's research-practice ecosystem creates hospital-ready AI solutions. Python-based AI solutions in healthcare are still difficult to implement, limiting their potential. Healthcare providers and AI developers must collaborate to establish clinician-specific AI models. Python can improve patient care by bridging AI and medicine. Python-driven AI development challenges and benefits doctors. AI can improve diagnosis, treatment, and healthcare systems but faces technical, ethical, and practical hurdles. Python's impact on medical AI must be properly researched to overcome these challenges and integrate AI into healthcare to improve patient outcomes. Addressing these issues will improve AI systems and assist healthcare workers in providing the best care in an information-driven culture.
2. Python's AI Development Importance. Python dominates AI development since it has TensorFlow, Keras, PyTorch, and Scikit-learn. These libraries' pre-built components simplify machine learning and deep learning. The simple syntax of Python enables healthcare practitioners, data scientists, and AI engineers to communicate.

12.2.1 Python Is Ideal for Medical AI

Python speeds up development, data analysis, visualisation, and machine learning model deployment. Pandas, Numpy, and SciPy help process medical data. Deep neural networks are needed for medical image processing, diagnosis, and prediction. Python frameworks PyTorch and Keras are popular for developing them.

12.3 Applications of Python and AI in Medicine

12.3.1 Imaging, Diagnosis

AI, particularly deep learning, has transformed medical imaging. Python and AI photo processing and classification speed up and improve disease diagnosis. TensorFlow or PyTorch CNNs analyse X-rays, MRIs, CT scans, and histopathology slides. These models detect tumours, fractures, and infections better than humans.

Python-powered mammography AI finds early cancer.

MRI diagnoses brain tumours and neurological disorders.

Diabetic retinopathy classification by retinal scans prevents blindness.

Pre-processing and segmenting medical images with OpenCV and Scikit-image finds regions of interest.

12.3.2 Predictive Analytics, Personalised Medicine

AI predicts future results using historical data, improving healthcare. Pandas and Dask can manage massive data sets, making Python excellent for medical predictive analytics. SVMs, Gradient Boosting, and Random Forest predict patient outcomes, hospital readmissions, disease outbreaks, and drug efficacy. Python has also improved personalised medicine, where AI models prescribe treatments based on genetics, lifestyle, and medical history. Genetic profiles affect cancer treatment, thus, customised drugs are essential. Genetic analysis, bioinformatics, and personalised therapy are offered by BioPython and PyCaret.

12.3.3 Healthcare NLP

Medical data, research articles, and clinical notes require NLP, a subset of AI that reads and evaluates human language. Unstructured text extraction techniques are often built with Python NLP tools like NLTK, SpaCy, and Hugging Face Transformers. Medicine uses NLP to enter clinical notes and extract structured data for study automatically.

Medical research: Discovering new trends, therapies, and fields via publications and trials.

12.5 Python's AI/Health Future

Patients may schedule appointments, check symptoms, and ask enquiries with Python-powered chatbots and virtual assistants.

12.3.4 AI-Driven Drug Discovery

Python-powered machine learning predicts drug molecule efficacy in AI-driven drug development. AI algorithms can find drugs faster utilising chemical structures, genetic data, and medical knowledge.

Python modules like RDKit for chemical informatics and TensorFlow for deep learning model molecular characteristics and pharmacological interactions. AI models predict drug-target protein interactions, saving lab time and money.

12.3.5 Robotics and Python in Medicine

Surgical and assistive robots use Python. AI-powered surgical robots are precise. Python with ROS (Robot Operating System) libraries program robot arms and control mechanisms and develop AI algorithms to improve robotic systems. Python creates surgical and mobility-impaired rehab robots. Robots improve recovery by personalising treatment.

12.4 Ethics and Issues

Python and AI have transformed medicine but raised ethical questions. AI-driven healthcare decisions cause accountability, transparency, and bias issues. Python developers and data scientists handling sensitive medical data must guarantee their AI models are ethical, objective, and explainable. Patient data privacy and anonymisation for AI algorithm training are challenges.

Lessen AI model bias from uneven or missing training data. Regulation and approval. Regulations may hinder medical AI system adoption.

12.5 Python's AI/Health Future

Python will thrive in AI medicine as reinforcement learning, machine learning, and quantum computing improve. Python will likely remain the healthcare AI language of choice because to its increasing community and healthcare-specific modules and capabilities. Reinforcement learning and real-time feedback will adjust AI models to clinical situations.

Federated Learning: Python-powered tool trains AI models with distributed data for privacy and resilience. Python produces healthcare quantum algorithms that can improve medication discovery and therapy.

12.6 Conclusion

Python affected medical AI. Its convenience and large library appeal to AI engineers, data scientists, and healthcare professionals. Drug discovery, tailored treatment, and diagnosis are evolving with Python-powered AI. Python will lead AI advances that improve patient outcomes, lower costs, and globalise healthcare. Medical AI will transform the twenty-first century. Python's simplicity, wide choice of libraries, and machine learning, data analysis, and automation applications enable these developments. In 'Python's Impact on Artificial Intelligence and Medicine', Python is crucial to AI innovation in medicine at the intersection of technology and healthcare. Doctors and AI researchers can utilise TensorFlow, Keras, Scikit-learn, and PyTorch to design strong algorithms for diagnostic and predictive analytics, drug creation, and customised treatments. Python's pros, disadvantages, and prospects in AI research and clinical practice are discussed. Python addresses healthcare efficiency, diagnostic errors, and therapy personalisation. Python democratises AI development, making healthcare breakthroughs easier. Python's ability to adapt to fast-changing healthcare needs deserves further study in medical AI.

Consequences

The chapter's findings impact doctors, AI developers, policymakers, and healthcare providers. Discovery has major effects. Python-based AI improves healthcare operations and patient care. Python-based AI can automate healthcare picture processing, data management, and administration. Correct diagnosis, timely treatment, and resource efficiency help hospitals.

1. For AI Researchers and Developers: Python's versatility and rising application in healthcare AI research. It stresses medical Python-based AI tool research. Python's success in healthcare suggests medical AI model makers should prioritise integration, scalability, and data protection for reliability.
2. For Policymakers and Regulations: Python facilitates medical AI tool creation, therefore regulations must react to ensure safe, ethical, and transparent AI systems. Healthcare AI blunders can kill, as shown in this chapter. Politicians should encourage AI-driven justice and innovation.
3. Python-based AI models speed up patient diagnosis and treatment. The chapter recommends medical professionals study Python and AI basics to collaborate with AI researchers and technologists. Understanding Python's role in AI-assisted diagnosis and therapy can help doctors make informed decisions as AI becomes more widespread in healthcare.

12.6 Conclusion

12.6.1 Importance

Python's AI research impacts medicine. Python helps medical research, patient outcomes, and operational efficiency in healthcare AI. These regions benefit from Python:

1. Democratising AI Development: Python's simplicity and popularity make AI in medicine easier for smaller hospitals to build and use. AI democratisation improves regional and economic healthcare fairness by increasing practitioner access.
2. Enabling Precision Medicine: Python-based AI models improve medical care by personalising it. Python algorithms improve precision medicine diagnosis and therapy by integrating genetic, environmental, and lifestyle factors. Avoiding unnecessary treatments and interventions improves patient outcomes and decreases healthcare costs with personalised care.
3. Healthcare Innovation Catalyst: Python is promising. Real-time patient monitoring, robotic surgery, and AI-driven drug development will use Python as AI progresses. Python will affect future healthcare tools and systems, claims the chapter.
4. Ethics and Privacy: Healthcare AI lacks fairness, transparency, and privacy. Python's explainable AI and data privacy libraries enable accurate, transparent models, overcoming ethical issues and developing healthcare professionals' and patients' AI trust. AI must be transparent to be widely used in sensitive medical contexts.
5. Global Health Impact: Finally, Python's AI and medicine advances global health. Python can process massive healthcare data from diverse populations to generate more accurate and representative AI models that eliminate regional health inequities. AI may be adapted to diverse healthcare systems, making it universal.

Python's Impact on AI and Medicine finishes with a comprehensive look at AI's healthcare impact. Python's scalability, affordability, and variety in handling crucial healthcare concerns make it essential for AI-based medicine. Python lets doctors diagnose, modify, and improve treatment with AI.

Python-based AI tool research is crucial for medicinal, technological, and legal reasons. Python improves systems and prepares for global medical care. Python is essential to AI and, health advances, and patient outcomes. As healthcare grows, Python will enable AI-driven solutions to maximise patient, practitioner, and enterprise benefits.

References

Akhlaghi, H., Freeman, S., Vari, C., McKenna, B., Braitberg, G., Karro, J., & Tahayori, B. (2024). Machine learning in clinical practice: Evaluation of an artificial intelligence tool after implementation. *Emergency Medicine Australasia, 36*(1), 118–124.

Allam, A. H., Eltewacy, N. K., Alabdallat, Y. J., Owais, T. A., Salman, S., & Ebada, M. A. (2024). Knowledge, attitude, and perception of Arab medical students towards artificial intelligence in medicine and radiology: A multi-national cross-sectional study. *European Radiology, 34*(7), 1–14.

Busch, F., Hoffmann, L., Truhn, D., Palaian, S., Alomar, M., Shpati, K., Makowski, M. R., Bressem, K. K., & Adams, L. C. (2024). International pharmacy students' perceptions towards artificial intelligence in medicine—A multinational, multicentre cross-sectional study. *British Journal of Clinical Pharmacology, 90*(3), 649–661.

Chanthati, S. R. (2024). Second version on a centralized approach to reducing burnouts in the IT industry using work pattern monitoring using artificial intelligence using MongoDB Atlas and Python. *World Journal of Advanced Engineering Technology and Sciences, 13*(1), 187–228.

Çubukçu, H. C., Topcu, D. İ, & Yenice, S. (2024). Machine learning-based clinical decision support using laboratory data. *Clinical Chemistry and Laboratory Medicine (CCLM), 62*(5), 793–823.

Evans, H., & Snead, D. (2024). Understanding the errors made by artificial intelligence algorithms in histopathology in terms of patient impact. *NPJ Digital Medicine, 7*(1), 89.

Fouladvand, S., Pierson, E., Jankovic, I., Ouyang, D., Chen, J. H., & Daneshjou, R. (2023). Session introduction: Artificial intelligence in clinical medicine: generative and interactive systems at the human-machine interface. In Pacific Symposium on Biocomputing 2024.

Harbi, M. R., & George, L. E. (2024). Evaluation of the classification of medical and laboratory services using a python algorithm and physical statistically. In AIP Conference Proceedings.

Javaid, A., Baviriseaty, S., Javaid, R., Zirikly, A., Kukreja, H., Kim, C. H., Blaha, M. J., Blumenthal, R. S., Martin, S. S., & Marvel, F. A. (2024). Trends in glucagon-like peptide-1 receptor agonist social media posts using artificial intelligence. *JACC: Advances, 3*(9_Part_2), 101182.

Khadka, R., Lind, P. G., Yazidi, A., & Belhadi, A. (2024). DREAMS: A python framework to train deep learning models with model card reporting for medical and health applications. arXiv preprint arXiv:2409.17815.

Kim, S., Kazmierski, M., Qu, K., Peoples, J., Nakano, M., Ramanathan, V., Marsilla, J., Welch, M., Simpson, A., & Haibe-Kains, B. (2024). Med-ImageTools: An open-source Python package for robust data processing pipelines and curating medical imaging data. *F1000Research, 12*, 118.

Lavrova, E., Primakov, S., Salahuddin, Z., Beuque, M., Verstappen, D., Woodruff, H. C., & Lambin, P. (2023). Precision-medicine-toolbox: An open-source python package for the quantitative medical image analysis. *Software Impacts, 16*, 100508.

Li, C., Ye, G., Jiang, Y., Wang, Z., Yu, H., & Yang, M. (2024). Artificial Intelligence in battling infectious diseases: A transformative role. *Journal of Medical Virology, 96*(1), e29355.

Nicholas, I., Kuo, H., Perez-Concha, O., Hanly, M., Mnatzaganian, E., Hao, B., Di Sipio, M., Yu, G., Vanjara, J., & Valerie, I. C. (2024). Enriching data science and health care education: Application and impact of synthetic data sets through the health gym project. *JMIR Medical Education, 10*(1), e51388.

Osuala, R., Skorupko, G., Lazrak, N., Garrucho, L., García, E., Joshi, S., Jouide, S., Rutherford, M., Prior, F., & Kushibar, K. (2023). Medigan: A Python library of pretrained generative models for medical image synthesis. *Journal of Medical Imaging, 10*(6), 061403–061403.

Pacheco, V. M. G., Paiva, J. P. Q., Furriel, B. C. R. S., Santos, P. V., Ferreira Junior, J. R., Reis, M. R. C., Tornieri, D., Ribeiro, G. A. S., Silva, L. O., & Nogueira, S. A. (2024). Pilot deployment of a cloud-based universal medical image repository in a large public health system: A protocol study. *PLoS ONE, 19*(8), e0307022.

Qureshi, H., Shah, Z., Raja, M. A. Z., Alshahrani, M. Y., Khan, W. A., & Shoaib, M. (2024). Machine learning investigation of tuberculosis with medicine immunity impact. *Diagnostic Microbiology and Infectious Disease, 110*(3), 116472.

References

Rath, K. C., Khang, A., Rath, S. K., Satapathy, N., Satapathy, S. K., & Kar, S. (2024). Artificial intelligence (AI)-enabled technology in medicine-advancing holistic healthcare monitoring and control systems. In *Computer vision and AI-integrated IoT technologies in the medical ecosystem* (pp. 87–108). CRC Press.

Restrepo, D., Quion, J. M., Do Carmo Novaes, F., Azevedo Costa, I. D., Vasquez, C., Bautista, A. N., Quiminiano, E., Lim, P. A., Mwavu, R., & Celi, L. A. (2024). Ophthalmology optical coherence tomography databases for artificial intelligence algorithm: A review. *Seminars in Ophthalmology.*

Shi, J., Bendig, D., Vollmar, H. C., & Rasche, P. (2023). Mapping the bibliometrics landscape of AI in medicine: Methodological study. *Journal of Medical Internet Research, 25*, e45815.

Siino, M. (2024). T5-medical at semeval-2024 task 2: Using t5 medical embedding for natural language inference on clinical trial data. In Proceedings of the 18th International Workshop on Semantic Evaluation (SemEval-2024).

Silva, L. O. D., Silva, M. C. B. D., Ribeiro, G. A. S., Camargo, T. F. O. D., Santos, P. V. D., Mendes, G. D. S., Paiva, J. P. Q. D., Soares, A. D. S., Reis, M. R. D. C., & Loureiro, R. M. (2024). Artificial intelligence-based pulmonary embolism classification: Development and validation using real-world data. *PLoS One, 19*(8), e0305839.

Victoria, A. H., Tiwari, R. S., & Ghulam, A. K. (2024). Libraries for Explainable Artificial Intelligence (EXAI): Python. In *Explainable AI (XAI) for sustainable development* (pp. 211–232). Chapman and Hall/CRC.

Visan, A. I., & Negut, I. (2024). Integrating artificial intelligence for drug discovery in the context of revolutionizing drug delivery. *Life, 14*(2), 233.

Williams, A. M., Liu, Y., Regner, K. R., Jotterand, F., Liu, P., & Liang, M. (2018). Artificial intelligence, physiological genomics, and precision medicine. *Physiological Genomics, 50*(4), 237–243.

Yang, R., Zeng, Q., You, K., Qiao, Y., Huang, L., Hsieh, C.-C., Rosand, B., Goldwasser, J., Dave, A., & Keenan, T. (2024). Ascle—A Python natural language processing toolkit for medical text generation: Development and evaluation study. *Journal of Medical Internet Research, 26*, e60601.

Zia, A., Aziz, M., Popa, I., Khan, S. A., Hamedani, A. F., & Asif, A. R. (2022). Artificial intelligence-based medical data mining. *Journal of Personalized Medicine, 12*(9), 1359.

Chapter 13
Web-Based Food Recommendation

13.1 Introduction

Technological advancement has enabled Internet users to perform numerous tasks. The majority of users use it for communicating with others, searching for information, and other purposes. The Internet also enables online sales and purchases of goods and services, including food delivery or ordering food online (Ergezer & Leblebicioğlu, 2016). E-commerce is on the rise as the number of internet users increases rapidly (Clement & Hunt, 2019). There are numerous benefits for online consumers. For instance, they can buy products or services online at any time and in any location (Anastasiadou et al., 2019). However, it may result in information overload, making it difficult for consumers to decide which product to purchase (Pederson, 2008).

To solve this problem, Recommendation Systems (RSs) can be used (Häubl & Trifts, 2000). Due to the accessible amount of data online, consumers have a variety of choices of products, services, and restaurants. Therefore, recommendation systems can not only save consumers time and money but also assist them in identifying their precise needs (Gupta et al., 2021). A recommendation system is a software programme that allows users to make personalised selections from among a vast number of available possibilities. This is accomplished by either covertly or overtly inquiring about the user's preference for a certain product, service, or vendor (Li & Karahanna, 2015). RSs have improved in their ability to accurately predict the preferences of customers as a direct result of the ongoing development of web-based technology. One example of a recommendation system that we have seen in our life is music and media platforms such as YouTube Music, Spotify, and iTunes that are

---

Supplementary Information The online version contains supplementary material available at https://doi.org/10.1007/978-981-96-8291-1_13.

constantly recommending songs to consumers based on their past choices and preferences. The overarching concept of recommendations is being maintained throughout this project, which includes the development of a web-based food recommendation system.

13.2 Problem Statement

Food selection is a complex habit that is influenced by a number of interconnected elements such as taste, monetary constraints, health concerns, and many more (Shipman, 2020). People were frequently unable to decide what to eat during this decade, a recurring occurrence. The diversity of accessible restaurants and cuisines may be one of the key reasons. When there are too many culinary options, it is simple to become overwhelmed. Because your brain is telling you to try anything and everything. This makes selecting the correct food more challenging, yet you will continue to fight for several minutes. Consequently, people spend more time contemplating where to eat than actually eating.

13.3 Research Question

The purpose of this project is to create a web-based food recommendation system that will aid in resolving the problem. The first factor we included in our website is mood as people make meal choices based on their moods and the feelings that certain foods elicit. Moreover, because various people have varied tastes, food category preferences were also included. In addition, a person's income will also influence their food choices, as it may alter their budget and level of spending. Therefore, our website provides restaurant recommendations depending on the user's mood, cuisine category choices, and budget. And the problem will be solved by the online web-based food recommendation system. Therefore, it could reduce the time needed to decide what to eat at mealtimes. Additionally, those who lack decisiveness may find this useful and convenient. To conclude, the research objectives of our project are:

- To provide food recommendation based on ones' mood, food category preferences, and budget
- To help people who are indecisive on what to eat
- To help people to save time while deciding what to eat

13.4 Research Objective

1. What types of methods and techniques have been applied to build a food recommendation system?
2. How can these food recommendation systems be classified based on the consumer decision-making process?
3. How do consumer choices on the factors (mood, food category preferences) affect the results of food recommendation?

13.5 Domain (Introduction)

13.5.1 Mood

A mood is a usually consistent emotional state that is frequently defined as pleasant or sad. A person's mood is sometimes referred to as their internal emotional state, which determines how they express themselves externally. Moods are wider and less concentrated than emotions, which are frequently more powerful and focused. Furthermore, they are not usually triggered by a single occurrence or experience. However, a lot of variables, such as hunger, weather, stress, food, weariness, and general health, may influence them, and mood may also influence all of the variables. As a result, food and mood can occasionally coexist. People choose meals based on their moods and the emotions that particular foods elicit. So, it can explain that mood is one of the major factors that would influence a person's attitude or preference towards their eating behaviour.

According to Shipman (2020), the research study is compatible with the other studies that show, buying habits for both traditional and European foods are influenced by one's mood. This is because college students usually have high levels of stress, depression, anxiety, and hopeless due to their environments and daily lifestyle. It was observed that people who take sweet, sour, and salty tastes food are expressed less 'happy' emotions while people who choose food with a bitter taste expressed lower 'calm' and 'contempt' emotions. Besides, people who express with an higher 'sad' and lower 'contempt' expressions were observed that they prefer a neutral taste. As a result, we may draw the conclusion that both food and mood can impact each other.

13.5.2 Food Category Choice

There are several food category options given in our daily lives. However, we recognise that a person's mood might influence their eating choices. According to Leeds et al. (2020) research, brain activity is linked to mood, and behaviour has been linked to nutrition and food choices. They stated that a complex connection of brain and gut activity is hypothesised to operate as a gateway for potential effects on mood, cognitive, and emotional processes, such as tryptophan and gut flora, excess sugar and fat consumption, nutrient function, and inflammatory responses. Thus, sugar and fat eating may temporarily enhance the endogenous-opioid receptor system and dopamine pathways in order to relieve stress and negative mood state. Immediate mood improvement from appetising meals might generate recurring and habitual coping mechanisms for mood management in the post-prandial phase (Leeds et al., 2020). Observational studies, cross-sectional data, and longitudinal research all point to a correlation between consuming fruits and vegetables and improving mental health outcomes. High sugar and fat consumption has been associated to depression, whereas Mediterranean pattern diets have been connected to improved long-term mental health conditions via reductions in inflammation and oxidative stress (Leeds et al., 2020). A plethora of research has found that consuming fruits and vegetables improves short-term well-being and positive affect, as well as improving long-term mental health, while other trials demonstrate a causal association between well-being and fruit and vegetable intake (Leeds et al., 2020).

13.5.3 Price

When deciding between numerous food alternatives, price is a crucial factor, especially for people with low-income levels. People with lower-income levels have been proven to be more aware of price and value than those with higher income levels. In other words, low-income levels are significantly more influenced by the cost of food while making food purchases. As people who have low-income levels cannot afford certain high price food such as Japanese food, Korean food, etc. Another intriguing finding is that women with dietary limitations are less sensitive to pricing than those without constraints. Recent studies on altering eating habits have led to the development of many economic ideas, such as lowering the cost of food items in order to lower prices (Simone, 2003). Food pricing and promotional campaigns are thus an important aspect of the eating environment. Recent research has used economic theory to change people's eating habits (Simone, 2003). Price reduction tactics encourage the consumption of specific foods by decreasing their real cost to other food options. For instance, price reductions of healthy food were made possible by corporate cooperation as a public health strategy to encourage consumption (Shipman, 2020).

13.6 Predictive Model

There is much research that was carried out where different types of models were built to recommend food and restaurants based on different types of factors. These factors include past orders (content-based filtering), ratings (collaborative filtering), location, nutrition, and many more.

In an article by Sawant and Pai (2015), a Yelp food recommendation system based on restaurant reviews from customers was suggested. The algorithm used in this journal to recommend eateries based on consumer preferences and the location was K-nearest neighbour clustering. Petrusel and Limboi (2019) had developed a model using sentiment analysis which can propose a restaurant based on both positive and negative customer feedback. Besides, a study was conducted by Maia and Ferreira (2018) to recommend restaurants and meals based on reviews from prior customers. Additionally, a food recommendation system based on nutrition and calories was introduced by Toledo et al. (2019) where the diets of the individuals were solely focused on, with no further considerations for taste or renowned restaurant food.

However, none of the above-mentioned research developed a model for recommending food based on a customer's mood. An individual's mood is extremely important when ordering meals because it influences many of our decisions, including what to eat. On our website, users must provide their basic personal information to register an account. Then, users must choose their mood, preferred food category and budget after making an account because that will determine what food stalls and restaurants are recommended to them. HyperText Markup Language HTML and PHP HyperText Pre-processor (PHP) are used to create our website while NLTK is used for building our predictive model.

13.7 Tools and Techniques

Python will be used to clean the extracted raw data and perform machine learning while Tableau is used to visualise the food choices data which allows us to spot trends and patterns. The front end (user interface) of the web page food recommendation system will be created using HTML and PHP in Visual Code Studio.

13.7.1 Python

Machine learning consists of algorithms that teach computers to carry out routine tasks in a natural and effortless manner (Haffner, 2016). Python will be utilised for machine learning because it is a simple, elegant language with a clear syntax that makes text manipulation and processing relatively simple. Additionally, a sizable development community contributes to the accessibility of a variety of documentation. Python is regarded as one of the programming languages that has developed the fastest in recent years. It is especially suited for rapid application development because of its high-level built-in data structures, dynamic typing, and dynamic binding. Additionally, it serves as a scripting language or 'glue language' to connect already existent components (Python, n.d.).

13.7.2 Python Libraries

Python coding includes using libraries, which are collections of built-in modules or functions that help to simplify and solve a variety of programming-related issues (van Rossum et al., 2017). To build a predictive model for our project, several libraries including Pandas and NLTK is required.

Pandas (Python data analysis) is the most well-known and commonly used Python library for data science. It has about 17,000 comments on GitHub and is frequently used for data analysis and cleaning. SciPy is particularly helpful for general data wrangling and cleaning, ETL (extract, transform, load) jobs for data transformation and storage (Saabith et al., 2021).

NLTK (Natural Language Toolkit) is one of the most popular Python libraries for natural language processing. Along with a collection of text processing libraries for categorization, tokenization, stemming, tagging, parsing, and semantic reasoning, wrappers for industrial-strength NLP libraries, and an active discussion forum. More than 50 corpora and lexical resources, including WordNet, are also easily accessible using NLTK's easy interfaces. It can perform secondary processing on the processing results in conjunction with the robust Python standard library and other third-party libraries (Li et al., 2019).

13.7.3 Tableau

Data visualisation is the use of computer-aided, interactive visual representations of abstract data (Card et al., 2007). This method enhances the usage of common data sources such as Excel spreadsheets by allowing users to discover trends and patterns that are not immediately apparent in a column of numbers (Datig & Whiting, 2018). In this project, Tableau will be utilised to display our dataset. Tableau is a visual analytics platform that allows consumers and organisations to maximise their data; transforming the way data is utilised to solve issues. Tableau is also widely considered as the most powerful, secure, and adaptable end-to-end analytics platform, including everything from data gathering to collaboration (Tableau, n.d.). Tableau is designed to enhance the analysis's flow and to increase the accessibility for individuals to data through visualisation. By using Tableau, information workers can create interactive visualisations via a desktop application that connects to an online data source or creates its own copy of data while working online. In addition, users can easily switch between these two versions (Wesley et al., 2011). Besides that, Tableau also assists companies in the deployment and scaling of a data-driven culture that delivers resilience and value with impactful outcomes (Tableau, n.d.). With the help of Tableau, it can assist in the creation of data that can be comprehended by experts at all levels of a business as well as allowing non-technical people to easily develop customised dashboards to the company.

13.7.4 HyperText Markup Language HTML

The HyperText Markup Language (HTML) is a set of markup symbols or codes that are inserted into a file to be displayed on the Internet. HTML is essentially a collection of short codes that are typed into a text file (Mughal, 2018). Web browsers are instructed by the tags on how to display the words and images on a webpage. For example, each individual piece of markup code that falls between '<' and '>' characters is referred to as an element, but many people refer to it as a tag (Cailliau & Ashman, 1999). Some elements are presented in pairs, indicating when a display effect will begin and end. The text has been saved as an HTML file, which can be viewed in a web browser. The browser reads the file and converts the text into a visible form as directed by the author's codes for visible rendering. HTML tags use markup to identify the text within them as a specific type of text. To draw attention to a specific word or phrase, markup text could take the form of bold or italic type (Burrows, 2000). HTML determines the structure of webpages. However, this structure is insufficient to create a visually appealing and interactive webpage. Thus, CSS and JavaScript can be used to make HTML more visually appealing and to add interactivity, respectively (Alnaqeib et al., 2010).

13.7.5 PHP HyperText Pre-Processor (PHP)

HyperText Pre-processor known as PHP is a popular general-purpose scripting language that can be embedded in HTML (Bala et al., 2022). PHP is a server-side scripting language that is open source and widely used by web developers (Siame & Kunda, 2017). PHP is mostly used to build web servers and it can be run both in the browser and from the command line. PHP is a server-side scripting language that is popular among web developers. It is also a general-purpose programming language that can be used to create a variety of projects, including graphical user interfaces. PHP scripts can range from simple one-line commands to complex functions (Favre & Jonsson, 2005). Some PHP-based websites generate nearly all their webpage content dynamically using a series of PHP scripts. While earlier versions of PHP were not object-oriented, PHP3 introduced class support, which included object attributes and methods (Siame & Kunda, 2017). Developers can create custom object libraries and import them into various PHP pages, just like in a compiled language.

13.8 BALC Framework

BALC framework consists of five steps such as identify domain, data extraction, data cleaning/preparation, predictive model, and visualisation/EDA. These steps will be further explained below:

13.8.1 Identify Domain

The main domain of our website is to help individuals who are unsure about where to eat and what to eat based on their current mood. Eating meals, as noted in the scientific review, may regularly influence a person's mood. People choose meals based on their moods and the emotions that particular foods elicit. As a result, mood is one of the important aspects that determine a person's attitude or inclination towards their eating behaviour. Choosing a meal based on an individual's tastes might improve tranquillity and affection while minimising wrath and anxiety. Furthermore, budget is an essential element that influences one's food habits, especially for low-income university students. People with lower-income levels have been proven to be more aware of price and value than those with higher income levels. Hence, mood and budget would be the factors that we would be considered when developing a 'Web-Based Food Recommendation System'.

13.8.2 Data Extraction

The primary dataset (Fig. 13.1), 'Food Choices Among College Students' which consists of 126 tuples (rows) and 61 attributes is extracted in CSV file format from **Kaggle**. The dataset is built from **126 United States (US) college students'** survey responses on **dietary habits, food choices, childhood favourites, and other information**. Due to the **categorical variables** in the dataset such as current diet and type of comfort food, the data is classified as qualitative data. In addition, the researcher of the dataset has assigned numerical codes or values to each type of response through the process of survey coding. This allows the feedback to be swiftly analysed to identify the most important insights or solutions.

A secondary dataset (Fig. 13.2) is added into our project in order to support the predictive model. The data is extracted from a **journal** with the title **'The Association among Emotions and Food Choices in First-Year College Students Using mobile-Ecological Momentary Assessments' by Ashurst et al.** and published by

13.8 BALC Framework

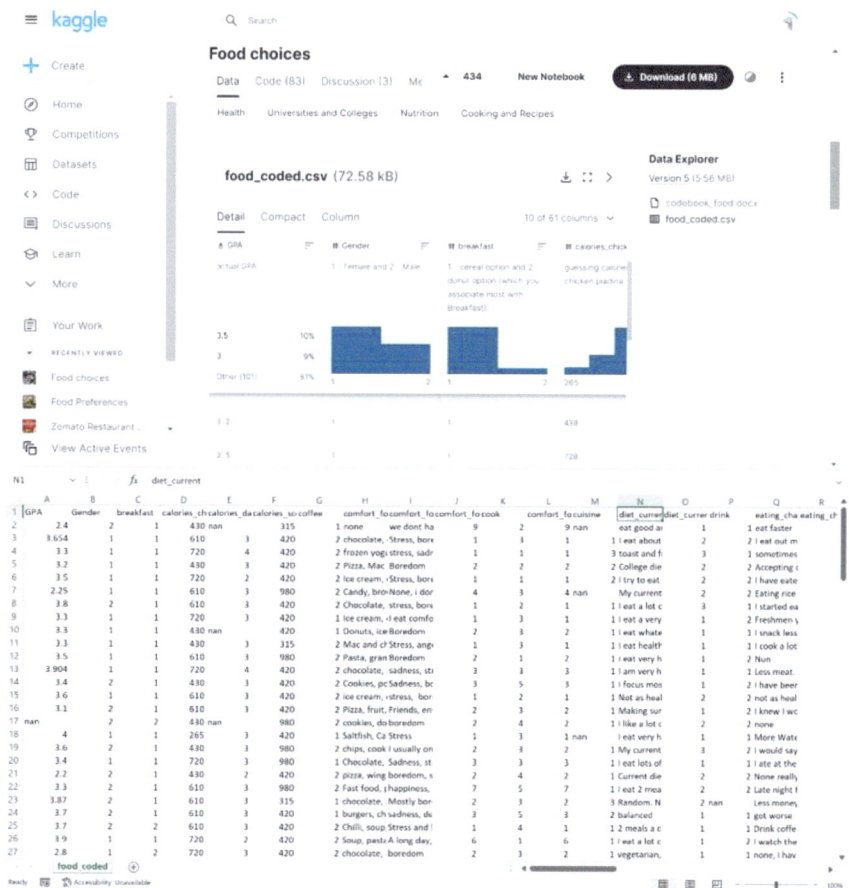

Fig. 13.1 Food choices dataset extracted from Kaggle

BMC Public Health in 2018. The table consists of 24 tuples (rows) and 4 attributes which were copied, pasted, and saved as CSV format in Microsoft Excel. The table shows the investigation on the **relationship between emotions and first-year college students' dietary preferences**. With mEMA (mobile Ecological Momentary Assessment) as the research methodology, the study carried out both within-person and between-person tests to determine the correlations between emotions and food choices. Positive and negative feelings had distinct connections to food choices while apathetic feelings were not connected to any (Ashurst et al., 2018).

Table 2 Generalized Estimating Equations Odds Ratios, (99% Confidence Intervals), and p-values for Between- and Within-Person Associations[a] of Emotions with Food Choices

Emotion	Food choice	Between-person		Within-person	
		OR (99% CI)	p-value	OR (99% CI)	p-value
Negative[b]	Sweets	1.5 (0.9, 2.5)	0.037	1.3 (0.8, 1.9)	0.168
	Salty snacks/fried foods	1.2 (0.6, 2.2)	0.552	1.0 (0.6, 1.5)	0.844
	Fruits/vegetables	1.3 (0.8, 2.2)	0.168	1.1 (0.8, 1.6)	0.298
	Pizza/fast food	1.2 (0.6, 2.2)	0.470	0.8 (0.5, 1.2)	0.134
	Sandwiches/wraps	1.0 (0.6, 1.7)	0.905	1.1 (0.7, 1.6)	0.551
	Meats/proteins	1.3 (0.8, 2.1)	0.184	**1.5 (1.0, 2.1)**	**0.004**
	Pasta/rice	1.3 (0.8, 2.3)	0.164	1.4 (1.0, 2.1)	0.022
	Cereals	1.6 (0.6, 4.1)	0.230	1.1 (0.6, 2.4)	0.627
Positive[b]	Sweets	1.5 (0.9, 2.4)	0.042	**1.7 (1.1, 2.6)**	**0.002**
	Salty snacks/fried foods	0.8 (0.5, 1.4)	0.383	1.5 (1.0, 2.2)	0.015
	Fruits/vegetables	1.5 (1.0, 2.4)	0.012	1.4 (1.0, 1.9)	0.012
	Pizza/fast food	0.8 (0.5, 1.3)	0.238	**0.6 (0.4, 1.0)**	**0.007**
	Sandwiches/wraps	1.0 (0.7, 1.6)	0.817	0.8 (0.5, 1.2)	0.130
	Meats/proteins	**1.8 (1.2, 2.8)**	**<0.001**	1.2 (0.8, 1.6)	0.222
	Pasta/rice	1.6 (1.0, 2.5)	0.013	1.0 (0.7, 1.5)	0.903
	Cereals	2.0 (0.8, 4.8)	0.052	1.0 (0.5, 1.9)	0.890
Apathetic[b]	Sweets	1.2 (0.6, 2.3)	0.398	1.3 (0.8, 2.2)	0.151
	Salty snacks/fried foods	2.0 (1.0, 3.9)	0.013	1.4 (0.9, 2.2)	0.076
	Fruits/vegetables	0.7 (0.4, 1.4)	0.190	1.0 (0.7, 1.5)	0.766
	Pizza/fast food	2.0 (1.0, 4.1)	0.017	0.8 (0.5, 1.4)	0.387
	Sandwiches/wraps	1.0 (0.5, 1.8)	0.862	0.7 (0.5, 1.2)	0.083
	Meats/proteins	0.7 (0.4, 1.3)	0.163	0.9 (0.6, 1.3)	0.364
	Pasta/rice	0.7 (0.4, 1.5)	0.274	0.8 (0.5, 1.2)	0.182
	Cereals	1.0 (0.3, 3.1)	0.967	1.6 (0.7, 3.7)	0.136

[a]Associations were adjusted for sex, day of the week, time of day and within-person clustering of responses
[b]Negative emotions included sad, stressed, and tired; Positive emotions included happy, energized, and relaxed; Apathetic emotions included bored and meh
Boldface indicates statistical significance at p<0.01

Fig. 13.2 Supportive dataset extracted from journal

13.8.3 Data Cleaning/Preparation

Since the dataset retrieved from Kaggle is unprocessed and raw, **Python** will be used to clean and prepare the data. Before cleaning, the raw data is loaded into **Jupyter Notebook** using the **pd.read_csv** function (Fig. 13.3).

With the help of the **drop ()** function, unnecessary columns like 'GPA,' 'breakfast,' and 'calories chicken' will be removed from the dataset. The **drop duplicates ()** function and **dropna ()** function will be used respectively to eliminate duplicates and Not a Number (NaN) values from the dataset. There will also be some columns renaming to prepare the data. The **rename ()** method, for instance, will rename 'comfort_food_reasons_coded' to 'mood.' Since the survey responses are coded, all the numerical values will be converted to categorical values. There are a total of 19 columns that have been changed to categorical values. For example, the raw data gender columns consist of values '1' and '2' where '1' represents 'Female' and '2' represents Male. After changing, the gender column only shows Female or Male.

The same steps such as loading data, removing unnecessary columns and NaN values are repeated for the supportive dataset. Additionally, the dataset values are rearranged from ascending to descending after cleaning. Some examples of Python code for data preparation and cleaning are demonstrated below (Please refer to Appendix 3 for the full Python Codes) (Figs. 13.4 and 13.5).

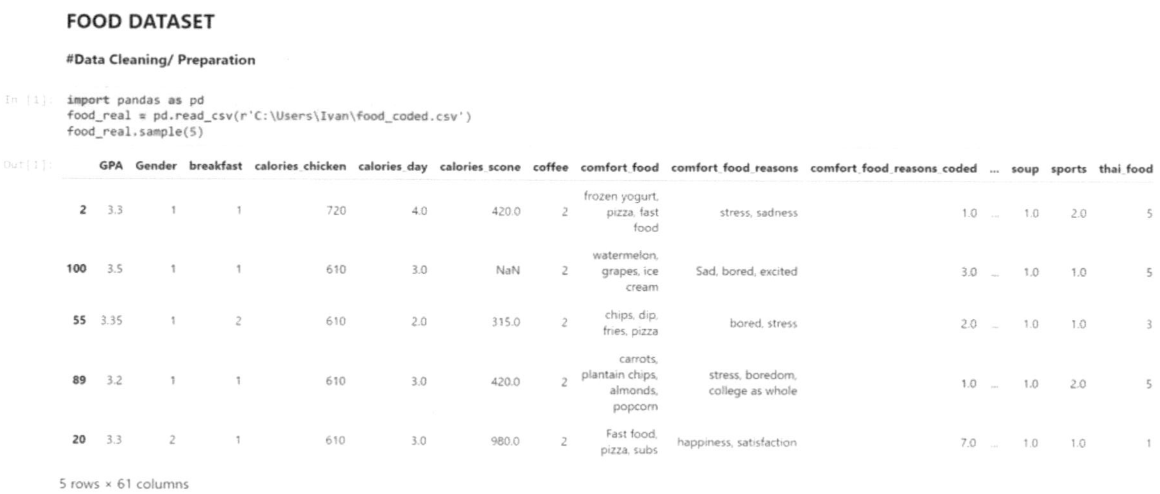

13.8 BALC Framework

FOOD DATASET

#Data Cleaning/ Preparation

```
In [1]: import pandas as pd
        food_real = pd.read_csv(r'C:\Users\Ivan\food_coded.csv')
        food_real.sample(5)
```

Out[1]:

	GPA	Gender	breakfast	calories chicken	calories day	calories scone	coffee	comfort food	comfort food reasons	comfort food reasons coded	...	soup	sports	thai food
2	3.3	1	1	720	4.0	420.0	2	frozen yogurt, pizza fast food	stress, sadness	1.0	...	1.0	2.0	5
100	3.5	1	1	610	3.0	NaN	2	watermelon, grapes, ice cream	Sad, bored, excited	3.0	...	1.0	1.0	5
55	3.35	1	2	610	2.0	315.0	2	chips, dip, fries, pizza	bored, stress	2.0	...	1.0	1.0	3
89	3.2	1	1	610	3.0	420.0	2	carrots, plantain chips, almonds, popcorn	stress, boredom, college as whole	1.0	...	1.0	2.0	5
20	3.3	2	1	610	3.0	980.0	2	Fast food, pizza, subs	happiness, satisfaction	7.0	...	1.0	1.0	1

5 rows × 61 columns

Fig. 13.3 Loading data into Jupyter Notebook

```
In [2]:  #Deleting Unnnecessary Columns (Dropping the column "", "", "" and saving the new dataset as "food_df")
         food_df=food_real.drop(['GPA','breakfast','calories_chicken','calories_day','calories_scone','coffee','cook',
                                 'comfort_food_reasons_coded.1','drink','eating_out','employment','ethnic_food',
                                 'father_education','father_profession','food_childhood','fries','fruit_day','greek_food',
                                 'indian_food','italian_food','life_rewarding','marital_status','meals_dinner_friend',
                                 'mother_education','mother_profession','persian_food','soup','thai_food','tortilla_calories',
                                 'turkey_calories','type_sports','vitamins','waffle_calories'],axis=1)

         #Removing the Duplicates
         food_df.duplicated().sum()
         food_df.drop_duplicates(inplace=True)

         #Remove the NaN values from the dataset
         food_df.isnull().sum()
         food_df.dropna(how='any',inplace=True)

         #Changing the column names
         food_df= food_df.rename(columns={'comfort_food_reasons':'list_3_moods','comfort_food_reasons_coded':'mood',
                                          'comfort_food':'food','diet_current_coded':'current_diet','fav_food':'fav_food_source',
                                          'fav_cuisine':'listed_fav_cuisine','fav_cuisine_coded':'fav_cuisine',
                                          'grade_level':'classification_of_student','pay_meal_out':'food_spending_level',
                                          'eating_changes_coded':'eating_better_worse',
                                          'eating_changes_coded1':'eating_habits_changes','ideal_diet_coded':'what_ideal_diet'})

         #Changing Numerical to Categorical

In [4]:  gender_toName = {
             1: "Female",
             2: "Male"
         }
         food_df['Gender']=food_df['Gender'].apply(lambda x: gender_toName[x])

In [5]:  mood_toName = {
             1.0: 'stress',
             2.0: 'boredom',
             3.0: 'depression/sadness',
             4.0: 'hunger',
             5.0: 'laziness',
             6.0: 'cold weather',
             7.0: 'happiness',
             8.0: 'watching tv',
             9.0: 'none'
         }
         food_df['mood']=food_df['mood'].apply(lambda x: mood_toName[x])

In [6]:  cuisine_toName = {
             1.0: 'American',
             2.0: 'Mexican.Spanish',
             3.0: 'Korean/Asian',
             4.0: 'Indian',
             5.0: 'American inspired international dishes',
             6.0: 'other'
         }
         food_df['cuisine']=food_df['cuisine'].apply(lambda x: cuisine_toName[x])
```

Fig. 13.4 Data cleaning and data preparation codes for main dataset

```
In [39]:  #Deleting Unnnecessary Columns (Dropping the column "", "", "" and saving the new dataset as "food_journal1"
          food_journal1=food_journal.drop(['Emotion'],axis=1)

          #Remove the NaN values from the dataset
          food_journal1.isnull().sum()
          food_journal1.dropna(how='any',inplace=True)

          #Sort values from the largest to smallest based on "WP OR(99% CI)"
          food_journal1.sort_values(by = ['WP OR(99% CI)'], ascending = [False])

          food_journal1
```

Fig. 13.5 Data cleaning and data preparation codes for supportive dataset

13.8.4 Predictive Model

The next step after data cleaning and processing is to build the predictive model. As our dataset originated from a survey that consists of open-ended questions, it is suitable for natural language processing. Therefore, **NLTK** will be used as the main library to build our predictive model. The figure below shows the libraries and packages that have to be imported or installed before creating our predictive model (Fig. 13.6).

13.8 BALC Framework

```
In [30]: import nltk
         nltk.download('wordnet')
         nltk.download('omw-1.4')

         nltk.download('stopwords')
         from wordcloud import WordCloud, STOPWORDS
         stopwords=set (STOPWORDS)
         from collections import Counter
         from nltk.corpus import stopwords
         stop = set (stopwords.words ('english'))
         stop.update(['.', ',',"=","'",'?','!',':', ';', '(', ')', '[', ']','{', '}',''])
         from nltk.stem import WordNetLemmatizer

         [nltk_data] Downloading package wordnet to
         [nltk_data]     C:\Users\Ivan\AppData\Roaming\nltk_data...
         [nltk_data]   Package wordnet is already up-to-date!
         [nltk_data] Downloading package omw-1.4 to
         [nltk_data]     C:\Users\Ivan\AppData\Roaming\nltk_data...
         [nltk_data]   Package omw-1.4 is already up-to-date!
         [nltk_data] Downloading package stopwords to
         [nltk_data]     C:\Users\Ivan\AppData\Roaming\nltk_data...
         [nltk_data]   Package stopwords is already up-to-date!
```

Fig. 13.6 Libraries and packages needed for predictive model

After installing those libraries and packages, we can start off with the predictive model codes. The **define** function is used to find and call a specific mood (stress, boredom, hungry, happy, sad, lazy) from the main dataset. Then, the frequency of occurrence for the type of food listed in that specific mood is counted (foodcount[a]) and the values will be sorted from ascending to descending order. The define function will be used again to find the three foods with the highest percentage of occurrence for a specific mood. As a result, the **top three foods for a mood will be listed out in the coding output.** The detailed coding is shown below (Please refer to Appendix 3 for the full Python Codes) (Fig. 13.7).

```python
def search_food(mood):
    lemmatizer = WordNetLemmatizer()
    foodcount = {}
    for i in range(77):
        temp = [temps.strip().replace('.','').replace(',','').lower() for temps in str(food_data["list_3_moods"][i]).split(' ') if temps.strip() not in st
        if mood in temp:
            foodtemp = [lemmatizer.lemmatize(temps.strip().replace('.','').replace(',','').lower()) for temps in str(food_data["food"][i]).split(',') if tem
            for a in foodtemp:
                if a not in foodcount.keys():
                    foodcount[a] = 1
                else:
                    foodcount[a] += 1
    sorted_food = []
    sorted_food = sorted(foodcount, key=foodcount.get, reverse=True)
    return sorted_food

def find_my_food(mood):
    topn = []
    topn = search_food(mood) #function create dictionary only for particular mood
    print("3 popular comfort foods in %s are:"%(mood))
    print(topn[0])
    print(topn[1])
    print(topn[2])
```

Fig. 13.7 Predictive model codes

13.8.5 Visualisation/EDA

Data analysts utilise exploratory data analysis (EDA) to study and investigate data sets and describe their essential properties, frequently using data visualisation approaches. It's a necessary stage in every study analysis. The major goal of an exploratory analysis is to thoroughly investigate the data necessary for distribution and to find any outliers or aberrant data. The EDA also aids in the detection of natural patterns in data and highlights critical findings. It will provide you with a fundamental knowledge of your data, including its distribution, null values, and much more. Typically, EDA is provided in the form of dashboards, allowing users to readily view and analyse data, and then use the visualisations to give vital insight into the performance of a model.

Tableau will be used to display the dataset in order to examine trends and patterns. As the Kaggle dataset contains categorical variables, it will be loaded into the Tableau dimension. Text variables, date variables, geographic place names, and discrete numeric variables are all examples of Dimensions in Tableau. For visualisation, graphical charts such as a pie chart, horizontal bar graph, vertical bar graph, scatter plot, box plot, and line graph will be employed. Figure 13.8, would be our dashboard based on the Kaggle dataset we used above.

Starting from the 1st graph in the dashboard, a table is shown with the total amount of people choosing different types of food. Based on the table, we understand a total of 64 participants, the highest amount, choose sweets from the above food choices. While Salty Snacks/Fried Food would be the second highest with a total amount

Fig. 13.8 Dashboard

13.8 BALC Framework

of 42, followed by 28 people with Pizza/Fast food. This means that most of the people prefer Sweet Foods, Salty Snacks/Fried Food, and Pizza/Fast food compared to others.

Next, spending level is also one of the factors that may affect food choices. Thus, we create a pie chart to analyse which spending level most college students would prefer. As you can see from the above pie chart in the dashboard, the respondents who choose spending level 2 have the highest amount among the three different spending levels with a total of 70.6%. While students who choose spending level 1 have a total of 16.6% and students who choose spending level 3 have 12.8%. To conclude this pie chart, we can focus more on spending level 2 with different or more variety of food choices while building our recommendation system as 70.6% of students prefer spending level 2.

Moving on to the line graph showing 'Mood Affecting Spending Level'. From this line graph, we can understand that mood can affect spending levels as the graph shows a huge change, especially during stress, boredom, and depression for three different spending levels. The line graph for three different spending levels has the same trend where the line goes upwards when it meets stress, boredom, and depression. However, the highest would still be spending level 2. More than 20 students would spend more when they are bored and 10+ students spend more when they are stressed. We can conclude that students would spend more when they have stress, boredom, and depression.

Besides, a bar chart would be generated to show how mood affects food choices. This is to help us understand which food choices people would choose when they have a certain mood. As we can see 'sweets' have the highest score in a different type of mood in the above bar chart in the dashboard. However, people who choose boredom have the highest percentage of choosing sweets food and the second highest would be 'salty snacks' food compared to others. Moreover, the second highest of people who would choose 'sweet' foods are those people who have stress. Hence, we can analyse that people who are bored and stressed would prefer sweet food.

Moreover, a box plot will be used to analyse food choices by gender. In the box plot, it shows a higher number of females choose sweet foods compared to males. While male has a higher percentage of salty foods compared to female. Other than sweet and salty foods, it shows a similar amount for both genders on the other types of foods. Thus, we can conclude that female prefers sweet food compared to male and male has a higher percentage of salty food compared to female. While other than sweet and salty food, both genders have an almost similar amount.

Lastly, a bar chart would be created to show an analysis of mood by gender. Based on our visualisation, we realise that female has a higher amount on having boredom, stress, and depression compared to male. Based on our literature review, females tend to show more emotions than males. Hence, it can conclude why female has a higher amount emotions compared to male.

13.9 SDLC Framework

SDLC is a five phases framework that includes planning and requirement analysis, design, development, integration, and testing, as well as deployment and maintenance. Below are the further explanations for each phase:

13.9.1 Planning and Requirement Analysis

The first step in our SDLC framework for our web-based food recommendation system is the planning and requirements analysis phase. In this phase, we aim to identify the problem and what issues we intend to tackle. After that, we must analyse what problem our system aims to solve and the feasibility of our intended system. We must take into considerations the time constraints of the project as well as what impact our system will have technically and if it solves the issue we intend to tackle. Thus, the problem that our web-based food recommendation system aims to tackle is to assist individuals in the local region of Sunway who have trouble deciding what to eat. Therefore, our system will allow users to choose their specified mood, category, and budget where we can then provide them restaurant recommendations based on these criteria. Furthermore, in our requirements analysis, we found that our webpages will need to support these decisions by providing multiple different pages of restaurant recommendations. It was also decided that an algorithm was necessary in order to provide the actual food recommendations based on the user's mood.

13.9.2 Design

The next step in our SDLC process is the design phase. In this phase, we will have to establish the logical model for the system to understand the overall system flow. Furthermore, we also develop an understanding of any technical hardware requirements. We established that an SQL database had to be developed to store user login info. Further, there was also a need to develop the logical model to understand the workflow of the website.

13.9 SDLC Framework

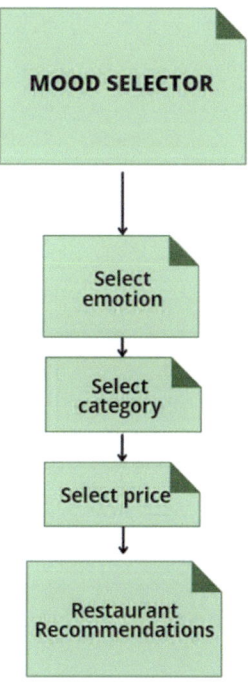

Our website will allow users to first select their emotions, then move on to a page that will let them select their food category based on what our algorithm recommended. Then they are given three different budget options—cheap, moderate, and expensive, where after choosing the budget, we will provide them with restaurant recommendations based on what our algorithm suggests. These restaurant recommendations will follow up with button that links to food panda where the users can directly place their order with the click of a button. The figures below demonstrate our website design.

Figure 13.9 demonstrates the login page where users can enter their email and password after registering to access our website.

Figure 13.10 is the homepage of our website where users now have access to view our header with a few options for them to view such as Home, Dashboard, and Analysis. There is also a button in the centre that takes them to the food recommendation service.

Figure 13.11 shows the available mood choice for our customers, where they are provided with 3 choices of moods being happy, sad, or bored.

Figure 13.12 comes after the mood selection where users will be given a choice of 3 options based on their different moods. The figure provides an example of our recommendations of a user that had selected the 'Sad' category.

Figure 13.13 represents our choices for budget where users are given a choice of 3 different budgets—cheap, moderate, and expensive.

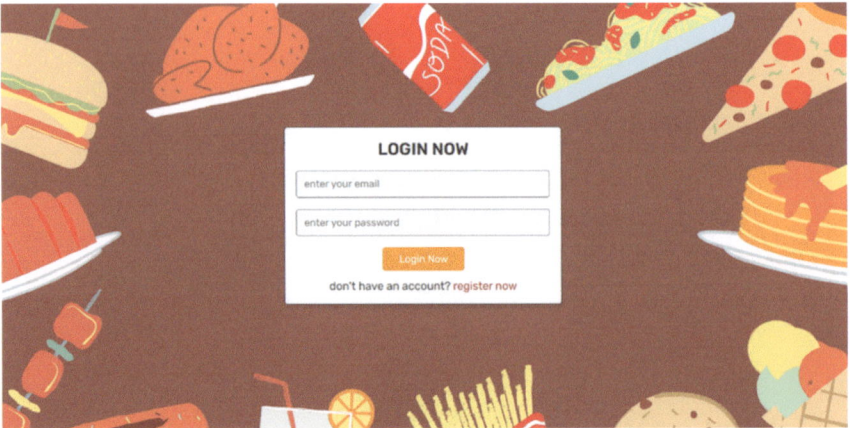

Fig. 13.9 Data flow diagram of recommender system

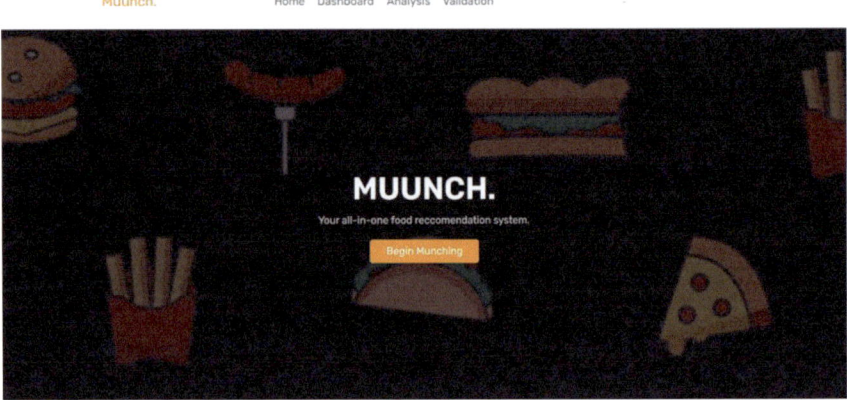

Fig. 13.10 User Login window

Lastly, Fig. 13.14 is the final page where users will be given the option of 5 restaurants that are based on their mood choice and budget.

13.9.3 Development

The next phase of our SDLC is the development phase. In this phase, we must develop the coding for the website and establish the database as well as the algorithm. For our SDLC, we primarily used PHP and CSS for the website and MySQL for the database that store the user's login info. The figure above is an example of the PHP

13.9 SDLC Framework

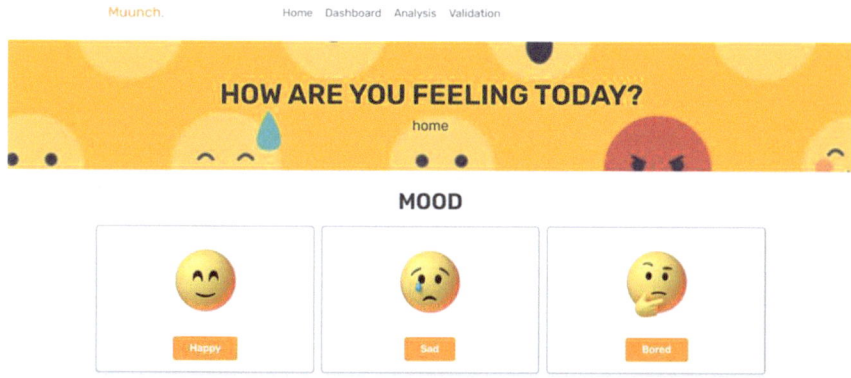

Fig. 13.11 Input of User Expression

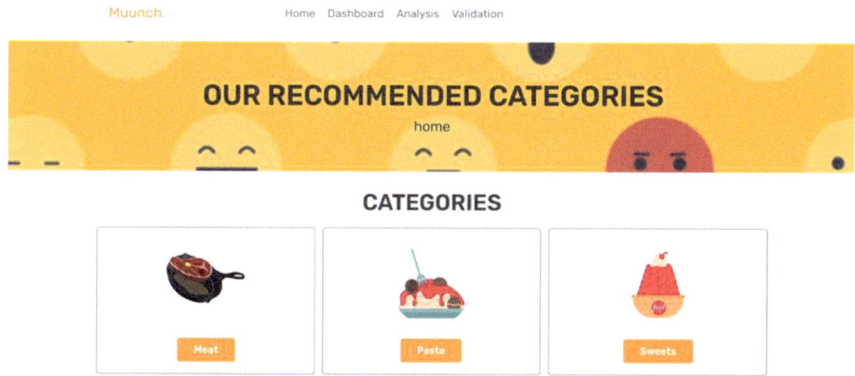

Fig. 13.12 Recommendation Based on Food Section

code used that links the food choices to the different category pages. In this phase, the database design will be transformed into a database system. First, a connection to the SQL data file will be created in Visual Code Studio. After creating a connection to the database, coding will be created for the login page, register page, header, footer, and so on. To create form layouts for the login and register page, '<div class=form container>' is used. This way, users can type in their email address and password into the form to log into their account. Once the coding for all pages is completed, the login page relative path will be copied to a clipboard, edited, and pasted on a web browser's search bar. Examples of coding for the webpage are shown in Fig. 13.15.

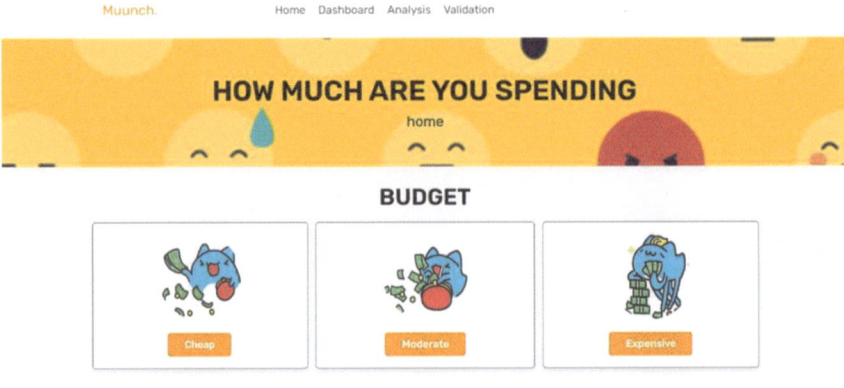

Fig. 13.13 Budget-based food recommendation

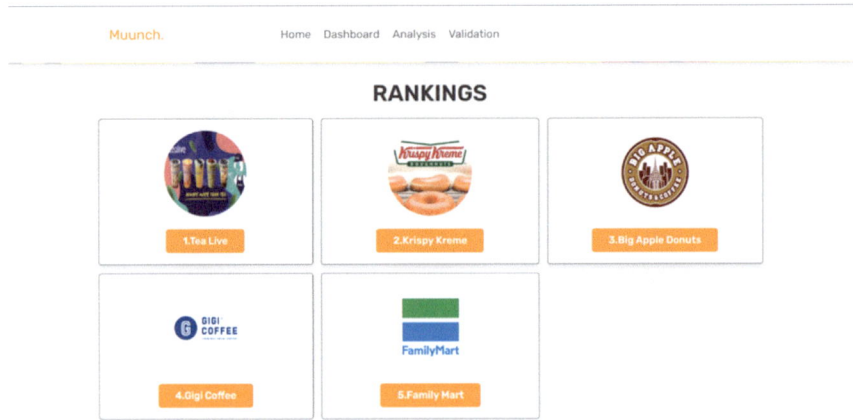

Fig. 13.14 Windows view of recommender welcome page

13.9.4 Integration and Testing

The next phase is the integration and testing phase where we can begin to taste the functionalities of the system and the system that we have developed will have to be tested. We decided the best way to conduct this is to establish a Google form to collect data from students around the Sunway University Area (Fig. 13.16).

We can then utilize this data to gauge the real-world accuracy of our system and whether the recommendations align with the consumers' expectations. For example, if the restaurants we have recommended in the price range match their expectation of what defines 'budget' or 'expensive' food.

13.9 SDLC Framework

```php
<?php

$conn = mysqli_connect('localhost','root','','shop_db') or die('connection failed');

?>
```

```html
<!-- custom css file link -->
<link rel="stylesheet" href="css/style.css">

</head>
<body>

<?php
if(isset($message)){
    foreach($message as $message){
        echo '
        <div class="message">
            <span>'.$message.'</span>
            <i class="fas fa-times" onclick="this.parentElement.remove();"></i>
        </div>
        ';
    }
}
?>

<div class="form-container">

    <form action="" method="post">
        <h3>login now</h3>
        <input type="email" name="email" placeholder="enter your email" required class="box">
        <input type="password" name="password" placeholder="enter your password" required class="box">
        <input type="submit" name="submit" value="login now" class="btn">
        <p>don't have an account? <a href="register.php">register now</a></p>
    </form>

</div>

</body>
</html>
```

```html
<?php
if(isset($message)){
    foreach($message as $message){
        echo '
        <div class="message">
            <span>'.$message.'</span>
            <i class="fas fa-times" onclick="this.parentElement.remove();"></i>
        </div>
        ';
    }
}
?>

<div class="form-container">

    <form action="" method="post">
        <h3>register now</h3>
        <input type="text" name="name" placeholder="enter your name" required class="box">
        <input type="email" name="email" placeholder="enter your email" required class="box">
        <input type="password" name="password" placeholder="enter your password" required class="box">
        <input type="password" name="cpassword" placeholder="confirm your password" required class="box">

        <input type="submit" name="submit" value="register now" class="btn">
        <p>already have an account? <a href="login.php">login now</a></p>
    </form>

</div>

</body>
</html>
```

Fig. 13.15 Examples of coding

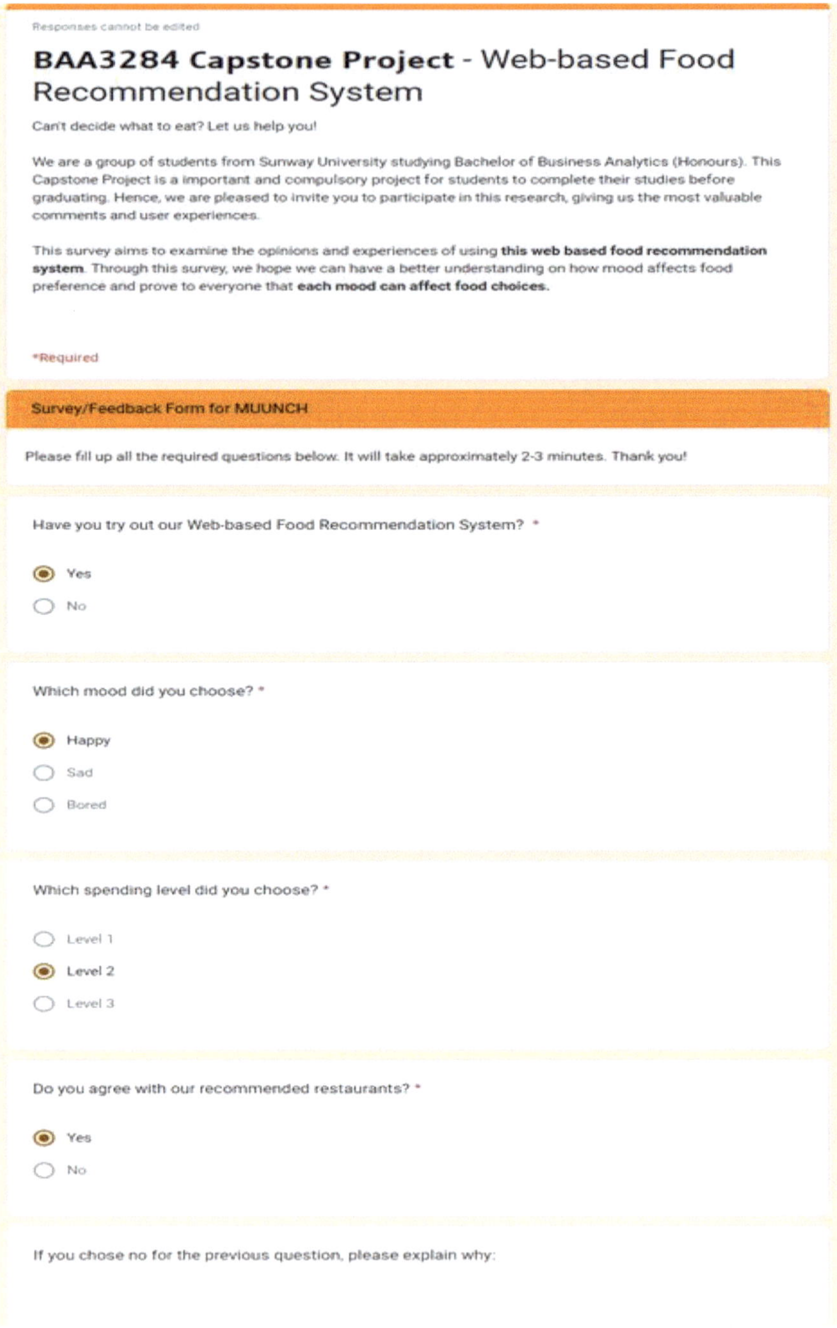

Responses cannot be edited

BAA3284 Capstone Project - Web-based Food Recommendation System

Can't decide what to eat? Let us help you!

We are a group of students from Sunway University studying Bachelor of Business Analytics (Honours). This Capstone Project is a important and compulsory project for students to complete their studies before graduating. Hence, we are pleased to invite you to participate in this research, giving us the most valuable comments and user experiences.

This survey aims to examine the opinions and experiences of using **this web based food recommendation system**. Through this survey, we hope we can have a better understanding on how mood affects food preference and prove to everyone that **each mood can affect food choices.**

*Required

Survey/Feedback Form for MUUNCH

Please fill up all the required questions below. It will take approximately 2-3 minutes. Thank you!

Have you try out our Web-based Food Recommendation System? *

- (•) Yes
- ( ) No

Which mood did you choose? *

- (•) Happy
- ( ) Sad
- ( ) Bored

Which spending level did you choose? *

- ( ) Level 1
- (•) Level 2
- ( ) Level 3

Do you agree with our recommended restaurants? *

- (•) Yes
- ( ) No

If you chose no for the previous question, please explain why:

Fig. 13.16 Example form

13.9.5 Deployment and Maintenance

The final phase of our system development life cycle is the deployment and maintenance of our model. The deployment of the system requires us to optimise the data present in the database and ensure that the database is fully operational and functional after the necessary UATs have been conducted. Once the database has been deployed, the maintenance of the database begins. The maintenance of our database will involve steps such as creating backups, consolidating data, and configuring log files. These maintenance steps will ensure our database will continuously operate accurately and efficiently even after it has been deployed.

13.10 Results from the Prediction Model

With the main dataset, prediction model was done to predict the three most popular foods that individuals eat during specific moods. For example, chocolate, ice cream, and chips are found as the top three most popular foods that individuals eat whenever they are stressed. As seen in the figures below, the results shown were for the **predicted food during moods such as stress, boredom, hungry, happy, sad, and lazy**. There were prediction errors for the mood lazy as the model could identify 1 type of food only. This means that whenever an individual is feeling lazy, they will eat burgers only (Fig. 13.17).

As the results from the prediction model of the main dataset are somewhat similar for each mood, the supportive dataset is brought into place. Instead of building another prediction model, the **food choices for a specific mood are chosen based on the top three within-person (WP) values.** It can be seen that top food choices for the negative mood (sad, stressed, tired) are meats or proteins, pasta or rice, and

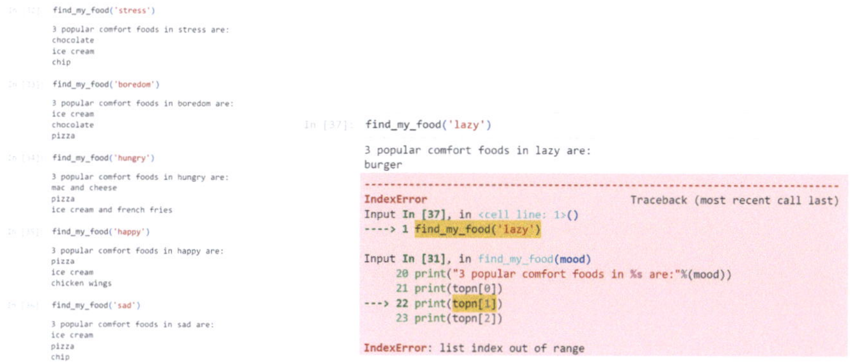

Fig. 13.17 Results from main dataset

sweets. Figure 13.18 show the detailed results for negative, positive, and apathetic moods.

In the end, we were able to create a prediction model with an **accuracy of 93.3%** (Fig. 13.19). This result was obtained from our Google Form survey completed by 30 randomly selected students in Sunway University. About **28 out of the 30 students** agreed on the food and restaurant recommendations that were provided to them in our website. Therefore, our recommended restaurants to users were in fact accurate.

```
In [40]: #Top 3 food choices for negative emotion
         food_negative= food_journal1.iloc[0:8]
         food_negative.head(3)
```

Out[40]:

	Mood	Food Choices	WP OR(99% CI)
1	Sad, stressed, tired	Meats/proteins	1.5 (1.0, 2.1)
2	Sad, stressed, tired	Pasta/rice	1.4 (1.0, 2.1)
3	Sad, stressed, tired	Sweets	1.3 (0.8, 1.9)

```
In [41]: #Top 3 food choices for positive emotion
         food_positive=food_journal1.iloc[8:16]
         food_positive.head(3)
```

Out[41]:

	Mood	Food Choices	WP OR(99% CI)
9	Happy, energized & relaxed	Sweets	1.7 (1.1, 2.6)
10	Happy, energized & relaxed	Salty snacks/fried foods	1.5 (1.0, 2.2)
11	Happy, energized & relaxed	Fruits/vegetables	1.4 (1.0, 1.9)

```
In [42]: #Top 3 food choices for apathetic emotion
         food_apathetic=food_journal1.iloc[17:24]
         food_apathetic.head(3)
```

Out[42]:

	Mood	Food Choices	WP OR(99% CI)
18	Boredom, meh	Salty snacks/fried foods	1.4 (09, 22)
19	Boredom, meh	Sweets	1.3 (0.8, 2.2)
20	Boredom, meh	Fruits/vegetables	1.0 (0.7, 15)

Fig. 13.18 Results from supportive dataset

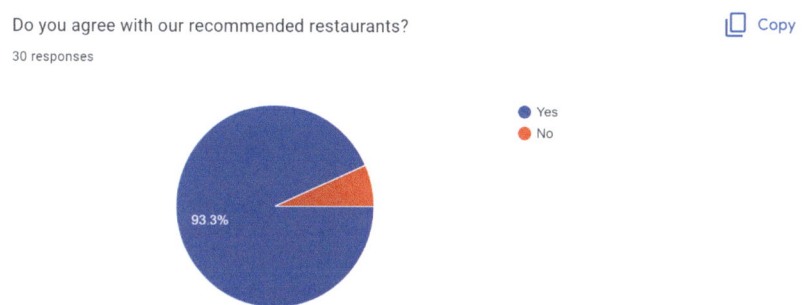

Fig. 13.19 Validation results obtained from Google Form

13.11 Results from the Web-User Interface

The responses we received from the users indicated that our website was easy to use and very intuitive. The goal of our web design was to keep it consistent and to make sure the buttons were laid out in a consistent manner. This goal was achieved as can be seen by the figure below as the website layout remains relatively consistent while also maintaining a level of interactivity as we avoided the use of static images for our website. We affirm that our web-user interaction has achieved our anticipated outcomes, enabling us to create an engaging website while ensuring the appropriate provision of food suggestions. (Fig. 13.20).

13.12 Instruction Manuals

The Instruction Manuals below provide a more thorough explanation of our website's (Muunch) navigation and coding. These guides were created with the intention to ease the users and developers to install, navigate, and comprehend the code:

User's guide: see Online Appendix
Developer's guide: see Online Appendix

13.13 Discussion of Contribution from the Results

From our results, we are able to find out the types of food that an individual craving for based on the specific mood by using the predictive model on our dataset. It has been discovered that one of the examples from our predictive model is chocolate, ice cream, and chips are the top three most popular foods that people eat when they are

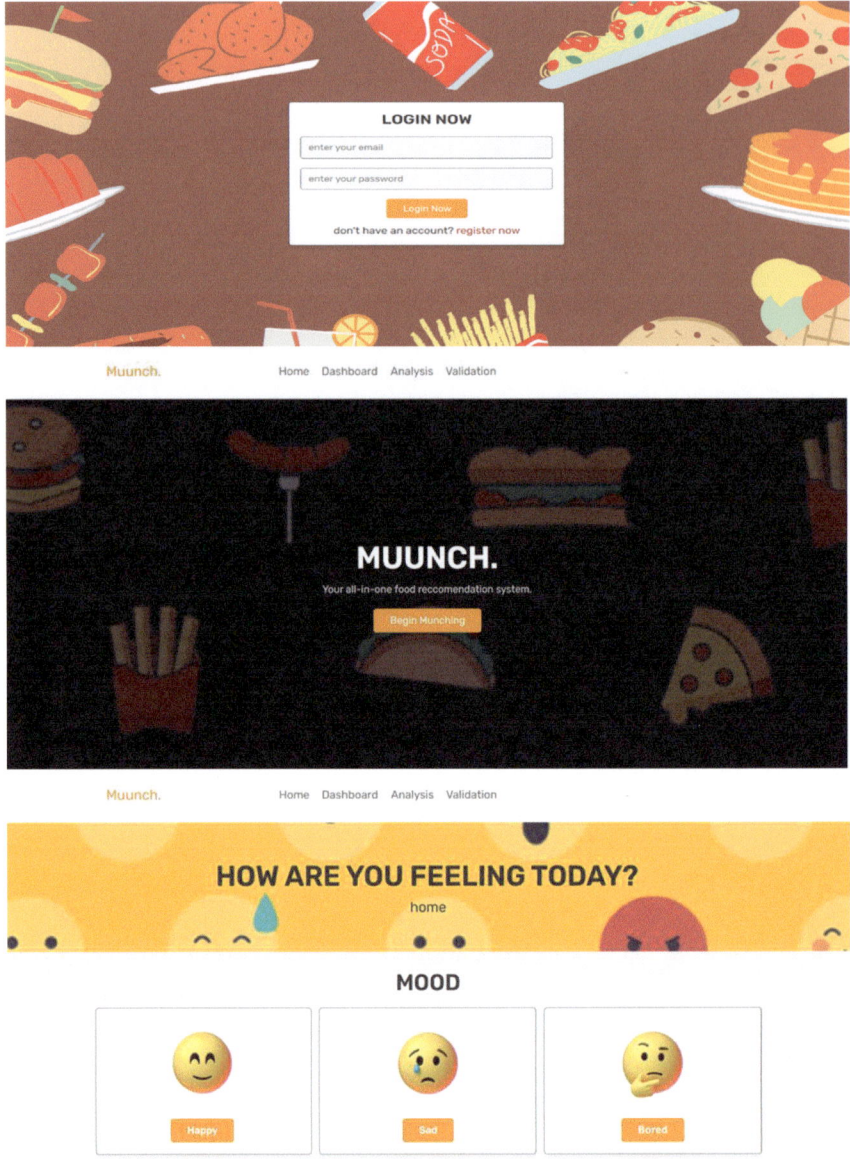

Fig. 13.20 Demonstration of website

13.13 Discussion of Contribution from the Results

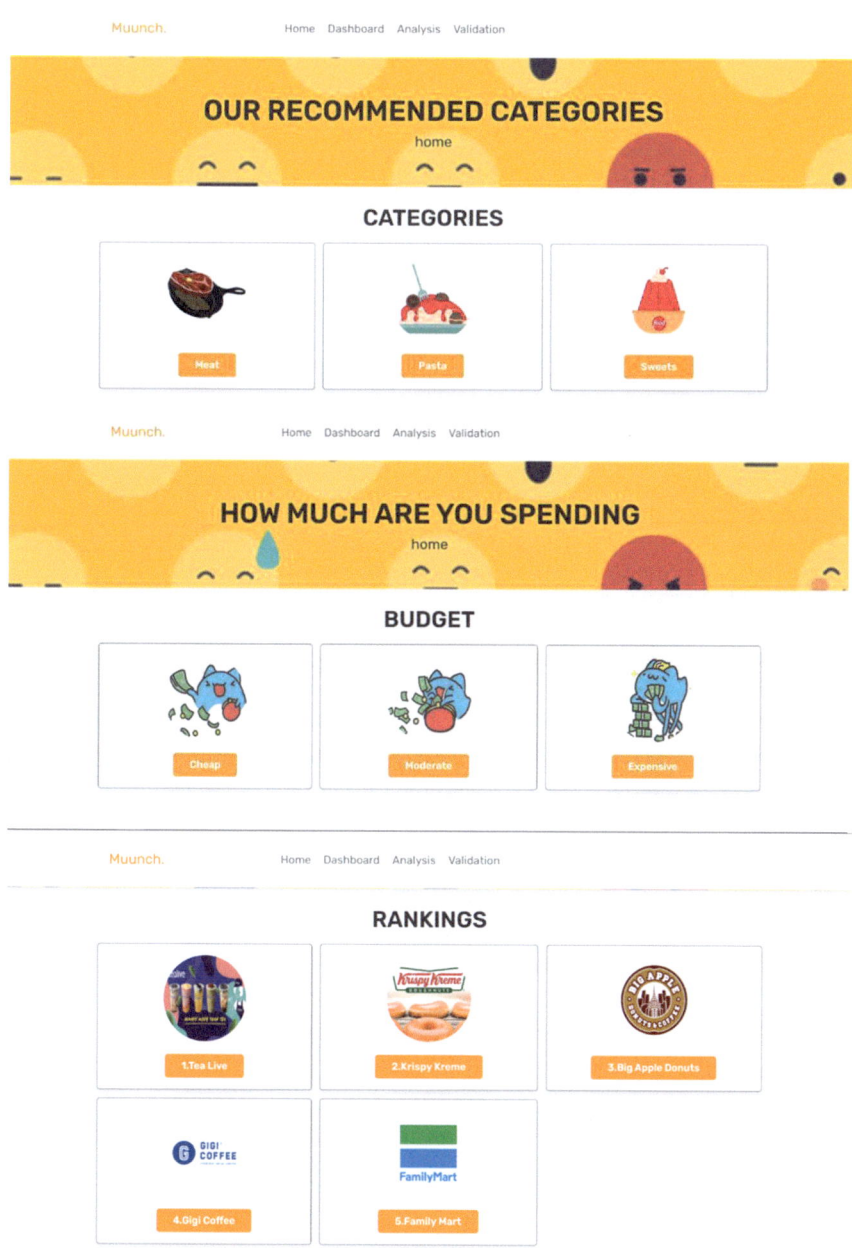

Fig. 13.20 (continued)

stressed. This demonstrated that whenever an individual was stressed, their preferred foods were chocolates, ice cream, and chips, as predicted by our predictive model. As for our problem statement of people spending more time thinking about where to eat rather than eating, the results allow us to build a website that recommends restaurants based on their mood, budget, and food types. As a result, it allows people to spend less time deciding where to eat by selecting restaurants recommended by our prediction model.

13.14 Future Work

Although the web-based food recommendation system is currently a prototype, we believe that by using advanced machine learning methods, we can develop a more accurate and dynamic prediction model. We were able to generate a predictive model during the process of our project, but we discovered that it is difficult to find many relevant datasets to generate a prediction model due to specific variables such as moods and budget.

Additionally, we are only able to target individuals in Sunway area only due to time constraints. We believe that if more time was given, we would be able to further improve our website and take in consideration of the feedback that we have obtained from our survey. For example, we might open to all users by recommending nearby restaurants in their current location. However, this process would need a much longer time to figure out and implement as it requires different variables like artificial intelligence, real-time data, etc. Furthermore, the user website interface could be developed for publishing, allowing us to successfully launch our project into the market by collaborating with Food Panda or Grab Food.

Appendix 1: Main Dataset

Appendix 2: Supportive Dataset

Supportive Data (Journal).csv

Appendix 3: Full Python Codes

Python Codes.pdf

Appendix 4: Google Survey Responses for Validation Purposes

Validation - Google Survey Responses.csv

Appendix 5: Tableau Link

https://public.tableau.com/app/profile/natasha.ngo.xue.er/viz/CapstoneDashboard_16683850332030/Dashboard5.

Appendix 6: Dashboard

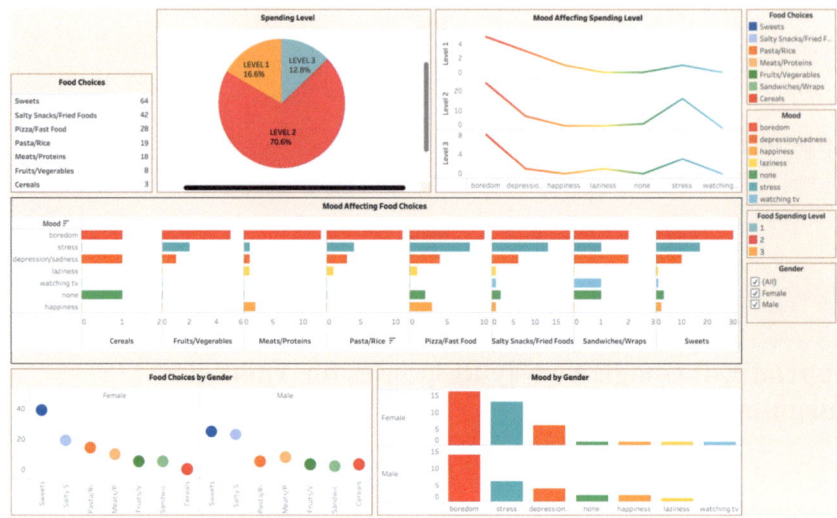

Appendix 7: Gantt Chart

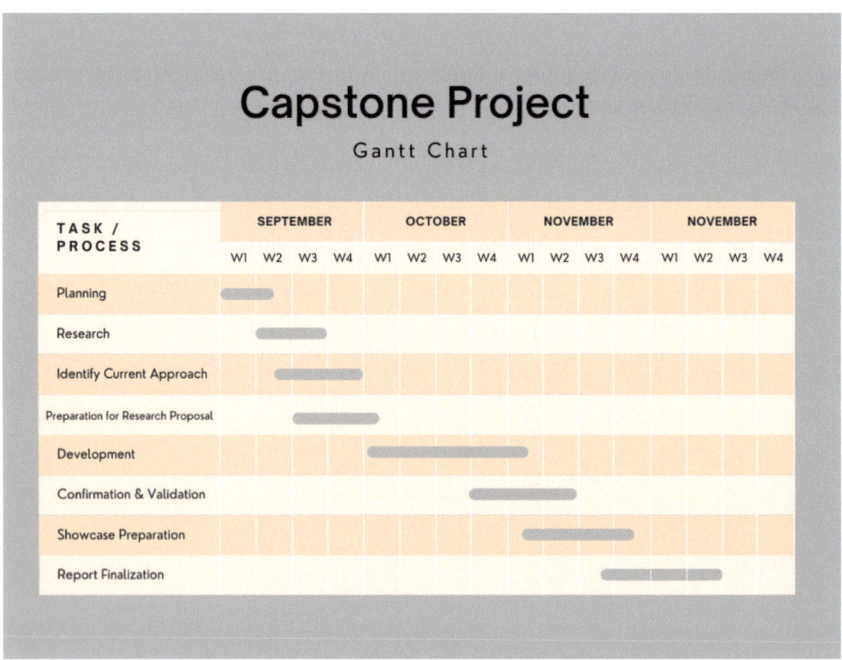

Appendix 8: Capstone Showcase Poster

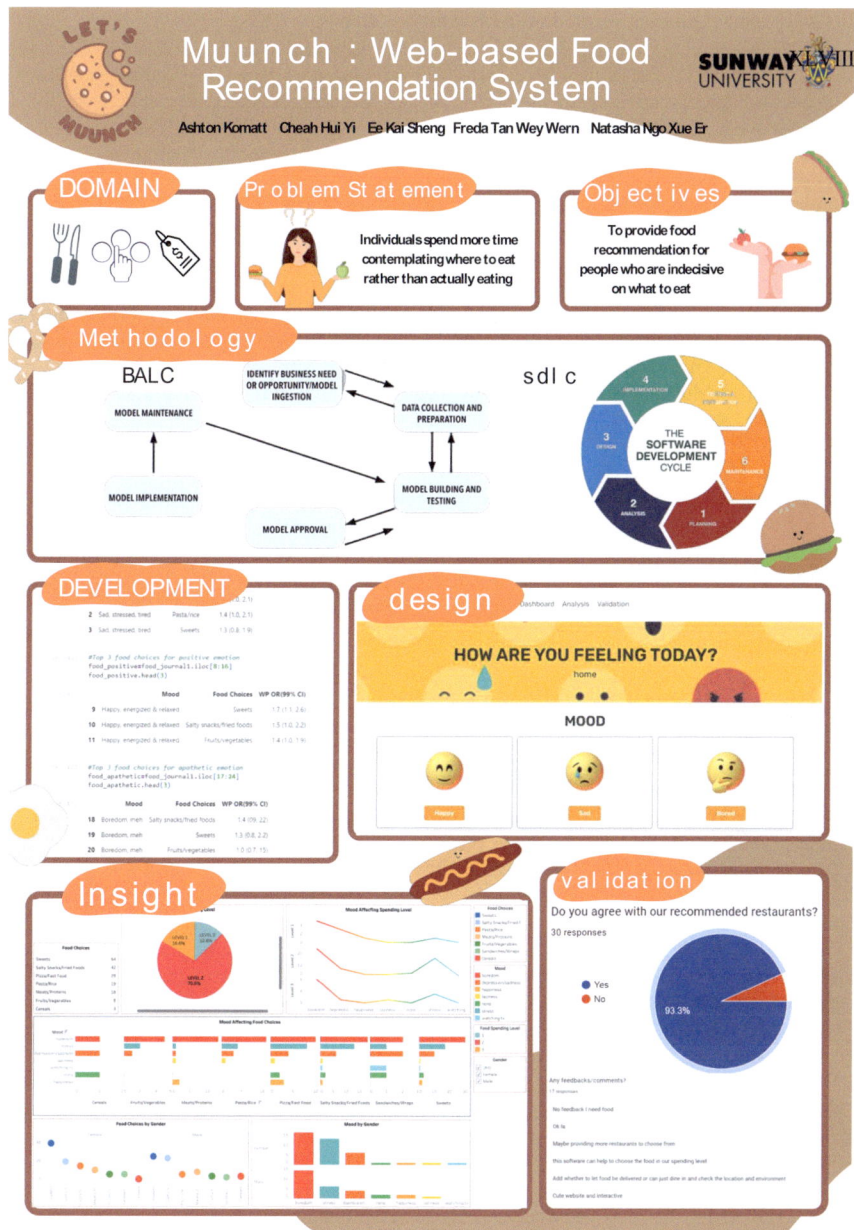

References

Alshammari, F. H., Alnaqeib, R., Zaidan, M. A., Hmood, A. K., Zaidan, B. B., & Zaidan, A. A. (2010). New Quantitative Study for Dissertations Repository System. *arXiv preprint* arXiv. 1006.4547

Alzubi, J., Nayyar, A., & Kumar, A. (2018). *Machine learning from theory to algorithms: An overview.* Paper presented at the Journal of physics: Conference series.

Anastasiadou, E., Lindh, C., & Vasse, T. (2019). Are consumers international? A study of CSR, cross-border shopping, commitment and purchase intent among online consumers. *Journal of Global Marketing, 32*(4), 239–254.

Ashurst, J., Van Woerden, I., Dunton, G., Todd, M., Ohri-Vachaspati, P., Swan, P., & Bruening, M. (2018). The association among emotions and food choices in first-year college students using mobile-ecological momentary assessments. *BMC Public Health, 18*(1), 573.

Bala, S., Garg, D., Thirumalesh, B. V., Sharma, M., Sridhar, K., Inbaraj, B. S., & Tripathi, M. (2022). Recent strategies for bioremediation of emerging pollutants: A review for a green and sustainable environment. *Toxics, 10*(8), 484.

Burrows, A. (2000). Supernova explosions in the universe. *Nature, 403*(6771), 727–733.

Burrows, C. J., & Muller, J. G. (1998). Oxidative nucleobase modifications leading to strand scission. *Chemical Reviews, 98*(3), 1109–1152.

Cailliau, R., & Ashman, H. (1999). Hypertext in the Web—A history. *ACM Computing Surveys (CSUR), 31*(4es), 35-es.

Card, D., Chetty, R., & Weber, A. (2007). The spike at benefit exhaustion: Leaving the unemployment system or starting a new job? *American Economic Review, 97*(2), 113–118.

Carins, J. E., & Rundle-Thiele, S. R. (2014). Eating for the better: A social marketing review (2000–2012). *Public Health Nutrition, 17*(7), 1628–1639.

Ceniccola, G. D., Holanda, T. P., Pequeno, R. S. F., Mendonça, V. S., Oliveira, A. B. M., Carvalho, L. S. F., de Brito-Ashurst, I. & Araujo, W. M. C. (2018). Relevance of AND-ASPEN criteria of malnutrition to predict hospital mortality in critically ill patients: A prospective study. *Journal of Critical Care, 44*, 398–403.

Clemens, M. A., & Hunt, J. (2019). The labor market effects of refugee waves: Reconciling conflicting results. *ILR Review, 72*(4), 818–857.

Datig, I., & Whiting, P. (2018). Telling your library story: Tableau public for data visualization. *Library Hi Tech News, 35*(4), 6–8.

Ergezer, H., & Leblebicioğlu, K. (2016). *Anomaly detection and activity perception using covariance descriptor for trajectories.* Paper presented at the Computer Vision–ECCV 2016 Workshops: Amsterdam, The Netherlands, October 8–10 and 15–16, 2016, Proceedings, Part II 14.

Favre, C., & Jonsson, M. (2005). Valuative analysis of planar plurisubharmonic functions. *Inventiones Mathematicae, 162*(2), 271–311.

Fischer-Preßler, D., Eismann, K., Pietrowski, R., Fischbach, K., & Schoder, D. (2020). Information technology and risk management in supply chains. *International Journal of Physical Distribution & Logistics Management, 50*(2), 233–254.

Gupta, S., Wang, W., Hayek, S. S., Chan, L., Mathews, K. S., Melamed, M. L., ... & Modersitzki, F. (2021). Association between early treatment with tocilizumab and mortality among critically ill patients with COVID-19. *JAMA internal medicine, 181*(1), 41–51.

Haffner, C., Malik, R., & Dichgans, M. (2016). Genetic factors in cerebral small vessel disease and their impact on stroke and dementia. *Journal of Cerebral Blood Flow & Metabolism, 36*(1), 158–171.

Häubl, G., & Trifts, V. (2000). Consumer decision making in online shopping environments: The effects of interactive decision aids. *Marketing Science, 19*(1), 4–21.

Lafuente, D. V. M., Catin, J. C. A., & Dagoc, M. G. R. (2023). Underlying motivations for food choices and their influence on healthy eating among millennials. *Journal of Tourism and Hospitality Management, 11*(2), 29–37.

References

Leeds, J., Keith, R., & Woloshynowych, M. (2020). Food and Mood: Exploring the determinants of food choices and the effects of food consumption on mood among women in Inner London. *World Nutrition, 11*(1), 68–96.

Li, J., Zou, B., Yeo, Y.H., Feng, Y., Xie, X., Lee, D.H., Fujii, H., Wu, Y., Kam, L.Y., Ji, F., & Li, X. (2019). Prevalence, incidence, and outcome of non-alcoholic fatty liver disease in Asia, 1999–2019: A systematic review and meta-analysis. *The Lancet Gastroenterology & Hepatology, 4*(5), 389–398.

Li, S. S., & Karahanna, E. (2015). Online recommendation systems in a B2C E-commerce context: A review and future directions. *Journal of the Association for Information Systems, 16*(2), 2.

Maia, C. F., Silva, B. R. S. D., & Lobato, A. K. D. S. (2018). Brassinosteroids positively modulate growth: physiological, biochemical and anatomical evidence using two tomato genotypes contrasting to dwarfism. *Journal of Plant Growth Regulation, 37*(4), 1099–1112.

Mughal, M. J. H. (2018). Data mining: Web data mining techniques, tools and algorithms: An overview. *International Journal of Advanced Computer Science and Applications, 9*(6).

Newby, L. K., Jesse, R. L., Babb, J. D., Christenson, R. H., De Fer, T. M., Diamond, G. A., Fesmire, F. M., Geraci, S. A., Gersh, B. J., Larsen, G. C., & Kaul, S. (2012). ACCF 2012 expert consensus document on practical clinical considerations in the interpretation of troponin elevations: a report of the American College of Cardiology Foundation task force on Clinical Expert Consensus Documents. *Journal of the American College of Cardiology, 60*(23), 2427–2463.

Nixon, P., Harrington, M., & Parker, D. (2012). Leadership performance is significant to project success or failure: A critical analysis. *International Journal of Productivity and Performance Management, 61*(2), 204–216.

Pai, S., & Sawant, N. (2017). Applications of new validated RP-HPLC method for determination of Indomethacin and its hydrolytic degradants using sodium acetate buffer. *Indian Journal of Pharmaceutical Education and Research, 51*(3), 388–392.

Pai, T. V., Sawant, S. Y., Ghatak, A. A., Chaturvedi, P. A., Gupte, A. M., & Desai, N. S. (2015). Characterization of Indian beers: chemical composition and antioxidant potential. *Journal of Food Science and Technology, 52*(3), 1414–1423.

Pederson, T. (2008). As functional nuclear actin comes into view, is it globular, filamentous, or both? *Journal of Cell Biology, 180*(6), 1061–1064.

Petrusel, M.-R., & Limboi, S.-G. (2019). *A restaurants recommendation system: Improving rating predictions using sentiment analysis.* Paper presented at the 2019 21st International Symposium on Symbolic and Numeric Algorithms for Scientific Computing (SYNASC).

Saabith, S., Vinothraj, T., & Fareez, M. (2021). A review on Python libraries and ides for Data Science. *International Journal of Research in Engineering and Science, 9*(11), 36–53.

Shipman, Z. D. (2020). Factors affecting food choices of millennials: How they decide what to eat? *Journal of Tourismology, 6*(1), 49–62.

Siame, A., & Kunda, D. (2017). Evolution of PHP applications: A systematic literature review. *International Journal of Recent Contributions from Engineering, Science & IT (iJES), 5*(1), 28–39.

Simone, A., Wells, G. N., & Sluys, L. J. (2003). From continuous to discontinuous failure in a gradient-enhanced continuum damage model. *Computer Methods in Applied Mechanics and Engineering, 192*(41-42), 4581–4607.

Toledo, R. Y., Alzahrani, A. A., & Martinez, L. (2019). A food recommender system considering nutritional information and user preferences. *IEEE Access, 7*, 96695–96711.

van Rossum, S. A., Tena-Solsona, M., van Esch, J. H., Eelkema, R., & Boekhoven, J. (2017). Dissipative out-of-equilibrium assembly of man-made supramolecular materials. *Chemical Society Reviews, 46*(18), 5519–5535.

Wesley, J. (2011). *The essential works of John Wesley.* Barbour Publishing.

Chapter 14
RateMyStay

14.1 Introduction

The recent rise of prominent hotel review platforms has transformed how travellers acquire information and select lodging. Platforms like TripAdvisor, Booking.com, and Agoda are crucial for insights regarding hotel quality and experiences. Nonetheless, these platforms possess certain limitations that hinder their capacity to deliver dependable and tailored reviews, ratings, and suggestions. These websites predominantly depend on text-based reviews, which may be biased and frequently neglect to capture the nuanced elements of the hotel experience (Schuckert et al. 2018). Our research is to investigate the shortcomings of conventional hotel review systems and to offer a more comprehensive and user-focused methodology for hotel evaluations and suggestions. Our research will concentrate on sentiment analysis, which will serve as our predictive model. Sentiment analysis approaches are frequently employed to extract sentiments and emotions from assessments, providing a more nuanced understanding of the consumer experience (Lee & Hosanagar, 2020). Employing sentiment analysis technologies and pertinent methodology, our study findings can profoundly influence travellers' hotel selections and enhance the whole hotel experience.

This project aims to address the shortcomings of conventional hotel review platforms. These systems occasionally have information overload and insufficient personalisation, hindering users' ability to obtain pertinent insights and locate lodgings that align with their own tastes. This project seeks to enhance the precision and pertinence of hotel recommendations by the integration of modern methodologies, including sentiment analysis and collaborative filtering, thereby improving the entire user experience and enabling informed decision-making.

Furthermore, our research endeavour employs iterative prototyping in accordance with the System Development Life Cycle (SDLC) to perpetually enhance the information system. The primary processes include data extraction, integration, loading, and visualisation. Advanced tools employed for an extensive hotel review platform include web scraping, Python sentiment analysis using TextBlob, PhpMyAdmin for database administration, HTML for intuitive website design, and Power BI for data visualisation. This methodology prioritises precision, eliminates untrustworthy assessments, and offers tailored recommendations. The findings provide a highly precise hotel rating system that incorporates comprehensive category analysis and allows consumers to make informed choices via intuitive visual representations.

14.2 Problem Statement and Summary of Solution

To counter these problems surrounding our domain to a greater extent, our capstone project has proposed a framework which revolves around sentiment analysis predominantly (which will be discussed further). Sentiment analysis is a potent method that enables us to examine the feelings and viewpoints stated in reviews, assisting us in producing more precise and trustworthy evaluations for each hotel. We can extract sentiments from textual reviews using the Text Blob library, and we can then utilize this information to enhance the overall rating system. Sentiment analysis is essential for refining the hotel rating system so that it remains more accurate, credible, and pertinent for users. Enhancing the user experience and fostering educated decision-making for consumers looking for hotels are our primary objectives with the inclusion of a complete sentiment-based rating, information summarization, and removal of inaccurate and skewed reviews.

Similar studies with the same objective have also proposed to conduct sentiment analysis on hotel reviews using various classification techniques, thereby comparing their performance. The identification of the need for sentiment analysis stems from literature reviews, which underscore sentiment analysis as a highly active research domain within Natural Language Processing (NLP). While sentiment analysis has been explored across different text datasets, there remains a dearth of research specifically focused on sentiment analysis using hotel reviews (Bai & Wang, 2022).

14.3 Research Questions

1. How can we develop a hotel rating system that assures the reliability and trustworthiness of reviews while diminishing the occurrence of skewed or biased opinions?
2. What approaches or algorithms can be used to successfully identify and filter out manipulated or biased reviews, hence maintaining the rating system's integrity?
3. How can we combat information overload on hotel review websites by creating clever processes for summarising and displaying reviews in a succinct and user-friendly manner?

4. What novel methodologies or technologies, such as natural language processing or sentiment analysis, may be used to extract relevant insights from reviews and ratings, therefore increasing the relevance and utility of the information offered to users?

14.4 Significance of Research

The research conducted on the domain of hotel review and rating systems holds significance in the hospitality sector and in the field of information technology. Travellers can make informed decisions on their hotel choices that leads more increased customer satisfaction if accurate and personalised ratings and recommendation systems are developed. Even though existing traditional hotel review and rating websites persist, this study aims to extend recommendations algorithms, data analysis methodologies with a minimalist yet functional approach that is user-centric. Eventually, enhancing the entire customer experience and assisting decision-making processes in the hotel industry.

The significance of our research can be derived from a simple hypothesis, which is **to address the needs of the hospitality and information technology sector**. Referring to a study with similar context conducted by (Chang et al., 2020), their research directly corresponds to the practical requirements of hotels, acknowledging the distinct attributes and demands across the hospitality sector. By encompassing a wide range of hotel reviews, their study customises the sentiment analysis model to cater to the industry's diverse needs. This underscores the applicability of sentiment analysis as a targeted solution, capable of elevating service quality and customer contentment across the entire spectrum of hotels.

14.5 Literature Review Introduction

The main purpose of this literature review is to thoroughly analyse the pertinent theoretical frameworks that correspond to the study objectives stated in the previous section. The forthcoming discourse will thoroughly explore a variety of subjects, including fields of study, Software Development Framework and Methodology, Business Analytical Tools and Technologies, Previous Research Approaches and Findings, Benefits and Challenges of Hotel Review Recommendation Systems, Empirical Evidence from Journal Articles, and culminate in a comprehensive conclusion.

14.6 Domain of Study

This domain of study for our literature review emphasises hotel review and recommendation systems and websites, specifically addressing shortcomings and limitations in standard hotel review systems and websites. The study investigates the use of sentiment analysis as an avenue to further enhance review reliability and accuracy, resulting in more neutral and thorough hotel evaluations. The results are intended to contribute to a more user-centric and trustworthy platform, allowing users and travellers to make more informed choices when booking hotels.

14.6.1 Hotel Review Websites

The significance of hotel review systems and their impact on travellers' decisions, influenced by online platforms and user-generated content, while acknowledging the potential limitations and biases.

14.6.2 Challenges Faced in the World Due to Issues with Hotel Review Systems

Table 14.1 shows hotel review systems' crucial role in decision-making is evident, but challenges like fake reviews, bias, and overemphasis on negatives need attention for fairness and credibility.

14.7 Software Development Framework and Methodology

14.7.1 System Development Life Cycle (SDLC): Iterative Process

14.7.1.1 SDLC Introduction

The Software Development Life Cycle, also known as the SDLC, is a methodical procedure that is utilised in the process of developing and updating software programs. It consists of a set of clearly defined phases that serve as a roadmap for software developers and other stakeholders for the entirety of the product's life cycle. The primary objective of the software development life cycle (SDLC) is to create high-quality software that satisfies user requirements in a manner that is consistent with the project's scope, budget, and schedule.

14.7 Software Development Framework and Methodology

Table 14.1 Challenges faced in the world due to issues with Hotel Review Systems SDLC

No	Author	Summary	Critical thinking
1.	Cheng et al. (2023)	The article discusses the importance of transparency in the process of generating digital advertisements, particularly in the context of online hotel booking. It focuses on how digital marketers can design transparency messages to address consumer concerns and potential backlash regarding the transparency of ad generation	• The article delves into the complexities of hotel review systems, recognizing their significance in informing consumers' decisions and enhancing transparency • It astutely highlights challenges like fake reviews, lack of uniformity in rating systems, and the disproportionate impact of negative feedback on hotel reputations • However, while discussing biases in reviews, the article could explore potential solutions to address these issues • The overemphasis on negative feedback's impact on hotel image underscores the need for platforms to ensure a balanced representation of reviews
2.	Márquez Reiter et al. (2023)	This article explores the intercultural dynamics and experiences of travelers who provide online reviews for Spanish hotel chains in two different overseas tourist destinations: the Caribbean and Mexico. The study delves into the interactions between tourists and the host country, focusing on both direct and indirect prior knowledge of the destination, as well as the knowledge gained through interactions during the visit	
3.	VASQUEZ et al. (2023)	The article discusses a study aimed at assessing the performance of Hotel Luna in Vigan City by analyzing customer satisfaction ratings obtained from online travel agents. The study utilizes the s SERVQUAL theory and associated variables to evaluate customer satisfaction levels and to improve the hotel's services based on customer feedback	

(continued)

Table 14.1 (continued)

No	Author	Summary	Critical thinking
4.	Roy et al. (2023)	This article discusses a study that applied Source Credibility Theory (SCT) to explore how source credibility factors (SCFs) influence travelers' electronic word of mouth (eWOM) and its impact on tourists' intentions to book hotels and share reviews	
5.	Martin-Fuentes et al. (2020)	This paper discusses a research study that focuses on the impact of various scales and methods used to collect reviews and ratings on online travel agencies (OTAs) and how these factors can influence hotels	
6.	Kuokkanen and Sun (2020)	This article discusses the topic of corporate social responsibility (CSR) initiatives and their impact on customers in the hospitality and tourism industry. While previous studies have indicated that CSR initiatives can have a positive effect on customers, the article highlights a research gap in the existing	
7.	Banerjee et al. (2019)	This article discusses a research paper that focuses s on the objective of distinguishing between authentic and fictitious user-generated hotel reviews	
8.	Zhou and Li (2023)	The article discusses how the flourishing tourism industry has led to an increased reliance on online travel reviews by travelers when booking accommodations	

SDLC Phases

Table 14.2 discusses the Software Development Life Cycle (SDLC), its iterative approach, and the significance of adaptable methods like Agile and Scrum in achieving efficient, user-focused software development. The Software Development Life Cycle (SDLC) includes the processes of determining and documenting software requirements, developing a project plan, transforming requirements into a technical blueprint, developing the software based on the design, testing it thoroughly for flaws, deploying it for end-user access, and providing ongoing maintenance and support to ensure functionality and security (Leloudas, 2023).

The Software Development Life Cycle (SDLC) may make use of several development approaches such as Waterfall, Agile, and DevOps, depending on the requirements of the project and the preferences of the team (Galin, 2019). The most important thing is to make sure that the development process is well-structured and that each phase features careful attention to detail (Figs. 14.1 and 14.2).

14.7.1.2 Introduction to Iterative Process

An iterative process is a method for developing software that divides the process of creating a software application into a series of successively smaller and more manageable steps known as iterations (Awati, 2023). An iterative process, as opposed to traditional linear processes, which require that each step be finished in the order that it was introduced, enables ongoing feedback, improvements, and revisions over the entirety of the development lifetime.

The software is built and deployed in increments using an iterative method. At each stage of the process, either new features are added or current features are improved. The steps of the standard Software Development Life Cycle (SDLC) are normally followed by each iteration. These phases include gathering requirements, designing the implementation, testing the implementation, and deploying the software (Akinsola et al., 2020). On the other hand, the iterative approach enables partial and incremental deliveries at the conclusion of each iteration, as opposed to waiting until the very end to hand over a product that has been built in its whole.

The iterative process involves the construction and delivery of software in small increments, providing value to users at each stage, while continuously involving stakeholders and users for feedback and adaptability, reducing risks by identifying and managing issues early on, and enabling the software to evolve and improve over time based on user input and changing requirements (Wan et al., 2023).

Agile and Scrum are two popular iterative approaches that place an emphasis on close cooperation, frequent communication, and the delivery of high-priority features early on in the development process.

The iterative method, in general, offers a more flexible, efficient, and responsive approach to the creation of software. This helps to ensure that the final result better matches the requirements of the users and the objectives of the project.

Table 14.2 Phases

No	Author	Summary	Critical thinking
1.	Leloudas (2023)	The article introduces the idea that software development is not a haphazard activity but a systematic process that involves several distinct phases	• SDLC Overview: The provided text outlines the Software Development Life Cycle (SDLC), which encompasses steps from software requirements determination to maintenance. It highlights the importance of a well-structured process and careful attention to detail
2.	Galin (2019)	The article provides an overview of what the chapter covers, focusing on different software development models, quality assurance integration, and a specific emphasis on the SDLC and spiral models	• Development Approaches: The SDLC can adopt different approaches like Waterfall, Agile, or DevOps based on project needs and team preferences
3.	Awati (2023)	The article provides an overview of iterative development as a technique that involves dividing a large software development process into smaller, manageable parts	• Iterative Process: The iterative process breaks software creation into smaller steps (iterations) allowing ongoing feedback, enhancements, and revisions. It contrasts with linear methods by enabling incremental deliveries, reducing risks, and promoting adaptation
4.	Akinsola et al. (2020)	The article provides insights into the significance of SDLC models, their applicability based on project characteristics, and the influence of organizational factors	
5.	Wan et al. (2023)	The article presents a control strategy tailored to the complexities of batch production in the SSC growth process for semiconductor manufacturing. The strategy combines predictive control, iterative learning control, and extended state observation to ensure that the produced SSCs meet the high standards required for electronic components	• Phases and Iterations: Each iteration within the iterative approach follows SDLC phases (requirements, design, testing, deployment). It delivers value sooner compared to waiting for full product completion • Agile and Scrum: Agile and Scrum are iterative methods emphasizing collaboration, communication, and early high-priority feature delivery for enhanced flexibility and responsiveness • Flexibility and Efficiency: The iterative approach offers flexibility, efficiency, and adaptability in software development, leading to a final product better aligned with user requirements and project objectives

Iterative Process Details

Table 14.3 shows the interplay between structured SDLC and flexible iterative methods demands a balanced approach, addressing risks, time, customer input, complexity, and team dynamics to achieve successful software development. In order

14.7 Software Development Framework and Methodology

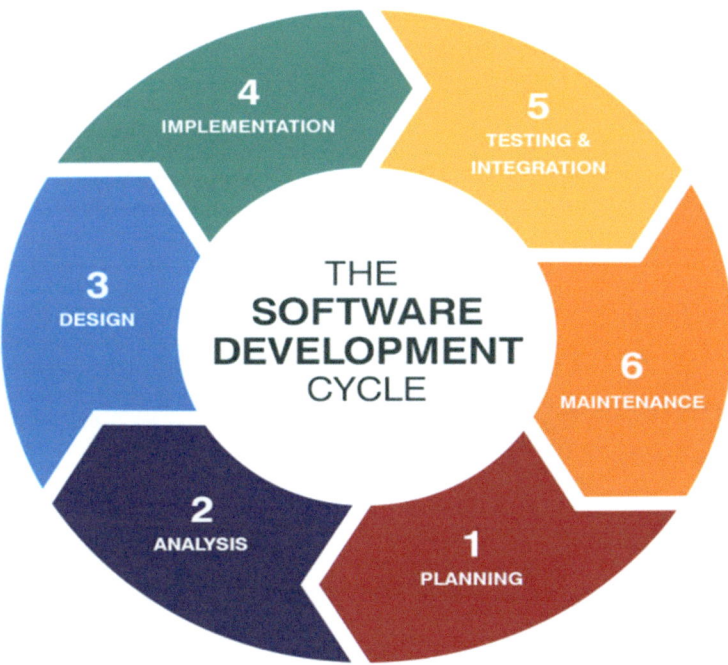

Fig. 14.1 System Development Life Cycle (SDLC) (Bwc, 2020)

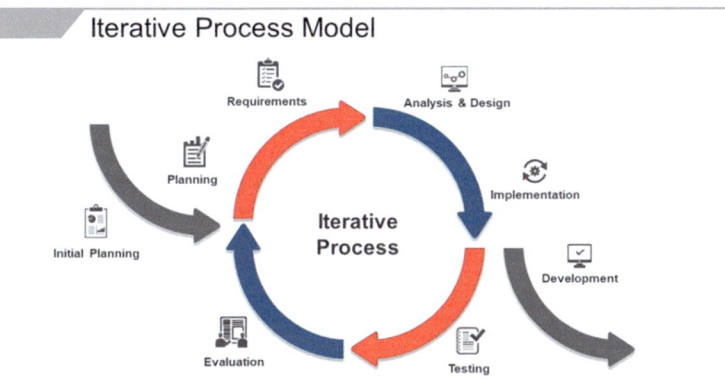

Fig. 14.2 Iterative process (Wan et al., 2023)

to achieve our objective of resolving the challenges outlined in the problem description, the iterative approach is essential to our hotel review recommendation system project. We will use an iterative approach to ensure consistent progress and will focus our efforts on the most important aspects of system development.

Table 14.3 Iterative process details

No	Author	Summary	Critical Thinking
1.	Zhu et al. (2023)	The main focus of the article is on addressing the challenges of identifying essential proteins in cells by using the iterative framework	• Flexibility vs. Structure: The SDLC and iterative processes highlight the tension between structured planning and flexibility. While SDLC provides a comprehensive roadmap, iterations prioritize adaptability. Balancing these approaches is crucial for dynamic projects • Risk Management: Iterative methods excel in risk identification and mitigation. Early stakeholder engagement aids in catching issues early However, SDLC's linear nature might cause late-stage surprises, necessitating a more integrated risk assessment strategy • Time and Cost: Iterations enable quicker value delivery, but managing constant changes can extend timelines. SDLC's structured phases may streamline progress but risk delayed feedback incorporation. Finding the right equilibrium is pivotal • Customer Involvement: Iterations engage users regularly, refining the software according to their evolving needs. SDLC's linear progression might miss evolving user expectations • Complexity: Complex projects may benefit from SDLC's organized approach. However, iterative processes might face challenges in maintaining coherence and integration when dealing with intricate systems • Team Dynamics: Iterations require strong collaboration and communication. SDLC might offer a more compartmentalized work environment. Teams need to adapt their approach based on their strengths and project demands
2.	Pan et al. (2022)	This article introduces a new approach called C-ILEO (Iterative Learning with Ensemble Operating) for addressing the challenges of imbalanced classification using machine learning	
3.	Badea and Popescu (2022)	The article presents comparative results between the implementation of LearnEval and an earlier study, indicating improved levels of system usability, grading validity, and student satisfaction	

(continued)

14.7 Software Development Framework and Methodology

Table 14.3 (continued)

No	Author	Summary	Critical Thinking
4.	Burton et al. (2020)	The primary focus of the article is on the iterative yti&ability testing cycle that was employed during the design process to create an effective and user-friendly console workstation for the aircraft carrier's tactical support center	
5.	Cai and Zhang (2022)	This article provides a detailed exploration of the iterative closest point (ICP) algorithm, focusing on its iterative process, parameter selection strategies, and the resulting rigid transformations between consecutive point clouds	
6.	Pei et al. (2023)	This article focuses on a control strategy for the tricalcium neutralization process (TNP), a significant recovery process within the context of citric acid production	

(continued)

Table 14.3 (continued)

No	Author	Summary	Critical Thinking
7.	Panwar et al. (2022)	This research article discusses a new iterative process called "MP iteration" and its applications in the context of fixed points of p-nonexpansive mappings in modular function spaces. The main focus of the article is on introducing and analyzing the properties of this iterative process and its convergence behavior	
8.	Zhai and Yang (2022)	This article presents a novel approach for time-varying process monitoring using iterative-updated semi-supervised nonnegative matrix factorizations (ISNMFs)	
9.	Petersen et al. (2023)	This article discusses the role of synthetic biology in engineering biocatalysis, cellular functions, and organism behavior, and emphasizes the importance of data-driven approaches in this field	

14.7.2 Sentiment Analysis

14.7.2.1 Introduction of Sentiment Analysis

Table 14.4 shows the sentiment analysis studies linguistic expressions of private states in context, vital due to the surge in opinion-rich digital data from social media. Challenges include context-dependent opinions, communication variations, and polarity complexities. Feature extraction gains importance for understanding implicit expressions.

14.8 Summary of Sentiment Analysis

Table 14.5 shows sentiment analysis grapples with terminology nuances, contextual subjectivity, individual communication variations, polarity-strength dynamics, recipient focus, and the expanding social media data landscape for accurate interpretation of evaluative language. In conclusion, this discipline which brings together academics from computer science, data mining, text retrieval, and computational linguistics, offers several options for both quantitative and qualitative studies. Taking on the hazy definition of sentiment and the complexities of its representation in text, it opens the door to creative applications of techniques already created for data mining and text analysis, as well as raising new problems that stimulate the development of more advance tools.

The Internet provides an infinite amount of different and opinionated text, although only a small portion of the existing domains have been studied. Product reviews— brief texts with a well-defined topic—have received a lot of attention. More broad writing, such as blog posts and webpages, has recently gained popularity. Even said, the area is still struggling with more complicated texts such as sophisticated political debates and formal works. Future work on improving existing strategies to handle more linguistic and semantic patterns will undoubtedly be appealing to both researchers and business users.

14.9 TextBlob

14.9.1 Introduction of TextBlob

Understanding and processing human language has become a vital part of a variety of applications ranging from sentiment analysis and language translation to information extraction and text classification in the fast-evolving discipline of Natural Language Processing (NLP). An open-source Python module called TextBlob is used to process textual data. To access its features and carry out simple NLP procedures, it provides

Table 14.4 Sentiment analysis

No	Author	Summary	Critical thinking
1.	Pang and Lee (2019)	This article discusses the evolution of information-gathering behavior, particularly the practice of seeking out and understanding the opinions of others	• Terminology Variation: Sentiment analysis is known by various names like subjectivity analysis, opinion mining, and evaluation extraction. These terms highlight its focus on extracting sentiments and opinions from text data
2.	Wiebe et al. (2004)	This article discusses the concept of subjectivity in natural language, which pertains to the use of language to express opinions, evaluations, and speculations	• Link to Affective Computing: Sentiment analysis is linked to affective computing, which involves recognizing and representing emotions in computers. This connection underscores its role in understanding emotional aspects of text • Subjective Elements: Subjective elements are linguistic expressions of personal states within a context. They often manifest as single words, phrases, or sentences and are key components of sentiment analysis • Sentiment Units: While whole documents have been analyzed for sentiment, the focus is generally on smaller linguistic units • Sentiment is typically believed to reside in these smaller components Interchangeable Terms: Sentiment and opinion are often used interchangeably due to their close relationship, as they both capture people's emotional responses and viewpoints • Interdisciplinary Influence: Sentiment analysis transcends computer science, extending its significance to management sciences and social sciences. This shift reflects its growing importance in understanding human behavior and decision-making • Digital Data Explosion: The rise of social media platforms and online communication has led to an abundance of opinionated digital data, making sentiment analysis more relevant than ever before • Challenges: Sentiment analysis faces challenges in interpreting opinion words across contexts and accounting for variations in communication styles • Polarity and Strength: Sentiment polarity (positive/negative) is distinct from sentiment strength (intensity of emotion). Recognizing these differences is essential for accurate analysis • Recipient Focus: Understanding the intended recipient of sentiment is crucial. Analysis often centers on products and movies, but attention to specific aspects within these is essential for deeper insights • Feature Extraction: Extracting relevant features from text has gained importance, especially due to available product review datasets. Features can be explicit or implicit in the text, contributing to sentiment understanding

(continued)

14.9 TextBlob

Table 14.4 (continued)

No	Author	Summary	Critical thinking
3	Turney and Littman (2003)	This article discusses the concept of semantic orientation, which pertains to the evaluative nature of words, indicating whether they have a positive or negative connotation	
4	Agarwal et al. (2011)	This article discusses sentiment analysis on Twitter data, introducing new features based on prior polarity and exploring the use of a tree kernel for analysis	
5	Liu (2012)	The book's content is organized into various chapters, covering topics such as document sentiment classification, sentence subjectivity, and sentiment classification, aspect-based sentiment analysis, sentiment lexicon generation, opinion summarization, analysis of comparative opinions, opinion search and retrieval, opinion spam detection, quality of reviews, and concluding remarks	
6.	Vinodhini and Chandrasekaran (2019).	This article discusses the prevalence and significance of sentiment analysis due to the abundance of opinion-rich web resources available in digital format, including discussion forums, review sites, blogs, and news articles	

(continued)

Table 14.4 (continued)

No	Author	Summary	Critical thinking
7.	Popescu and Etzioni (2005)	This paper presents a system called Opine, which addresses the common issue faced consumers when making product choices based on online reviews	
8.	Liu et al. (2005)	This paper highlights the significance of the internet as a valuable resource for collecting consumer opinions, particularly through various online platforms like customer review websites, forums, discussion groups, and blogs	
9.	Liu (2011)	The book aims to cover key tasks and techniques within Web mining, which can be categorized into three main areas: structure mining, content mining, and usage mining. It focuses on both theoretical aspects and practical applications, presenting a comprehensive overview of the field	

a simple API. On textual data, TextBlob carries out a variety of operations, including noun phrase extraction, sentiment analysis, classification, translation, etc. (Bandgar, 2022). Its user-friendly approach allows both novice and professional developers to dig into the field of NLP, boosting their apps with language comprehension skills (He & Zheng, 2019) (Fig. 14.3).

14.9.2 Workflow of TextBlob

1. **Cleaned Data**

   Use the TextBlob library to clean and preprocess the text data by removing special characters, punctuation, and irrelevant information. Next, convert all text to lowercase to ensure consistency in the analysis (Fig. 14.3).

2. **TextBlob Library**

   Apply the TextBlob library to calculate sentiment scores for each text entry. Extract sentiment polarity scores (ranging from -1 to 1) to determine the positivity or negativity of the text. Next, compute subjectivity scores (ranging from 0 to 1) to measure the objectivity or subjectivity of the text.

3. **Sentiment Scores**

14.9 TextBlob

Table 14.5 Summary of sentiment analysis

No	Author	Summary	Critical thinking
1.	Bandgar (2022)	The article discusses the concept of sentiment analysis and introduces TextBlob, an open-source Python library for processing textual data.	• Semantic Ambiguity: The diverse terminologies used in sentiment analysis underscore the challenge of interpreting subjective language. Shifting definitions like opinion, sentiment, and affective computing can lead to inconsistent analysis if not carefully defined
2.	He and Zheng (2019)	The article discusses the application of sentiment analysis in analyzing online social media data, particularly in the context of health-related content like tweets and forum posts	• Contextual Subjectivity: Evaluative expressions heavily depend on context. What's positive in one situation might be negative in another. This context sensitivity requires sophisticated models that can grasp nuanced meaning shifts
3.	Hinduja et al. (2022)	The article discusses the use of social media platforms as an ecosystem of social sensors for monitoring mental health, treating each user as a "social sensor cloud"	• Individual Variation: Sentiment communication varies among individuals, and classical text processing assumptions may not hold. Variations in expression style, culture, and language intricacies pose challenges for creating universally accurate sentiment models
4.	Suanpang et al. (2021)	The article discusses a study focused on using sentiment analysis, specifically utilizing the TextBlob package, for a tourism business case study in Thailand with the goal of revitalizing the tourism industry after the impact of the COVID-19 pandemic	• Polarity vs. Strength: The interplay between sentiment polarity and strength complicates analysis. Distinguishing between strong opinions on average items and weak opinions on exceptional items necessitates nuanced understanding
5.	Gupta (2023)	This article provides an overview of using the TextBlob library in Python for Natural Language Processing (NLP). NLP involves extracting meaningful information from human language, and TextBlob is a powerful tool that simplifies various NLP tasks. The article highlights the advantages of using TextBlob and demonstrates how to perform different NLP tasks using this library	• Recipient Focus: Identifying the target of sentiment (product features, aspects) enhances the applicability of sentiment analysis. Efficiently extracting these elements from text aids in generating more insightful results • Expanding Data Landscape: The exponential growth of opinionated digital data from social media adds complexity. Navigating this evolving landscape requires continuous adaptation and expansion of sentiment analysis techniques

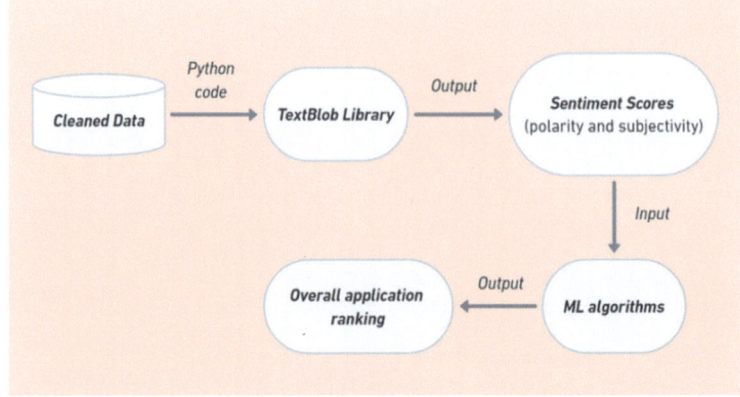

Fig. 14.3 Workflow of TextBlob (Kuzminykh, 2022)

Analyse the preprocessed text data to determine the popularity of each application. Next, implement a method to count occurrences or measure engagement (e.g. likes, comments) related to each application in the text data.

4. **Machine Learning Algorithms**

   Choose suitable ML algorithms (e.g. linear regression, decision trees, and random forests) to predict sentiment scores or subjectivity based on extracted features from the text data. Next, train the ML models using labelled data to improve accuracy in sentiment analysis and subjectivity prediction.

5. **Overall Application Ranking**

   Combine the popularity scores, sentiment polarity scores, and subjectivity scores to create an overall ranking for each application. Optionally, apply weighted averaging to give different importance to popularity, sentiment, and subjectivity scores. Finally, generate the final ranking, which reflects the applications' overall performance based on sentiment and popularity.

14.9.3 How TextBlob Enhances Sentiment Analysis for Hotel Reviews

Our study uses TextBlob as a potent tool to improve sentiment analysis for hotel evaluations. How to use TextBlob is as follows:

1. **Sentiment Analysis:**

   The process of sentiment analysis is made simpler by TextBlob's user-friendly API, making it available to developers with varied levels of linguistics or NLP expertise. TextBlob accurately translates sentiments in a variety of languages, including the domain-specific and informal language used in hotel reviews, thanks to a pre-trained sentiment vocabulary and integration with NLTK.

14.10 PHP (Hypertext Preprocessor)

14.10.1 Introduction of PHP

Table 14.6 shows PHP's journey from basic templating to dynamic scripting showcasing its adaptability. Integrated with HTML, PHP facilitates dynamic web content creation, although competition from newer technologies remains. PHP (Hypertext Preprocessor) is a widely used server-side scripting language that has played a pivotal role in shaping the modern web (Chris, 2021). Developed by Rasmus Lerdorf in 1994, PHP was initially designed for small-scale web applications and templating purposes (Alih & Ogala, 2019). However, over the years, it has evolved into a robust and feature-rich programming language, powering some of the most prominent websites and applications on the internet (The PHP Group, 2023).

What sets PHP apart is its ability to seamlessly blend with HTML, making it an ideal choice for building dynamic and interactive webpages (Simplilearn, 2023). PHP scripts are embedded directly within HTML code, allowing developers to create a mix of static content and dynamic elements that can adapt to user input and data processing (Khan, 2021). Over the years, PHP has undergone significant improvements, with each new version introducing performance enhancements, security upgrades, and new language features.

14.10.2 Features of PHP

Table 14.7 highlights PHP's strengths: open-source nature, cross-platform compatibility, server-side scripting, database integration, OOP support, ease of learning, extensibility, community backing, improved speed, and security features. Lincopinis et al. (2023) demonstrate some of PHP's most notable features.

1. **Open Source**

   PHP is an open-source language that is freely available under the PHP Licence. This facilitates developer access and supports a broad and active community contributing to its development.
2. **Cross-Platform**

   PHP can run on a variety of operating systems, including Windows, Linux, Unix, and macOS, making it versatile and easy to utilise in a variety of settings. It is also interoperable with most web servers, including Apache and Nginx, making application deployment easier.

Table 14.6 PHP

No	Author	Summary	Critical thinking
1.	The PHP group (2023)	The article discusses the history and evolution of the PHP programming language, highlighting its origins, milestones, and significant changes over the years	• Legacy and Evolution: PHP's transformation from a simple templating language to a powerful scripting language illustrates its adaptability. The language's evolution highlights its ability to meet changing demands in web development
2.	Simplilearn (2023)	This article provides an overview of PHP (Hypertext Preprocessor), an open-source server-side scripting language used for dynamic web development. It emphasizes PHP's enduring popularity and dominant presence in the web development landscape, despite its age	• Integration and Ease: PHP's integration with HTML streamlines dynamic web content creation. However, this tight integration might pose challenges in terms of code maintainability and separation of concerns
3.	Alih and Ogala (2019)	This article focuses on PHP (Hypertext Preprocessor) in the context of web development. It aims to delve into the concept of programming and how it relates to web development using PHP	• Competing Technologies: While PHP has maintained its relevance, it faces competition from modern web frameworks and languages that offer more structured and efficient development processes
4.	Chris (2021)	This article provides an overview of PHP (Hypertext Preprocessor), an open-source server-side scripting language commonly used for web development. It discusses PHP's Python for Business Analytfcft istory, features, advantages, and use cases, and provides a tutorial on writing a simple "Hello World" program in PHP	
5.	Khan (2021)	The article provides an introduction and overview of PHP (Hypertext Preprocessor), a scripting language commonly used for creating dynamic and interactive websites. It explains various aspects of PHP, its applications, and how to get started with PHP programming	

14.10   PHP (Hypertext Preprocessor)   123

14.7   Features of PHP

No	Author	Summary	Critical thinking
1.	Lincopinis et al. (2023)	The article provides an overview of the PHP programming language, its history, applications, advantages, disadvantages, syntax, popularity, and more	• Versatility and Accessibility: PHP's open-source nature encourages collaboration, fostering a strong developer community. Its cross-platform compatibility and integration with major web servers ensure wide applicability
• Dynamic Web Development: PHP's server-side scripting enhances dynamic web content generation. However, the tight blend of PHP and HTML can pose challenges in terms of code maintainability and separation of concerns
• Database Interaction: PHP's database integration Database Interaction: PHP's database integration facilitates efficient data handling, a crucial aspect of the hotel review system. This allows for effective storage, retrieval, and analysis of scraped reviews
• OOP and User-Friendly Syntax: PHP's support for OOP promotes reusable code for intricate data processing logic. Its user-friendly syntax C-based languages, simplifies development without compromising effectiveness
• Extensibility and Community: PHP's extensibility via third-party libraries and the vast developer community aids in streamlining processes and problem-solving, ensuring ongoing language development
2.	Siame and Kunda (2019)	The article provides a review of research work conducted on the evolution of PHP applications that have gained widespread use over time	
3.	Crettenand (2019)	This book is designed to help PHP developers improve their code quality, testability, and readability by incorporating modern functional programming techniques. It aims to provide a solid foundation in functional programming concepts and methodologies, guiding readers step-by-step to architect more robust and maintainable code	
4.	Jevremovic (2019)	The article discusses the issue of protecting PHP scripts from unauthorized use, copying, and modifications. It highlights that current flython for Business AnaWssolutions primarily involve obfuscators working at the source code level, but they often lack substantial protection	
5.	Letarte et al. (2019)	This article discusses the dynamic nature of websites, which often consist of a combination of static content and programs that interact with relational databases as a backend	

3. **Server-side Scripting**

   PHP executes code on the server side rather than the client side, where the browser is located. The server can now generate HTML output, which improves the production of dynamic webpages, form processing, and database interactions.

4. **Database Integration**

   As a server-side scripting language, PHP allows developers to interface with databases, save and retrieve data, and conduct operations such as table creation and data modification.

5. **Object-Oriented Programming (OOP)**

   PHP supports object-oriented programming (OOP), which allows developers to construct reusable and maintainable code. Inheritance and polymorphism are OOP concepts that improve code organisation and readability (Siame & Kunda, 2019).

6. **Easy to Learn**

   PHP is well-known for its user-friendliness, despite its strict language. Its syntax is comparable to C, making it easier to learn for developers who have prior experience with C-based languages (Crettenand, 2019).

7. **Extensibility**

   PHP can be extended using third-party libraries and extensions, increasing the language's functionality. This enables developers to reuse existing code and quickly solve common problems (Prokofyeva & Boltunova, 2017).

8. **Large Community**

   PHP has a huge and active developer community that provides access to help, tools, and support when needed.

9. **Speed**

   After the release of version 7.x, PHP's processing speed improved significantly, making it faster than many other programming languages. This is critical for critical web applications requiring great performance.

10. **Security**

    PHP includes several pre-defined functions for data encryption and security. The language is intended to be more secure, and developers can supplement security using third-party apps (Jevremovic, 2019). Changes in security attributes, such as access control privileges, may be tracked by watching and analysing differences in security models retrieved from various versions of an application (Letarte et al., 2019).

14.10 PHP (Hypertext Preprocessor)

14.10.3 How PHP Enhances Dynamic Web Development and Data Processing in Our System

Our hotel review recommendation system relies heavily on PHP (Hypertext Preprocessor), which helps with dynamic web creation and effective data processing. The use of PHP is explained in the following:

1. **Server-Side Scripting:** PHP performs code execution on the server before transmitting the HTML output to the client's browser. This is known as server-side scripting. As a result, the system can successfully handle hotel reviews by generating dynamic webpages, processing form data, and interacting with databases.
2. **HTML Integration:** PHP integrates well with HTML, enabling programmers to include PHP scripts directly in HTML code. With the help of this integration, dynamic and interactive webpages may be made, allowing PHP code to effectively change data and adapt to user input.
3. **Database Integration:** PHP, a server-side programming language, provides database interaction, including data storing and retrieval. This capability is crucial for handling and analysing the hotel reviews that have been scraped in order to produce insights for users and company owners.
4. **Object-Oriented Programming (OOP):** Thanks to PHP's support for OOP, programmers may create reusable, maintainable code. This arrangement improves the readability of the code and makes it simpler to handle the intricate logic needed for data processing and analysis.
5. **User-Friendliness:** PHP's syntax is simple and simple to learn, especially for programmers who are accustomed to C-based languages. The development team can create system-specific code that is effective and efficient because of its simplicity.
6. **Extensibility:** PHP's extensibility helps to improve the functioning of the system. Developers can use a wide selection of tools to streamline procedures and address typical problems in data processing and web development by integrating third-party libraries and extensions.
7. **Large Community Support:** PHP enjoys the backing of a sizable and vibrant developer community, which offers helpful materials, tools, and support. This community-driven methodology guarantees PHP's ongoing development and progress as a dependable web development language.

14.11 Summary for PHP

In summary, PHP is open-source, cross-platform, server-side scripting, database integration, support for object-oriented programming, ease of learning, extensibility with third-party libraries, a big community, speed, and built-in security mechanisms. These characteristics all contribute to PHP's popularity and efficiency as a programming language for web development.

14.12 Power BI

14.12.1 Introduction of Power BI

Table 14.8 shows that Power BI's transformative influence on business intelligence is evident through improved decision-making. Its ongoing evolution and AI integration underline its role in reshaping data utilisation for businesses. Power BI, a groundbreaking product of Microsoft, has significantly revolutionised business analytics since its introduction in 2014. It offers a suite of business analytics tools that allow users to visualise data and share insights across an organisation or embed them in an application or a website (Becker & Gould, 2019). This cloud-based tool has reshaped how businesses approach data-driven decision-making.

Power BI emerged as a self-service business intelligence tool when Microsoft first introduced it as an add-in for Office 365 in 2014. The launch was a response to the need for intuitive tools that could facilitate data analysis for decision-makers with limited technical skills Becker and Gould (2019). The standalone, cloud-based version, known as Power BI Services, and the desktop application, Power BI Desktop, were introduced a year later in 2015.

14.12.2 How Power BI Empowers Data Visualisation and Decision-Making

In our hotel review recommendation system, Power BI is crucial in enabling data visualisation and data-driven decision-making. Here are some examples of how Power BI is used:

1. **Interactive Visualisations:** Power BI provides interactive visualisations that make it easy for users to explore and engage with data. Users may build meaningful reports and dashboards with little technical assistance thanks to drag-and-drop features and dynamic filters.
2. **Data Integration:** Power BI makes it easy to combine data from several sources, like as databases, spreadsheets, and cloud services. This thorough data gathering

14.12 Power BI

Table 14.8 Power BI

No	Author	Summary	Critical thinking
1.	Becker and Gould (2019)	The article talk about introduces Microsoft's Power BI software and associated functionality built into recent versions of Microsoft's Excel	• Enhanced Decision-Making: Power BI's impact lies in its role in data-driven decision-making. Its evolving features and AI integration broaden its potential • Dependency and Adaptation: Businesses relying heavily on Power BI must adapt to its updates. Its transformative power hinges on effective integration and user proficiency
2.	Becker, L. T., & Gould, E. M. (2019)	The article talk about use Power BI to combine, analyze, visualize, and share data from the wide variety of data sources encountered in library operations	
3.	Kim (1982)	The article talk about nesting of query blocks to an arbitrary depth	
4.	Chaudhuri et al. (2011)	The article talk about Business Intelligence (BI) is a collection of decision support technologies for the enterprise aimed at enabling knowledge workers	
5.	Ding (2023)	The article talk about Power BI is a suite of business analytics tools to analyze data and share insights. Monitor your business and get answers quickly with rich dashboards available on every device	

procedure makes sure that all pertinent facts are accessible for analysis and decision-making.

3. **Data Transformation and Modelling:** Power BI's data analysts can shape, clean, and transform input data into structured models using tools like Power Query and DAX functions. These data models provide the framework for creating engaging dashboards and producing insightful data.
4. **Collaboration and Sharing:** Users can publish and distribute reports and dashboards with coworkers and stakeholders using Power BI's cloud-based service. Through collaboration, the organisation's many divisions and levels can make decisions based on data.
5. **Scheduled Data Refresh:** Power BI offers options for scheduled data refresh to guarantee data accuracy and freshness. Decision-makers will always have access to the most recent data using this functionality for analysis and reporting.

14.13 Web Scraper

14.13.1 Introduction of Web Scraper

Table 14.9 shows the web scraping's evolution, challenges with dynamic websites, standardisation, ethics, and AI advancements collectively influence its role in data extraction and insights generation from the expanding online data landscape. Looking forward, advancements in artificial intelligence and machine learning are poised to shape the future of web scraping technologies. These technologies could facilitate more sophisticated data extraction processes, streamline data analysis, and enhance prediction models. The result would be a more nuanced and insightful understanding of available data (Zhai & Liu, 2020)]. Furthermore, as online data continues to grow exponentially, web scraping technologies' importance and application scope are also expected to expand (Vargiu & Urru, 2019).

14.13.2 The Challenges and Ethical Concerns in Web Scraping

Table 14.10 shows the web scraping's challenges span dynamic websites, standardisation, ethics, and technical complexity. It enables a hotel recommendation system by collecting, preprocessing, and generating insights from diverse review sources.

14.13.3 How Web Scraper Enables Data Extraction and Analysis

Our hotel review recommendation system relies heavily on web scraping, which makes it possible to efficiently extract and analyse data from numerous sources. The use of web scraping is described in the following:

1. **Data Collection:** Web scraping is an effective method for obtaining copious amounts of data from review websites for hotels like Agoda, TripAdvisor, and Booking.com. We ensure that the system has access to a wide variety of hotel evaluations by methodically collecting data from these sources.
2. **Data Preprocessing:** In order to organise and clean up the retrieved data for analysis, preprocessing is frequently necessary. Using web scraping, we can eliminate extraneous details, special characters, and inconsistencies to produce accurate data that is ready for further analysis.
3. **Insights Generation:** Web scraping makes it possible to extract insightful information from the gathered hotel evaluations. The system may discover trends,

14.13 Web Scraper

Table 14.9 Web scraper (introduction)

No	Author	Summary	Critical thinking
1.	Fkih and Omri (2020)	The article talks about the standards of the "semantic web" which allows the data to be shared and reused between several applications, it became necessary to model web text documents with a vision based on the concepts and exploit available linguistic resources	• Evolution from Internet Growth: Web scraping's evolution is intertwined with the internet's complexity and data explosion. It emerged as a solution to effectively extract and manipulate vast online information • Enhancing Techniques: Various techniques like APIs, DOM parsing, and regular expressions have been developed to enhance web scraping's effectiveness and efficiency, catering to diverse navigation and extraction needs • Dynamic Website Challenges: The changing structures of dynamic websites pose obstacles in consistent scraping. Management strategies are essential to handle data volume and maintain usability • Standardization Issues: Lack of uniformity in web pages demands scraping tools to accurately interpret unique elements and structures, contributing to technical complexities • Ethical and Privacy Concerns: Bulk data extraction raises ethical questions around user privacy and data misuse, emphasizing responsible scraping practices • Ethical and Privacy Concerns: Bulk data extraction raises ethical questions around user privacy and data misuse, emphasizing responsible scraping practices • AI and ML's Influence: AI and ML advancements hold potential to elevate scraping processes, enhancing extraction, analysis, and predictive capabilities • Growing Significance: The exponential growth of online data underscores web scraping's importance, with its scope expected to expand alongside data proliferation
2.	Kinne and Axenbeck (2019)	The article talks about apply this tool in a large-scale pilot study to provide information on the data source	
3.	Saurkar et al. (2019)	This article talks about web scraping is very imperative technique which is used to generate structured data based on available unstructured data on the web	
4.	Ferrara et al. (2019)	This article talks about providing a structured and comprehensive overview of the literature in the field of Web Data Extraction	
5.	Ipeirotis et al. (2019)	This article talks about present algorithms that improve the existing state-of-the-art techniques, enabling the separation of bias and error	

Table 4.10 Web scraper (summary)

No	Author	Summary	Critical thinking
1	Weiss et al. (2019)	This article study about provides an authoritative, comprehensive survey of the concepts, principles, and methods of text mining	• Dynamic Website Challenges: Navigating evolving website structures presents hurdles for consistent web scraping. Effective strategies are essential for managing the overwhelming volume of data • Standardization and Technical Complexity: Lack of uniformity in web pages complicates scraping. Diverse website elements require accurate interpretation, contributing to technical intricacies. • Ethical Concerns: Bulk data extraction raises ethical questions about privacy and misuse. Responsible practices are crucial to address user concerns and data security • AI and ML Potential: Advancements in AI and ML promise to refine web scraping processes, enhancing extraction, analysis, and prediction capabilities for more insightful data understanding. • Hotel Recommendation System: Web scraping is pivotal in data extraction for the hotel recommendation system. It enables diverse data • Data Variety and Accuracy: Scraping from multiple sources diversifies hotel review data, enhancing the system's capacity to provide comprehensive and objective recommendations
2	Khder (2021)	This article study about web scrapping is a technology that allow us to extract structured data from text such as HTML	
3	Zhai and Liu (2020)	This article study about studies the problem of extracting data from a web page that contains several structured data records.	
4	Vargiu and Urru (2019)	This article study about web scraping is the set of techniques used to automatically get some information from a website instead of manually copying it	
5	Marlina and Purwandari (2019)	This article study about It was further analysed to develop strategies to implement RDM services in Indonesia, which suggest provision of national policy and IT/IS infrastructure, as well as improvement of research data awereness among reseachers	

patterns, and feelings that assist in suggesting appropriate hotels and giving feedback to business owners by analysing sentiments, ratings, and feedback offered by users.
4. **Real-Time Data Updates:** The system makes sure that the suggestions and insights are based on the most recent and up-to-date information by routinely updating the scraped data (every two weeks or monthly), which increases the relevance and accuracy of the recommendations.
5. **Data Diversity:** Web scraping enables us to collect information from a variety of hotel review websites, broadening the range of reviews and comments that are available for study. This variety improves the system's capacity to offer thorough and objective recommendations.

14.13.4 Summary for Web Scrapper

Web scraping has become an indispensable tool in today's data-driven world, enabling individuals and businesses to make sense of the vast and complex digital landscape. However, as it continues to evolve and become more sophisticated, the challenges and ethical implications it presents need to be adequately addressed to harness its full potential effectively and responsibly.

14.14 Visual Studio

14.14.1 Introduction of Visual Studio

Table 14.11 shows Visual Studio's growth into a powerful IDE for web development is evident through its integration of HTML, JavaScript, and Bootstrap, offering comprehensive features and collaboration with JavaScript libraries, propelling efficient and streamlined development processes. Microsoft's Visual Studio, a comprehensive Integrated Development Environment (IDE), has been a game-changer in the field of web development. With robust support for key web technologies like HTML, JavaScript, and Bootstrap, it has become a one-stop solution for developers worldwide. This literature review aims to delve into Visual Studio's evolution in web development, its functionality, the challenges it faces, and future prospects.

Visual Studio's journey began with its launch in 1997, and it has since matured into a powerful tool in web development, thanks to its robust support for web technologies such as HTML, JavaScript, and later, Bootstrap (Dumas et al., 2019). Its integrative capabilities, combined with its intuitiveness and advanced debugging features, have redefined the landscape of web development, making the process more efficient and streamlined (Amann et al., 2019).

HTML, the fundamental building block of webpages, provides the necessary structure, while JavaScript, a scripting language, adds interactivity to these pages

Table 14.11 Visual studio

No	Author	Summary	Critical thinking
1.	Dumas et al. (2019)	This book offers a comprehensive introduction to the fundamental structures and applications of a wide range of contemporary coding operations	• Evolution and Integration: Visual Studio's inception in 1997 marked the beginning of its journey towards becoming a robust IDE for web development. Its integration of HTML, JavaScript, and Bootstrap showcases its adaptability and relevance • Comprehensive Toolset: Visual Studio's support for essential web technologies empowers developers with a consolidated solution. Its rich features, from syntax highlighting to advanced debugging, enhance efficiency. • Efficiency and Streamlining: Visual Studio's intuitive interface and debugging capabilities redefine web development, making it more efficient and user-friendly, potentially reducing development time. • JavaScript's Role: The seamless integration of JavaScript libraries and frameworks accentuates Visual Studio's potential. Pre-built code aids interactive feature development and enhances productivity • Future Outlook: The ongoing evolution of Visual Studio is expected to align with emerging web technologies, expanding its capabilities and influence in shaping web development landscapes
2.	Amann et al. (2019)	This books talks about Integrated Development Environments (IDEs) provide a convenient standalone solution that supports developers during various phases of software development	
3.	Alonso et al. (2003)	emphasis on what could be done with Web services in the future often makes us lose track of what can be really done with Web services today and in the short term	
4.	Wilton and McPeak (2020)	This book talks about shows you how to work effectively with JavaScript frameworks, functions, and modern browsers, and teaches more effective coding practices using HTML	
5.	Negrino and Smith (2020)	This research paper talks about a static program analysis infrastructure that can infer detailed and sound type information for JavaScript programs using abstract interpretation	

14.14 Visual Studio

(Alonso et al., 2003). Visual Studio offers an extensive range of features for these technologies, including syntax highlighting, auto-completion, and integrated debugging, which significantly simplify the web development process (Wilton & McPeak, 2020).

The power of Visual Studio in web development is further amplified by its collaboration with JavaScript libraries and frameworks, which offer pre-written JavaScript code to support the development of interactive features (Negrino & Smith, 2020).

14.14.2 Incorporating Bootstrap: Mobile-First, Responsive Design

Table 14.12 shows Visual Studio's integration of Bootstrap, coupled with challenges like learning curve and resource usage, is balanced by its adaptability, continuous development, and potential to align with emerging web trends.

The integration of Bootstrap, a popular open-source CSS framework, into Visual Studio marked a significant turning point. Bootstrap, which offers HTML and CSS-based design templates and optional JavaScript extensions, facilitates the creation of mobile-first, responsive web designs (Collins, 2019). The integration of this framework with Visual Studio has extended the IDE's capabilities, allowing developers to create modern and aesthetically pleasing web designs with relative ease (Frain, 2019).

Despite the advantages that Visual Studio offers, it is not without its challenges. The learning curve can be steep for beginners due to its extensive features and complex, integrated environment (Halvorson, 2019). Moreover, compared to lightweight IDEs, Visual Studio can be resource-intensive, affecting performance on lower-end hardware (Larsen, 2019).

Emerging trends in web development present new opportunities for Visual Studio. As JavaScript frameworks like React and Vue.js gain popularity, improving Visual Studio's support and integration with these technologies could further cement its position as a leading tool in web development (Sells & Flanders, 2020).

Microsoft's continuous updates to Visual Studio, including the launch of Visual Studio Code and Visual Studio 2019, reflect the company's commitment to adapting to developers' evolving needs. This active development ensures that Visual Studio remains relevant and well-equipped to meet future web development challenges (Suryanarayana et al., 2022).

Table 14.12 Incorporating bootstrap: Mobile-first, responsive design

No	Author	Summary	Critical thinking
1	Collins (2019)	Learn to use JavaScript to create web applications that are dynamic and interactive, and add advanced features, including audio, video, SVG, and drag and drop capabilities	• Bootstrap Integration: Visual Studio's inclusion of Bootstrap enhances its capabilities, allowing developers to create responsive, mobile-first designs with ease. • Learning Curve and Resource Intensiveness: Visual Studio's extensive features pose a steep learning curve for beginners, and its resource-intensive nature may affect performance on lower-end hardware. • Adapting to Trends: The rising popularity of JavaScript frameworks like React and Vue.js presents opportunities for Visual Studio to strengthen its support and integration, ensuring its relevance. • Active Development: Microsoft's updates, including Visual Studio Code and Visual Studio 2019, showcase its commitment to addressing evolving developer needs and equipping the IDE for future challenges
2	Frain (2019)	A responsive web design, built with HTML5 and CSS3, allows a website to 'just work' across multiple devices and screens	
3	Halvorson (2019)	Teach yourself the essential tools and techniques for Visual Basic 2010-one step at a time	
4	Larsen (2019)	HTML and CSS are the two core programming languages that you need to know in order to build web pages, and this beginner book introduces you to both. Providing step-by-step guidance on best practices and techniques	
5	Sells and Flanders (2020)	To experience the full spectrum of functionality and extensibility, Mastering Visual Studio .NET provides you with the practical depth and detail needed to best put—features to work	
6	Suryanarayana et al. (2022)	Helps developers or software engineers understand mistakes made while designing, what design principles were overlooked or misapplied, and what principles need to be applied properly to address those smells through refactoring	

14.15 Methodology

14.15.1 Introduction of Methodology

In this chapter, the methodologies of the research project will be defined and discussed in depth. The tools used in this project will also be discuss, including a description of the applied framework and a concise examination of the results and analysis.

14.16 Framework

14.16.1 Information Gathering

In this stage is where we had started brainstorming and gathering information with team members to start our project. The goal of this stage is to identify which direction we should take, and which step we need to take to proceed. After discussion, we have identified few factors that we will address:

1. Challenges faced by hotel customers
2. The hotel review system issues
3. Objective of study

After gathering the information needed for our project, we identified that many consumers have encountered difficulties in making informed decisions about hotels due to the abundance of fake and unreliable reviews. As a result, user trust in online hotel reviews has been compromised.

14.16.1.1 To Tackle This Issue

We developed the following solutions to address the issues faced by hotel guests and enhance the reliability of our hotel review recommendation system:

1. Sentiment Analysis: We used sentiment analysis to identify and filter out fraudulent, untrustworthy, or altered reviews from the scraped reviews. We can determine the validity and legitimacy of any review by analysing its emotion.
2. Data Cleaning and Preprocessing: To remove any irrelevant or duplicated reviews from the dataset, we used data cleaning techniques. In addition, we standardised the review structure to improve the accuracy of sentiment analysis (Figs. 14.4, 14.5, and 14.6).

Data Cleaning and Preprocessing
Sample Data
Clean Data

```
In [1]: import pandas as pd

        # read data
        reviews_df = pd.read_csv("../input/Hotel_Reviews.csv")
        # append the positive and negative text reviews
        reviews_df["review"] = reviews_df["Negative_Review"] + reviews_df["Positive_Review"]
        # create the label
        reviews_df["is_bad_review"] = reviews_df["Reviewer_Score"].apply(lambda x: 1 if x < 5 else 0)
        # select only relevant columns
        reviews_df = reviews_df[["review", "is_bad_review"]]
        reviews_df.head()
```

	review	is_bad_review
0	I am so angry that i made this post available...	1
1	No Negative No real complaints the hotel was g...	0
2	Rooms are nice but for elderly a bit difficul...	0
3	My room was dirty and I was afraid to walk ba...	1
4	You When I booked with your company on line y...	0

Fig. 14.4 Data cleaning and preprocessing

```
reviews_df = reviews_df.sample(frac = 0.1, replace = False, random_state=42)
```

Fig. 14.5 Text preprocessing with NLTK (Natural Language Toolkit) in Python

'No Negative' will show up in our data if the person doesn't leave any negative feedback. This is also true for the 'No Positive' default setting for positive comments. These parts have to be taken out of our books.

The Next Step is to Clean up the Text Data Using Different Steps

In the process of cleaning up textual data, we utilize a specialised 'clean_text' function that performs several essential tasks. Firstly, the text is converted to lowercase to ensure uniformity. Next, the function tokenizes the text, breaking it down into individual words while removing punctuation marks. Words that are not pertinent to the analysis and contain numbers are filtered out, along with common stop words such as 'the', 'a', and 'this'. Additionally, parts of speech (POS) tags are assigned to each word using the WordNet collection of words, providing valuable insights into the grammatical structure. Lastly, the function employs lemmatization to transform words into their root form, enabling a more meaningful representation of the data (Fig. 14.7 and 14.8).

```
# remove 'No Negative' or 'No Positive' from text
reviews_df["review"] = reviews_df["review"].apply(lambda x: x.replace("No Negative", "").replace("No Positive", ""))
```

Fig. 14.6 NLTK-based Python script for text cleaning and POS tagging

```python
# return the wordnet object value corresponding to the POS tag
from nltk.corpus import wordnet

def get_wordnet_pos(pos_tag):
    if pos_tag.startswith('J'):
        return wordnet.ADJ
    elif pos_tag.startswith('V'):
        return wordnet.VERB
    elif pos_tag.startswith('N'):
        return wordnet.NOUN
    elif pos_tag.startswith('R'):
        return wordnet.ADV
    else:
        return wordnet.NOUN

import string
from nltk import pos_tag
from nltk.corpus import stopwords
from nltk.tokenize import WhitespaceTokenizer
from nltk.stem import WordNetLemmatizer

def clean_text(text):
    # lower text
    text = text.lower()
    # tokenize text and remove puncutation
    text = [word.strip(string.punctuation) for word in text.split(" ")]
    # remove words that contain numbers
    text = [word for word in text if not any(c.isdigit() for c in word)]
    # remove stop words
    stop = stopwords.words('english')
```

Fig. 14.7 Snippet for text preprocessing using NLTK, including POS tagging, stopword removal, tokenization, and lemmatization

14.16.2 Data Storage

– The cleansed data has been stored in Excel, which functions as the project's database.
– As additional reviews are gathered over time, the system may append new data to the current Excel file.
– After storing our cleaned data in Excel, we utilised PHPMyAdmin to manage our database, storing pertinent information about hotels and their reviews.

```
    text = [x for x in text if x not in stop]
    # remove empty tokens
    text = [t for t in text if len(t) > 0]
    # pos tag text
    pos_tags = pos_tag(text)
    # lemmatize text
    text = [WordNetLemmatizer().lemmatize(t[0], get_wordnet_pos(t[1])) for
t in pos_tags]
    # remove words with only one letter
    text = [t for t in text if len(t) > 1]
    # join all
    text = " ".join(text)
    return(text)

# clean text data
reviews_df["review_clean"] = reviews_df["review"].apply(lambda x:
clean_text(x))
```

Fig. 14.8 Visualization source code

14.17 Dataset Page

Figures 14.9 and 14.10 is the page which shows the data of RateMyStay.

Lastly, by clicking the dataset it will navigate us to a new page. In this page, the side navigation bar contains home, dashboard, hotel reviews data entry, hotel review data entry with multiple tables and hotel data file upload.

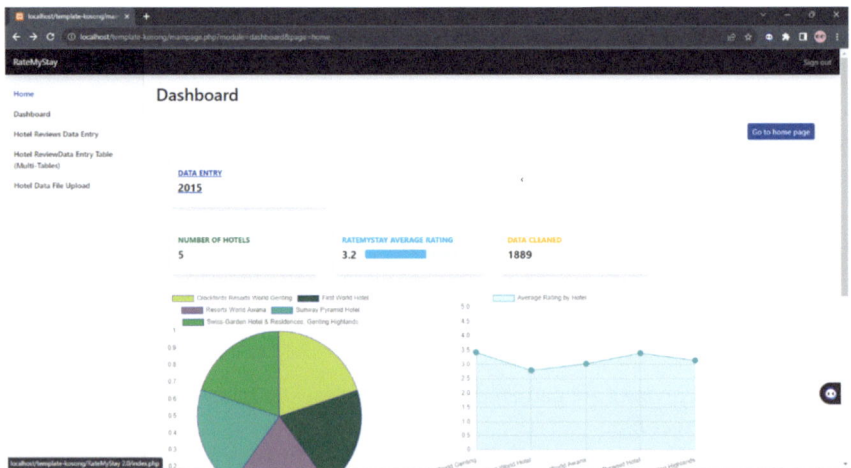

Fig. 14.9 Visual representations via a pie chart and line graph

14.18 Future Work

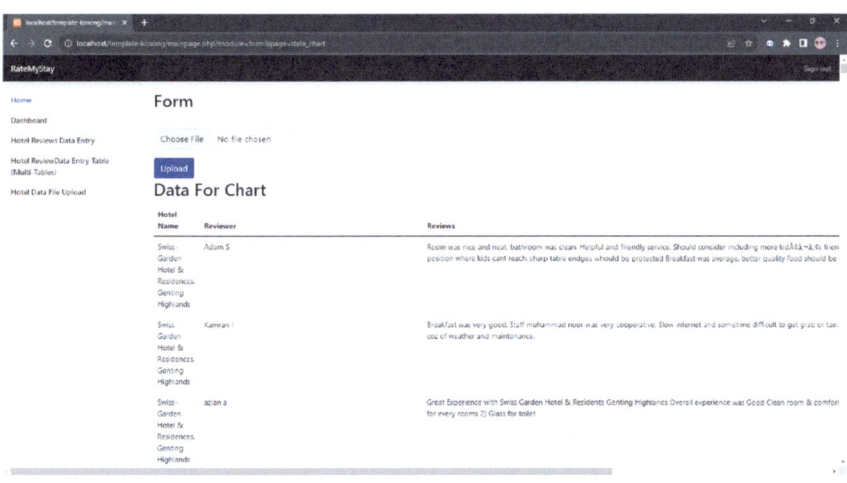

Fig. 14.10 Web application interface

14.18 Future Work

A partnership with Tourism Malaysia would encourage a win–win situation. Our project can help Tourism Malaysia make educated decisions about tourism planning and promotion by delivering important predictive analytics and insights. This data-driven strategy would aid in the optimization of marketing campaigns, the efficient allocation of resources, and the enhancement of the overall tourism experience for visitors. We would follow stringent data privacy and security measures to safeguard the confidentiality of sensitive information in order to ensure the success of this relationship. We recognise the importance of data integrity and protecting the privacy rights of both hoteliers and travellers. As we progress with this joint initiative, we hope that our prediction model will become a vital element of Tourism Malaysia's decision-making processes. We can help to more efficient resource management and better respond to the demands of tourists by precisely anticipating hotel occupancy during different seasons, thereby promoting Malaysia as a favoured destination for travellers globally.

Finally, future collaboration with Tourism Malaysia to get hotel occupancy data would considerably improve our project's predictive power. We hope to create a robust tool that benefits both the tourist sector and travellers by combining sentiment analysis of hotel reviews with occupancy statistics. As we strive for excellence and innovation, our collaboration has the potential to transform how tourism is managed and promoted in Malaysia, producing a win–win situation for all stakeholders.

References

Akinsola, J. E., Ogunbanwo, A. S., Okesola, O. J., Odun-Ayo, I. J., Ayegbusi, F. D., & Adebiyi, A. A. (2020). Comparative analysis of software development life cycle models (SDLC). *Intelligent Algorithms in Software Engineering*, 310–322. https://doi.org/10.1007/978-3-030-51965-0_27

Agarwal, A., Xie, B., Vovsha, I., Rambow, O., & Passonneau, R. J. (2011, June). Sentiment analysis of twitter data. In *Proceedings of the workshop on language in social media (LSM 2011)* (pp. 30-38).

Alonso, G., Casati, F., Kuno, H., & Machiraju, V. (2003). *Web Services: Concepts, architectures and applications.*

Alih, S. O., & Ogala, E. (2019). Concept of Web Programming, an overview of PHP Vol. 1. *International Journal of Scientific and Engineering Research, 10*(12). https://www.researchgate.net/publication/350789280_Concept_of_Web_Programming_An_Overview_of_PHP_Vol_1

Amann, S., Proksch, S., Nadi, S., & Mezini, M. (2019). A study of visual studio usage in practice. *O'Reilly & Associates, Inc.* https://doi.org/10.1109/saner.2016.39

Amueller. (2023). *GitHub - amueller/word_cloud: A little word cloud generator in Python.* GitHub. https://github.com/amueller/word_cloud

Awati, R. (2023, June 13). *What is iterative development?: Definition from TechTarget.* Software Quality. https://www.techtarget.com/searchsoftwarequality/definition/iterative-development#:~:text=Iterative%20development%20is%20a%20way,that%20build%20upon%20each%20other.

Badea, G., & Popescu, E. (2022). Learneval peer assessment platform: Iterative development process and evaluation. *IEEE Transactions on Learning Technologies, 15*(3), 421–433. https://doi.org/10.1109/tlt.2022.3185423

Bai, N., Wang, L., Xue, Y., Wang, Y., Hou, X., Li, G., ... & Guo, C. F. (2022). Graded interlocks for iontronic pressure sensors with high sensitivity and high linearity over a broad range. *Acs Nano, 16*(3), 4338–4347.

Banerjee, S., Chua, A. Y. K., & Kim, J. (2019). Distinguishing between authentic and fictitious user-generated hotel reviews. *2015 6th International Conference on Computing, Communication and Networking Technologies (ICCCNT).* https://doi.org/10.1109/icccnt.2015.7395179

Banerjee, S., & Chua, A. Y. K. (2019). Trust in online hotel reviews across review polarity and hotel category. *Computers in Human Behavior, 90*, 265–275. https://doi.org/10.1016/j.chb.2018.09.010

Bandgar, S. (2022). Sentiment analysis using TextBlob—Analytics Vidhya—Medium. *Medium.* https://medium.com/analytics-vidhya/sentiment-analysis-using-textblob-ecaaf0373dff

Becker, L. T., & Gould, E. M. (2019). Microsoft Power BI: Extending Excel to manipulate, analyze, and visualize diverse data. *Serials Review, 45*(3), 184–188. https://doi.org/10.1080/00987913.2019.1644891

Burton, N., Weaver, M., Smith, J., & Hall, K. (2020). Foam, wood, metal: An iterative process for console usability testing. *Proceedings of the Human Factors and Ergonomics Society Annual Meeting, 50*(23), 2502–2506. https://doi.org/10.1177/154193120605002308

Bwc, A. (2020). Software Development Life Cycle (SDLC). *Big water consulting.* https://bigwater.consulting/2019/04/08/software-development-life-cycle-sdlc/

Cai, L., & Zhang, J. (2022). Process analysis and effectiveness evaluation of iterative closest point algorithm. *International Conference on Mechanisms and Robotics (ICMAR 2022).* https://doi.org/10.1117/12.2652696

Caya, A. (2018). *Mastering The Faster Web with PHP, MySQL, and JavaScript.*

Chang, C. L., McAleer, M., & Wong, W. K. (2020). Risk and financial management of COVID-19 in business, economics and finance. *Journal of Risk and Financial Management, 13*(5), 102.

Chris, K. (2021). What is PHP? The PHP programming language meaning explained. *freeCodeCamp.org.* https://www.freecodecamp.org/news/what-is-php-the-php-programming-language-meaning-explained/

References

Chakraborty, U. (2019). Perceived credibility of online hotel reviews and its impact on Hotel Booking Intentions. *International Journal of Contemporary Hospitality Management, 31*(9), 3465–3483. https://doi.org/10.1108/ijchm-11-2018-0928

Chaudhuri, S., Dayal, U., & Narasayya, V. (2011). An overview of business intelligence technology. *Communications of the Acm, 54*(8), 88–98. https://doi.org/10.1145/1978542.1978562

Cheng, J., Chen, B., & Huang, Z. (2023). Collective-based ad transparency in Targeted Hotel Advertising: Consumers' regulatory focus underlying the crowd safety effect. *Journal of Retailing and Consumer Services, 72*, Article 103257. https://doi.org/10.1016/j.jretconser.2023.103257

Collins, M. J. (2019). Pro HTML5 with CSS, JavaScript, and Multimedia. *In Apress eBooks*. https://doi.org/10.1007/978-1-4842-2463-2

Crettenand, G. (2019). *Functional PHP*.

Ding, D. K. (2023). Power BI Service. In *Apress eBooks* (pp. 87–114). https://doi.org/10.1007/978-1-4842-9239-6_3

Dumas, J., Roch, J., Tannier, E., & Varrette, S. (2019). Foundations of coding: compression, encryption, Error-Correction. In *HAL (Le Centre pour la Communication Scientifique Directe)*. French National Centre for Scientific Research. https://hal.science/hal-00765802

Ferrara, E., De Meo, P., Fiumara, G., & Baumgartner, R. (2019). Web data extraction, applications and techniques: A survey. *Knowledge Based Systems, 70*, 301–323. https://doi.org/10.1016/j.knosys.2014.07.007

Fkih, F., & Omri, M. N. (2020). Hidden data states-based complex terminology extraction from textual web data model. *Applied Intelligence, 50*(6), 1813–1831. https://doi.org/10.1007/s10489-019-01568-4

Frain, B. (2019). *Responsive Web Design with HTML5 and CSS3*.

Fuhrer, C., Solem, J. E., & Verdier, O. (2021). *Scientific Computing with Python: High-performance scientific computing with NumPy, SciPy, and pandas*. Packt Publishing.

Galin, D. (2019). From SDLC to agile—Processes and quality assurance activities. In *John Wiley & Sons, Inc. eBooks* (pp. 635–666). https://doi.org/10.1002/9781119134527.app4

Gupta, J., Liverman, D., Prodani, K., Aldunce, P., Bai, X., Broadgate, W., ... & Verburg, P. H. (2023). Earth system justice needed to identify and live within Earth system boundaries. *Nature Sustainability, 6*(6), 630–638.

Halvorson, M. (2019). *Microsoft® Visual Basic® 2010 Step by step*.

Hinduja, S., Afrin, M., Mistry, S., & Krishna, A. (2022). Machine learning-based proactive social-sensor service for mental health monitoring using twitter data. *International Journal of Information Management Data Insights, 2*(2), Article 100113. https://doi.org/10.1016/j.jjimei.2022.100113

He, L., & Zheng, K. (2019). How do general-purpose sentiment analyzers perform when applied to health-related online social media data? *Studies in Health Technology and Informatics, 264*, 1208–1212. https://doi.org/10.3233/shti190418

Ipeirotis, P. G., Provost, F., & Wang, J. (2019). Quality management on Amazon Mechanical Turk. *In Proceedings of the ACM SIGKDD Workshop on Human Computation*. https://doi.org/10.1145/1837885.1837906

Jevremovic, A. (2019). One solution for protecting PHP source code. *Singidunum Journal of Applied Sciences*. https://doi.org/10.15308/sinteza-2014-616-619

Khder, M. A. (2021). Web scraping or Web crawling: State of art, techniques, approaches and application. *International Journal of Advances in Soft Computing and Its Applications, 13*(3), 145–168. https://doi.org/10.15849/ijasca.211128.11

Kinne, J., & Axenbeck, J. (2019). Web Mining of Firm Websites: A framework for web scraping and a pilot study for Germany. *Social Science Research Network*. https://doi.org/10.2139/ssrn.3240470

Khan, A. (2021). What is PHP programming & basic PHP scripts. *The Official Cloudways Blog*. https://www.cloudways.com/blog/how-to-start-with-php/

Kim, W. (1982). On optimizing an SQL-like nested query. *ACM Transactions on Database Systems, 7*(3), 443–469. https://doi.org/10.1145/319732.319745

Kuokkanen, H., & Sun, W. (2020). Social desirability and cynicism biases in CSR surveys: An empirical study of hotels. *Journal of Hospitality and Tourism Insights, 3*(5), 567–588. https://doi.org/10.1108/jhti-01-2020-0006

Kuzminykh, N. (2022). NLP with Python: Sentiment analysis|Level up coding. *Medium.* https://levelup.gitconnected.com/simple-nlp-in-python-2cb3243239d3

Larsen, R. (2019). *Beginning HTML and CSS.*

Leloudas, P. (2023). Software development life cycle. *Introduction to Software Testing, 35–55,.* https://doi.org/10.1007/978-1-4842-9514-4_3

Letarte, D., Gauthier, F., & Merlo, E. (2019). Security model evolution of PHP web applications. *2011 Fourth IEEE International Conference on Software Testing, Verification and Validation.* https://doi.org/10.1109/icst.2011.36

Li, H., Yong, L., Tan, C. W., & Hu, F. (2020). Comprehending customer satisfaction with hotels. *International Journal of Contemporary Hospitality Management, 32*(5), 1713–1735. https://doi.org/10.1108/ijchm-06-2019-0581

Lincopinis, D., Apiag, C. P., & Cadiz, E. B. (2023). A review on PHP programming Language. *ResearchGate.* https://www.researchgate.net/publication/371166635_A_Review_on_PHP_Programming_Language

Liu, B., Hu, M., & Cheng, J. (2019). Opinion observer. *WWW '05: Proceedings of the 14th International Conference on World Wide Web.* https://doi.org/10.1145/1060745.1060797

Liu, B. (2019a). *Web data mining: Exploring hyperlinks, contents, and usage data.* Springer Science & Business Media.

Liu, B. (2019b). Sentiment analysis and opinion mining. *Synthesis Lectures on Human Language Technologies, 5*(1), 1–167. https://doi.org/10.2200/s00416ed1v01y201204hlt016

Liu, F., Grundke-Iqbal, I., Iqbal, K., & Gong, C. X. (2005). Contributions of protein phosphatases PP1, PP2A, PP2B and PP5 to the regulation of tau phosphorylation. *European Journal of Neuroscience, 22*(8), 1942–1950.

Liu, M., Yin, X., Ulin-Avila, E., Geng, B., Zentgraf, T., Ju, L., ... & Zhang, X. (2011). A graphene-based broadband optical modulator. *Nature, 474*(7349), 64-67.

Liu, L., Johnson, H. L., Cousens, S., Perin, J., Scott, S., Lawn, J. E., ... & Black, R. E. (2012). Global, regional, and national causes of child mortality: an updated systematic analysis for 2010 with time trends since 2000. *The lancet, 379*(9832), 2151–2161.

Loria, S. (2019). *TextBlob: Simplified text processing.* Retrieved from https://textblob.readthedocs.io/en/dev/

Marlina, E., & Purwandari, B. (2019). Strategy for research data management services in Indonesia. *Procedia Computer Science, 161,* 788–796.

Márquez Reiter, R., Hidalgo Downing, R., & Iveson, M. (2023). Global expectations, local realities: All-inclusive hotel reviews and responses on TripAdvisor. *Contrastive Pragmatics,* 1–33. https://doi.org/10.1163/26660393-bja10086

Martin-Fuentes, E., Mellinas, J. P., & Parra-López, E. (2020). Online travel review rating scales and effects on hotel scoring and competitiveness. *Tourism Review, 76*(3), 654–668. https://doi.org/10.1108/tr-01-2019-0024

Negrino, T., & Smith, D. (2020). *JavaScript and Ajax for the web.*

NLTK Project. (2023). *Sentiment Intensity Analyzer.* Retrieved from https://www.nltk.org/api/nltk.sentiment.html

Oliphant, T. E. (2006). *Guide to NumPy.* Trelgol Publishing.

Pan, T., Pedrycz, W., Yang, J., Wu, W., & Zhang, Y. (2022). A new classifier for imbalanced data with iterative learning process and ensemble operating process. *Knowledge-Based Systems, 249,* Article 108966. https://doi.org/10.1016/j.knosys.2022.108966

Pang, B., & Lee, L. (2019). *Opinion mining and sentiment analysis.*

Panwar, A., Morwal, R., & Kumar, S. (2022). Fixed points of ρ-nonexpansive mappings using MP iterative process. *Advances in the Theory of Nonlinear Analysis and Its Application, 6*(2), 229–245. https://doi.org/10.31197/atnaa.980093

References

Pedregosa, F., Varoquaux, G., Gramfort, A., Michel, V., Thirion, B., Grisel, O., Blondel, M., Prettenhofer, P., Weiss, R., Dubourg, V., Vanderplas, J., Passos, A., Cournapeau, D., Brucher, M., Perrot, M., & Duchesnay, E. (2011). SciKit-Learn: Machine learning in Python. *HAL (Le Centre Pour La Communication Scientifique Directe)*. https://hal.inria.fr/hal-00650905

Pei, S., Zhao, Z., Liu, F., Miao, M., Jin, S., Sun, F., & Shi, G. (2023). Iterative Learning Control for tricalcium neutralization process with initial disturbance. *Chemical Engineering & Technology, 46*(5), 1028–1038. https://doi.org/10.1002/ceat.202200571

Petersen, S., Levassor, L., Pedersen, C. M., Madsen, J., Hansen, L. G., Zhang, J., Haidar, A. K., Frandsen, R., Keasling, J. D., Weber, T., Sonnenschein, N., & Jensen, M. K. (2023). *Literate Programming for Iterative Design-Build-Test-Learn Cycles in Bioengineering*. https://doi.org/10.1101/2023.06.18.545451

Popescu, A., & Etzioni, O. (2005). Extracting product features and opinions from reviews. *HLT '05: Proceedings of the Conference on Human Language Technology and Empirical Methods in Natural Language Processing*. https://doi.org/10.3115/1220575.1220618

Prokofyeva, N., & Boltunova, V. (2017). Analysis and practical application of PHP frameworks in development of web information systems. *Procedia Computer Science, 104*, 51–56. https://doi.org/10.1016/j.procs.2017.01.059

Python Software Foundation. (2023). *Matplotlib documentation*. Retrieved from https://matplotlib.org/stable/contents.html

Roy, G., Datta, B., Mukherjee, S., Eckert, A., & Dixit, S. K. (2023). How online travel reviews sources affect travelers' behavioral intentions? Analysis with source credibility theory. *Tourism Planning and Development, 1–31*. https://doi.org/10.1080/21568316.2023.2229296

Saurkar, A. V., Pathare, K. G., & Gode, S. A. (2019). An overview on web scraping techniques and tools. *International Journal on Future Revolution in Computer Science & Communication Engineering, 4*(4), 363–367. http://www.ijfrcsce.org/index.php/ijfrcsce/article/view/1529

Schuckert, M., Kim, T. T., Paek, S., & Lee, G. (2018). Motivate to innovate: How authentic and transformational leaders influence employees' psychological capital and service innovation behavior. *International Journal of Contemporary Hospitality Management, 30*(2), 776–796.

Sells, C., & Flanders, J. (2020). *Mastering visual studio*. In O'Reilly & Associates, Inc. eBooks.

Siame, A., & Kunda, D. (2019). Evolution of PHP applications: A systematic literature review. *International Journal of Recent Contributions from Engineering, Science & IT, 5*(1), 28. https://doi.org/10.3991/ijes.v5i1.6437

Simplilearn. (2023). What is PHP: The best guide to understand its concepts. *Simplilearn.com*. https://www.simplilearn.com/tutorials/php-tutorial/what-is-php#what_is_php

Suanpang, P., Jamjuntr, P., & Kaewyong, P. (2021). SENTIMENT ANALYSIS WITH A TEXTBLOB PACKAGE IMPLICATIONS FOR TOURISM. *Journal of Management Information and Decision Sciences, Suppl.Special Issue 6, 24*, 1–9. https://www.abacademies.org/articles/sentiment-analysis-with-a-text-blob-package-implications-for-tourism.pdf

Suryanarayana, G., Samarthyam, G., & Sharma, T. (2022). *Refactoring for software design smells: Managing technical debt*. https://dl.acm.org/citation.cfm?id=2755629

Turney, P. D., & Littman, M. L. (2019). *Measuring praise and criticism: Inference of semantic orientation from association*. ACM Transactions on Information Systems (TOIS)

The PHP Group. (2023). History of PHP. *PHP*. https://www.php.net/manual/en/history.php.php

Vargiu, E., & Urru, M. (2019). Exploiting web scraping in a collaborative filtering- based approach to web advertising. *Artificial Intelligence Research, 2*(1). https://doi.org/10.5430/air.v2n1p44

Vasquez, J. G., Cantimbuhan, N., Po, W. A., & Deogracias, E. (2023). Travel agencies' WEBPORTAL perception based on customer review in Hotel Luna, Vigan City. *Quantum Journal of Social Sciences and Humanities, 4*(1), 11–23. https://doi.org/10.55197/qjssh.v4i1.178

Vinodhini, G., & Chandrasekaran, R. (2019). Sentiment analysis and opinion mining: A survey. *International Journal of Advanced Research in Computer Science and Software Engineering, 2*(6), 283–292. https://www.researchgate.net/publication/265163299

Wan, Y., Liu, D., & Ren, J.-C. (2023). Iterative Learning-based predictive control method for electronic grade silicon single crystal batch process. *IEEE Transactions on Semiconductor Manufacturing, 36*(2), 239–250. https://doi.org/10.1109/tsm.2023.3266220

Weiss, S. M., Indurkhya, N., Zhang, T., & Damerau, F. J. (2019). *Text mining: Predictive methods for analyzing unstructured information.*

Wiebe, J. M., Wilson, T., Bruce, R., Bell, M., & Martin, M. (2019). *Learning subjective language. Computational Linguistics*

Wilton, P., & McPeak, J. (2020). *Beginning JavaScript.*

Zhou, R., & Li, S. (2023). A study on the persuasive function of metadiscourse in hotel responses to negative reviews on TripAdvisor. *English Language Teaching, 16*(6), 55. https://doi.org/10.5539/elt.v16n6p55

Zhai, L., & Yang, H. (2022). A Time-varying process monitoring approach based on iterative-updated semi-supervised Nonnegative Matrix Factorizations. *The Canadian Journal of Chemical Engineering, 101*(5), 2566–2578. https://doi.org/10.1002/cjce.24716

Zhai, Y., & Liu, B. (2020). Web data extraction based on partial tree alignment. *International Journal on Future Revolution in Computer Science & Communication Engineering.* https://doi.org/10.1145/1060745.1060761

Zhu, Y., Wang, L., Zhang, Z., Pei, H., & Wang, X. (2023). An iterative model for identifying essential proteins based on the wholeprocess network of protein evolution. *Current Bioinformatics, 18*(4), 359–373. https://doi.org/10.2174/1574893618666230315154807

Chapter 15
Integration of AI and Machine Learning

15.1 Introduction

The junction of artificial intelligence (AI) with machine learning (Jayakody et al.) is one of the major technological revolutions transforming industries all around (Adel, 2023). Artificial intelligence—which entails machines copying human thinking processes—and machine learning, a subset of artificial intelligence targeted at developing algorithms enabling computers to learn from data and provide predictions based on data—have been the sources of individual innovation across sectors.

15.1.1 Problem Statement

AI and ML present opportunities and challenges. Integration is difficult, but these technologies boost operational efficiency, decision-making, and innovation (Anaba et al., 2024). Large datasets, scalability issues, AI-ML system setup and maintenance, and ethical issues, including algorithmic bias and data privacy, are major issues. The research lacks best practices for merging ethics and innovation with these technologies (Tariq et al., 2021). This study addresses these concerns by studying AI/ML integration implementation variables and sectoral effects.

15.2 Literature Review

Many sectors are studying and using AI-ML. AI can perform human tasks, including visual perception, speech recognition, decision-making, and translation (ZainEldin et al., 2024). AI subset machine learning (Jayakody et al.) lets computers learn from data and improve without scripting. Healthcare, finance, manufacturing, and others benefit from this technology. This literature review covers AI-ML integration's uses, problems, and effects. Early computer science and AI developments inspired AI-machine learning integration. Early AI systems were logical. The inability to learn from new data hindered these systems. A significant change came with the introduction of machine learning algorithms in the 1980s and 1990s, which let systems evolve. More complex artificial intelligence systems capable of learning from vast volumes of data have been made possible by major developments in neural networks, support vector machines, and decision trees. Artificial intelligence and machine learning integration have sped in recent years thanks to developments in large data availability and processing capability.

They researched distributed machine learning systems that underlined the need for scalable solutions to meet the growing computing requirements of AI-ML integration (Aminizadeh et al., 2024). Businesses, society, and the economy depend greatly on how artificial intelligence and machine learning are combined. Integrating artificial intelligence and machine learning can inspire creativity, increase efficiency, and generate fresh income sources for companies. Organisations must also embrace new business models, reskill their employees, and invest in new technologies. Companies that effectively combine artificial intelligence and machine learning can increase production and profitability, according to a 2018 study by Bughin et al.; yet, the advantages are not shared equally; early adopters get a competitive advantage. From a societal standpoint, the combination of artificial intelligence and machine learning could help to solve major issues such as poverty, climate change, and access to healthcare. Still, it also brings social and ethical questions like employment displacement, privacy, and prejudice (Nazeer, 2024). According to the literature, stakeholders and legislators should cooperate to create systems guaranteeing the fair and responsible application of artificial intelligence and machine learning (Butt, 2024). Economically, combining artificial intelligence and machine learning is projected to be very important for the increase in world GDP. Rising consumer demand and increasing productivity are driving development. However, the advantages of artificial intelligence-machine learning integration will rely on how successfully nations and businesses embrace these technologies. Integration of artificial intelligence-machine learning is revolutionising sectors, driving creativity, and generating fresh prospects. On data management, system complexity, and ethical issues, it does, however, also present major difficulties. Review of the literature emphasises the requirement of companies implementing best practices for AI-ML integration with an eye towards scalability, openness, and ethical responsibility. Future business, society, and the economy will be shaped by their integration as artificial intelligence and machine learning develop. More studies are required to investigate the long-term effects of artificial intelligence-machine learning integration and create structures that guarantee these technologies' responsible and fair application.

15.2.1 Theoretical Framework

Several theoretical models help one to grasp the confluence of artificial intelligence and machine learning:

TAM: Technology Acceptance Model: This paradigm clarifies user acceptance and technology usage. This implies that the two main elements influencing a person's choice to accept a new technology are perceived usefulness and perceived simplicity. Within the framework of artificial intelligence and machine learning integration, TAM can help one comprehend the elements influencing acceptance and implementation in companies.

Everett Rogers developed the Diffusion of Innovations (DOI) Theory, which clarifies why, how, and how fast new ideas and technology spread over civilisations. Comparative benefits, interoperability, complexity, trialability, and observability help one to grasp the dissemination of artificial intelligence and machine learning technologies across sectors and the elements influencing their acceptance. RBV: Resource-Based View This structure emphasises the tools and resources companies need to reach a competitive advantage. The integration of artificial intelligence and machine learning can be considered a strategic resource that can improve a company's capacity and generate a lasting competitive advantage.

Theory of socio-technical systems: This paradigm stresses the interdependence of technical and social elements in organisations. This is especially true for AI and ML integration since it emphasises the importance of considering both technology (such as system design and functionality) and human components (such as user training and organisational culture) to guarantee successful implementation. Based on theories, literature review, and problem, this study constructs the theoretical framework of this study.

15.3 Methodology

This work investigates artificial intelligence and machine learning integration using a mixed-method approach. In the quantitative phase, 200 professionals from manufacturing, finance, healthcare, retail, and other fields analyse their AI and machine learning integration skills (Gurcan et al., 2023). The poll examines the pros, cons, and AI/ML integration's impact on company performance. Twenty AI and machine learning experts are interviewed in the qualitative phase to identify integration best practices, problems, and solutions. An online survey platform collects quantitative data from intentionally sampled participants to ensure sector and role diversity. AI and machine learning integration experts are chosen for qualitative video interviews. Descriptive statistics, correlation, regression, and other quantitative data analysis tools uncover AI-ML integration variables. The thematic analysis finds integration-related qualitative issues.

15.4 Discussion

AI and ML improve operational efficiency, predictive analytics, and customer experience. Companies using these technologies report improved decision-making, process automation, and data-driven insights. Data privacy, algorithmic bias, huge data sets, AI and machine learning difficulty, and data privacy are also covered. Theoretical frameworks yield debate results. TAM encourages the adoption of AI and machine learning by emphasising usefulness and simplicity. The diffusion of innovation (DOI) theory explains how these technologies spread across industries and their benefits and compatibility with existing systems. The paper discusses AI and ML ethics and advises companies to plan for algorithmic discrimination, data privacy, and job automation. Sociotechnical systems theory promotes technology-human integration to integrate AI and machine learning.

15.5 Conclusion

Artificial intelligence and machine learning can change industries. To determine how integration influences execution, this study explores its merits, cons, and effects. The report recommends strategic planning, lifelong learning, and ethical AI methods to maximise AI and ML integration. Companies using AI and ML will increase efficiency, decision-making, and innovation. Data management, system complexity, and ethics must be handled for these benefits. Future studies should address AI and machine learning integration best practices, long-term consequences, and ethics.

References

Adel, A. (2023). Unlocking the future: Fostering human–machine collaboration and driving intelligent automation through industry 5.0 in smart cities. *Smart Cities, 6*(5), 2742–2782.

Aminizadeh, S., Heidari, A., Dehghan, M., Toumaj, S., Rezaei, M., Navimipour, N. J., & Unal, M. (2024). Opportunities and challenges of artificial intelligence and distributed systems to improve the quality of healthcare service. *Artificial Intelligence in Medicine, 149*, Article 102779.

Anaba, D. C., Kess-Momoh, A. J., & Ayodeji, S. A. (2024). Digital transformation in oil and gas production: Enhancing efficiency and reducing costs. *International Journal of Management & Entrepreneurship Research, 6*(7), 2153–2161.

Butt, J. (2024). Analytical Study of the World's First EU Artificial Intelligence (AI) Act. *International Journal of Research and Publications, 5*(3).

Gurcan, F., Ayaz, A., Menekse Dalveren, G. G., & Derawi, M. (2023). Business intelligence strategies, best practices, and latest trends: Analysis of scientometric data from 2003 to 2023 using machine learning. *Sustainability, 15*(13), 9854.

Jayakody, C., Malalgoda, C., Amaratunga, D., Haigh, R., Liyanage, C., Witt, E., & Fernando, N. (2022). Approaches to strengthen the social cohesion between displaced and host communities. *Sustainability, 14*(6), 3413.

Nazeer, M. Y. (2024). Algorithmic Conscience: An In-Depth Inquiry into Ethical Dilemmas in Artificial Intelligence. *International Journal of Research and Innovation in Social Science, 8*(5), 725–732.

Tariq, M. U., Poulin, M., & Abonamah, A. A. (2021). Achieving operational excellence through artificial intelligence: Driving forces and barriers. *Frontiers in Psychology, 12*, Article 686624.

ZainEldin, H., Gamel, S. A., Talaat, F. M., Aljohani, M., Baghdadi, N. A., Malki, A., & Elhosseini, M. A. (2024). Silent no more: A comprehensive review of artificial intelligence, deep learning, and machine learning in facilitating deaf and mute communication. *Artificial Intelligence Review, 57*(7), 188.

Chapter 16
Automotive Prices Analytics

16.1 Introduction

The primary concern of sellers overcharging is immediately addressed by our concentration on predictive technologies. Our system seeks to recommend fair and reasonable prices by means of a methodical study of large datasets and pattern recognition, thereby serving as a defence against potential exploitation. Another challenge in the used car market is the abundance of choices provided by these existing systems. While variety of suggestions can be beneficial, an excessive number of options might lead to indecision or dissatisfaction, making it challenging for users to navigate and compare effectively. Our proposed system aims to reduce the number of recommendations by suggesting the top 5 cars with the lowest mileage and the best condition. This research as an anticipatory reaction to the problems facing the used automobile industry. The used automobile market by contributing to the larger conversation about enhancing transaction fairness and transparency through the integration of machine learning, data analysis, and consumer-centric design.

16.1.1 Problem Statement

The problem here is that customers do not have easy access to full information about the factors that affect used car prices. Customers frequently do not know how important these factors should be when making judgements about what to buy. To lessen this, the system can include an instructional element that provides information on the variables influencing used car costs, enabling consumers to make better decisions. This problem statement emphasises how the used automobile market lacks a systematic and cohesive system, which causes uncertainty among consumers and impedes a smooth buying process. One way to solve this problem is to provide a centralised, organised, and user-friendly platform that makes it easier to search for, assess, and buy second-hand cars. This methodical approach makes the market more reliable and effective. Making educated selections regarding purchasing used automobiles can be difficult for consumers, especially when taking their preferences and budget into account. Creating an intuitive interface that streamlines the decision-making process is one way to find a solution. Interactive tools, distinct choice classification, and tailored recommendations based on personal preferences and financial constraints are a few examples of this.

16.1.2 Research Objectives

Customers may, for instance, enter their budget, desired features, and other specifications, and the system would suggest cars that fit those specifications. The system could also be used to provide consumers with information about the market value of a vehicle. This information could help consumers negotiate a fair price with sellers. The project's objectives can be surmised as:

The primary objective of this project is to build a predictive pricing model that considers all relevant measurable variables to estimate the prices of used cars accurately (James & Smith, 2019). This enables customers to have a better understanding of the fair market value for a given vehicle. The recommendation algorithm of DriveSmart puts the needs of its users first by grouping and filtering results according to two important criteria: the lowest mileage and the best condition of the car. This deliberate focus guarantees that consumers obtain succinct and customised recommendations that tackle typical issues encountered on alternative platforms. DriveSmart provides consumers with a top 5 recommendation list and simplifies the decision-making process by emphasising longevity and high standards. This strategy highlights the platform's dedication to offering useful and reliable recommendations in the used automobile market while also saving time and improving the customer experience overall.

In addition to the predictive model, a user-friendly interface be developed for customers to interact with the system (Chen & Wang, 2018). This interface allows users to input their car's details and receive an estimated price, making the pricing information easily accessible. Historical data on used car sales be collected, organised, and stored for analysis (Johnson & White, 2020). This data serves as the foundation for training the predictive model and determining coefficients and intercepts for the pricing algorithm. The pricing algorithm be based on linear regression, providing transparency and clarity in how car prices are calculated (Lee & Kim, 2017). The algorithm be explained to users, making it comprehensible and trustable.

16.2 Literature Review

According to Dairu and Shilong (2021), XGBoost, recognised as an ensemble learning technique, has garnered substantial attention due to its efficacy and superior performance across diverse machine learning tasks, particularly in regression and classification problem domains. The investigation accentuates its noteworthy computational advantages, demonstrating a comparative computational efficiency approximately ten times faster than alternative ensemble learning methodologies, concurrently requiring reduced computational resources. This efficiency bears significance, particularly in the handling of expansive datasets or intricate models, as it accelerates both the training and prediction procedures, thereby diminishing computational time and associated expenses. Furthermore, empirical findings within the study assert XGBoost's proficiency in augmenting the pace of model execution alongside bolstering predictive accuracy. Empirical results and experimentation within the study corroborate the assertion that the proposed sales forecasting model, rooted in the principles of XGBoost, evidence substantial enhancements in computational efficiency and prediction accuracy when juxtaposed with alternative methodologies. This amalgamation of heightened computational efficiency and elevated predictive accuracy renders XGBoost an enticing prospect across varied domains, notably in circumstances necessitating rapid model deployment and precise predictions, exemplified in applications like retail sales forecasting, financial prognostication, and analogous domains.

In order to achieve better performance for the prediction model, a study conducted by Cui et al. (2022) found that combining two machine learning algorithms, XGBoost and LightGBM, has helped improve the accuracy of existing deep learning models. The XGBoost algorithm has been developed to operate with big and complex datasets and can be applied to both regression and classification tasks. LightGBM is a distributed high-performance framework for classification, regression, and ranking applications using decision trees which is similar to XGBoost. Cui et al. (2022) have further stated that following the addition of XGBoost + LightGBM iterative process, the effects of the random forest, XGBoost model, LightGBM model, and depth residual network have significantly improved by over 12%. This demonstrates that the algorithm framework is universal and generalisable, and that the iterative process suggested in this literature may be applied to other models to significantly improve the prediction performance of other models.

Author	Summary	Critical thoughts
Hamunen (2016) Challenges in Adopting a DevOps Approach to Software Development and Operations	The author discusses several challenges in the traditional agile development framework and how DevOps overcomes these problems	The DevOps approach may be suitable to be implemented into our project as it solves most of the challenges possessed by the traditional agile development method

(continued)

(continued)

Author	Summary	Critical thoughts
Akbar et al. (2022) Towards Successful DevOps: A Decision-Making Framework	A new software development approach called DevOps emphasises cooperation between the teams working on development and operations to create a shared set of objectives, procedures, and resources. Experts in the software industry view DevOps as a cultural movement that supports the development environment in terms of efficient control, responsibility, and communication	Agile software development is improved by the DevOps methodology, which blends development and operations

Hamunen (2016) has discussed the challenges in a traditional agile development framework and how the DevOps framework overcomes these challenges. The DevOps approach may be suitable to be implemented into our project as it solves most of the challenges possessed by the traditional agile development method.

Akbar et al. (2022) stated that DevOps is a contemporary method in software development that highlights teamwork between development and operations teams. The goal is to create shared objectives, practices, and tools. It's seen as a cultural shift in the software industry, promoting better organisation, accountability, and communication among developers. This approach improves Agile software development by smoothly combining development and operations, making workflows more efficient overall.

16.3 Research Methodology

The table below illustrates the overview of Drive Smart's intended system functionalities and the individual purposes of each of these. The functions summarised in this table include the home page, car recommendation quiz, car price calculator, and the analysis (dashboard) page.

Functions	Purpose
Home page	Provides an interactive and visually appealing webpage that is user-friendly
Car Recommender Quiz	Connects to machine learning model to generate top 5 best car recommendations (using lowest mileage and best condition) based on the keyed in user preferences

(continued)

16.3 Research Methodology

(continued)

Functions	Purpose
Car Price Calculator	Connects to machine learning model to accurately generate the predicted car price based on the type of car and its specific conditions keyed in by the user
Analysis (Dashboard)	Showcases the real-time and interactive PowerBI dashboard for a comprehensive overview of how the data is visualised and utilised with the most significant parameters

The DriveSmart online application can be accessed through the home page. The home page is the first intended system function; it aims to provide a visually appealing and dynamic interface for users. The home page is a smooth introduction to the platform's capabilities and sets the tone for a positive user experience. It is designed to be both efficient and engaging.

A crucial function that improves the user's experience is the Car Recommender Quiz, which links to an advanced machine learning model. Using the user's preferences as a basis, this model prioritises cars in the top five best conditions and with the lowest mileage. The quiz makes sure that consumers obtain data-driven, personalised recommendations for vehicles that are catered to their individual needs and preferences by utilising sophisticated algorithms.

Another function is the second quiz. This tool works with the machine learning model to provide precise price estimates for cars based on user input conditions in the Car Price Calculator. The calculator offers consumers insightful information about the projected price range by considering a number of parameters, including the type of car and its particular circumstances. This helps users make well-informed decisions during the car-buying process.

Lastly, the final function would be the dynamic, real-time PowerBI dashboard included in the Analysis area to give customers a thorough understanding of how data is displayed and used across the platform. Important factors are displayed in this interactive dashboard, giving customers insights into price dynamics, market trends, and other pertinent data. The dashboard is a useful tool for data-driven decision-making in addition to increasing user engagement.

16.3.1 Data Visualisation

The provided table details the visual representation methods adopted for this project. In particular, bar charts have been chosen to display rankings, and pie charts are utilised to depict overall percentages. These visualisations are employed to offer a straightforward snapshot of the dataset, facilitating a more accessible understanding of the information presented.

In contrast, the pie chart is harnessed for presenting percentages holistically. This visualisation method proves particularly effective in providing a comprehensive overview of the dataset. By visually conveying proportions and distributions, the pie chart aids in offering a holistic understanding of the composition of data categories. This visual representation is invaluable for determining the relative importance of different components within the dataset, fostering a straightforward and intuitive understanding of the overall data structure. Therefore, the integration of bar charts and pie charts provides a strong and adaptable method for visualising and analysing data within the system.

16.3.2 Pre-Development Preparations

Prior to commencing the development process, it is essential to undertake several crucial preparation measures. First and foremost, it is crucial to clearly state and describe the project objectives, clarifying the precise goals and desired results that the system aims to achieve. This initial phase guarantees that the team's actions and goals are in line with the intended objectives throughout the development process. Moreover, implementing a performance evaluation workflow that clearly outlines the order of events and interactions inside the system enhances the effectiveness and efficiency of the appraisal process.

Furthermore, it is essential to have a thorough comprehension and mastery of the specific tools and procedures designated for the development process. This involves a comprehensive examination and proficiency in the tools to be used, guaranteeing that the team is well-prepared for smooth implementation.

Moreover, it is crucial to create prototypes for the user interface (UI) to offer stakeholders an initial focus of the system's layout, features, and operations. These prototypes allow stakeholders to assess the system's capabilities and provide valuable input. The iterative feedback process aims to detect and correct any defects in the UI design and improve the system's usability, accessibility, and overall user experience.

Thorough planning and preparation are essential for building a website focused on price prediction and car recommendation. They provide a dependable basis for its establishment. This approach ensures that the resulting system aligns with and surpasses the expectations of stakeholders.

16.3.3 Design

The data flow diagram (DFD) depicts the complex operation of the recommender and predictor system for the price of second-hand cars. The data transmission is initiated when users enter their car preferences or details via the front-end user interface which is the webpage. The data that is input by the user is subsequently processed using the Python web framework Flask. Following processing, the data is transferred to the machine learning model (MLM), which employs the XGBoost algorithm to conduct the analyses such as classification and filtering. The Model Output presents the outcomes obtained from the analysis conducted by the MLM, offering users

16.3 Research Methodology

predictions or classifications in accordance with their car preferences. Concurrently, the Flask application engages in communication with the local drive, which signifies Data Output. This may involve the retrieval of the unprocessed or processed data, ensuring a smooth integration into the system. The data input from users, in conjunction with the collaborative interaction between Flask and the XGBoost model, is fundamental to hosting a functional and interactive webpage and enabling a streamlined operation of the system. The data flow diagram effectively illustrates the coordinated series of operations, emphasising the cyclical flow of user inputs and to the MLM to produce well-informed predictions through data processing.

16.3.4 Function Workflows

This section discusses all the individual function workflows for the home page, the Car Recommender Quiz, and the Car Price Calculator. The function workflows help illustrate the information and visual aspects required to be displayed for each page.

Home Page

The homepage of Drive Smart incorporates a comprehensive navigation bar facilitating seamless traversal across distinct sections, notably encompassing 'About', 'Our Services', 'Analysis', 'Featured Cars', 'Our Team', and 'Contact'. This intuitive design enhances user experience by providing facile access to diverse segments of the interface. The crux of our system lies in the implementation of Quiz 1 (recommender) and Quiz 2 (price predictor) nestled within the 'Our Services' section. These quizzes are conveniently accessible via designated text boxes, each intricately linked to Quiz 1 and Quiz 2, respectively. To enable users to engage with these quizzes and obtain personalised outcomes, an API orchestrates seamless integration between the homepage, quiz interfaces, and ensuing results. The synergy of JavaScript and CSS further augments the visual aesthetics of the homepage, enhancing its overall appeal and user engagement.

Car Price Recommender Quiz 1

The main function of this quiz is to execute the car recommendations based on the user inputs. The results generated need to be presented in an organised and readable manner in order of top 5. This is necessary to increase the user-friendly aspect of the web design and results generation. The recommendation results being loaded onto the same page as the Quiz is intentional to reduce waiting time and help provide a consolidated approach.

The information for these recommendations is presented in individual columns for each car recommendation with additional information such as the year, make, and model being listed underneath. The development of this was done using CSS and JavaScript to consolidate the results and streamline the results loading time.

Car Price Calculator Quiz 2

The primary function for the car price calculator quiz 2 is to present the predicted price of the car upon user input of the information. Therefore, the page is intentionally structured to present a simple and straightforward calculator. The results are generated to be displayed in a large blue block below the calculator in order to mimic how actual calculator's work. This was done using CSS and basic JavaScript. The simplicity of this page helps users utilise it in a fast and effective manner owing to a streamlined user experience.

16.3.5 Development

The developmental phase comprises two fundamental components that collectively constitute a comprehensive process. The primary aspect involves model development, a sophisticated stage encompassing meticulous data preparation and code formulation. This stage entails the intricate crafting and refinement of the algorithmic framework, involving the assimilation, curation, and preparation of pertinent datasets. It encompasses a nuanced interplay of activities such as data cleaning, feature engineering, and model fine-tuning, culminating in the establishment of a robust predictive machine learning model. Concurrently, this phase entails the development of code structures utilising programming languages and frameworks to architect the algorithmic framework, ensuring its coherence and functional integrity.

Concurrently, the developmental phase integrates another pivotal dimension: webpage development. This facet centres on the meticulous crafting and construction of webpages that constitute the essential interface within our system. These webpages serve as the conduit for user interaction, demanding meticulous attention to design, layout, and functional considerations. From the aspects of user experience (UX) design to user interface (UI) development, this segment necessitates a seamless fusion of aesthetic appeal with practical usability. It encompasses the implementation of front-end technologies, including HTML, CSS, and JavaScript, among others, to materialise an intuitive and user-friendly interface.

16.3.5.1 Model Development

Overview

This overview outlines the systematic computational approach developed for analysing and creating Drive Smart's car recommendation & price prediction system. It commences by meticulously preparing the data, involving encoding categorical variables via scikit-learn's LabelEncoder and carefully curating essential features. Subsequent stages focus on training and assessing an XGBoost regression model, enabling predictions of vehicle prices based on selected attributes. Rigorous evaluation through metrics like Mean Squared Error (MSE), R-squared (R2), and Mean

Absolute Error (MAE) validates the model's predictive capabilities. Moreover, the process involves crafting functional tools for practical implementation and generating personalised recommendations. These functionalities empower users to filter vehicle data and receive tailored suggestions based on specific parameters such as manufacturer, age range, and mileage. The workflow culminates in presenting refined datasets and condensed insights, spotlighting top vehicle recommendations aligned with user-defined criteria like mileage and condition. This structured approach presents a robust framework for exhaustive vehicle data analysis and custom-tailored recommendation systems.

16.3.5.2 Data Preparation

The dataset utilised in this development was obtained from Kaggle which is the US used car price dataset, which initially contained 18 columns and 426,853 rows of unique car data. These columns include the region, state, price, year, manufacturer, model, condition, cylinders, fuel, odometer, title status, transmission, drive, size, type, paint colour, latitude, and longitude. During the data cleaning process, only the relevant columns such as price, year, manufacturer, model, condition, fuel type, mileage, and transmission were kept, reducing the total number of columns to 9. After retaining the relevant columns, Google Colaboratory was used to remove any missing values and outliers to help improve the reliability of the dataset, keeping only 18,218 rows of unique values.

Exploratory Data Analysis

The above dashboard is designed to showcase the cleaned data on second-hand users curated from the research papers. It prioritises the top 20 manufacturers most relevant to the second-hand market. The dashboard also filters the age and mileage data to enhance the visual clarity, focusing on the most clustered segments. It also categorises the cars into the most popular types, namely, pickup, sedan, hatchback, and SUV, providing an analysis on the second-hand car market dynamics (Fig. 16.1).

The inclusion of a correlation heatmap serves as an additional layer of analytical depth, shedding light on the relationship between the second-hand car data variables. Specifically, the heatmap highlights the correlation between price and age (-0.51) and mileage (-0.37). These coefficients signify a negative relationship indicating that as the age or mileage increases, the price of the car in relation tends to decrease. This insight not only confirms previous expectations but also quantifies the degree of influence these factors have on pricing dynamics in the second-hand car market (Fig. 16.2).

The Python-generated bar chart serves as compelling visual evidence on the pivotal role of the five key elements that shape the dynamics of the second-hand

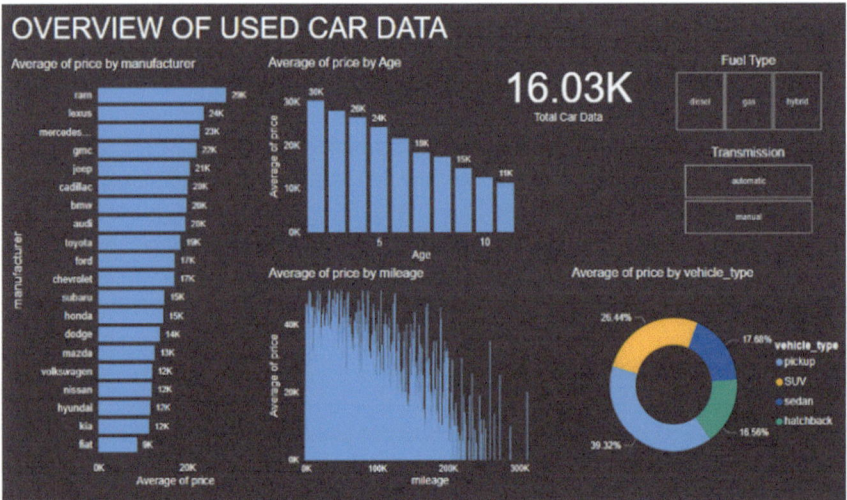

Fig. 16.1 Exploratory data analysis in power BI

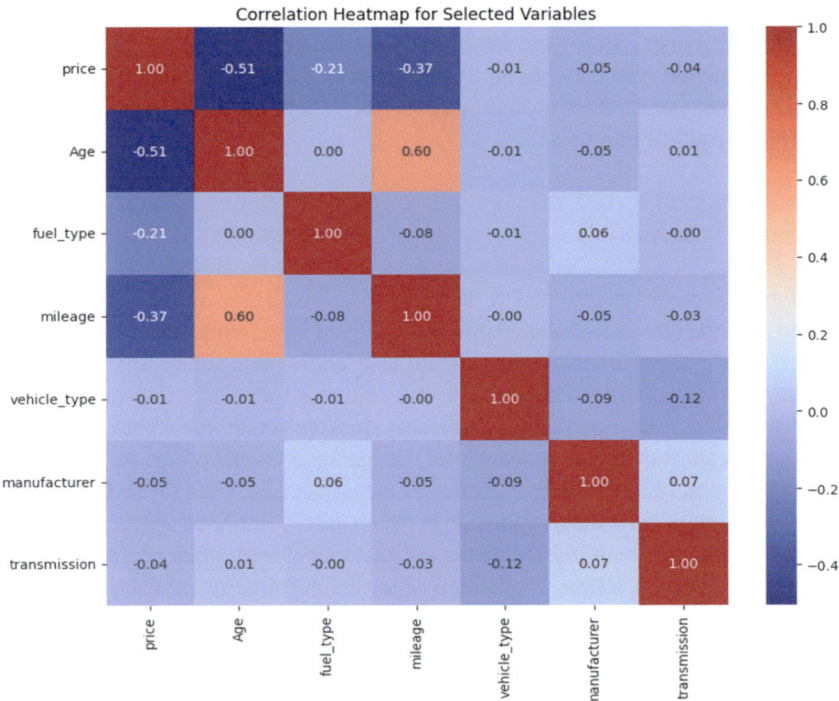

Fig. 16.2 Correlation Heatmap of US car price dataset

16.3 Research Methodology

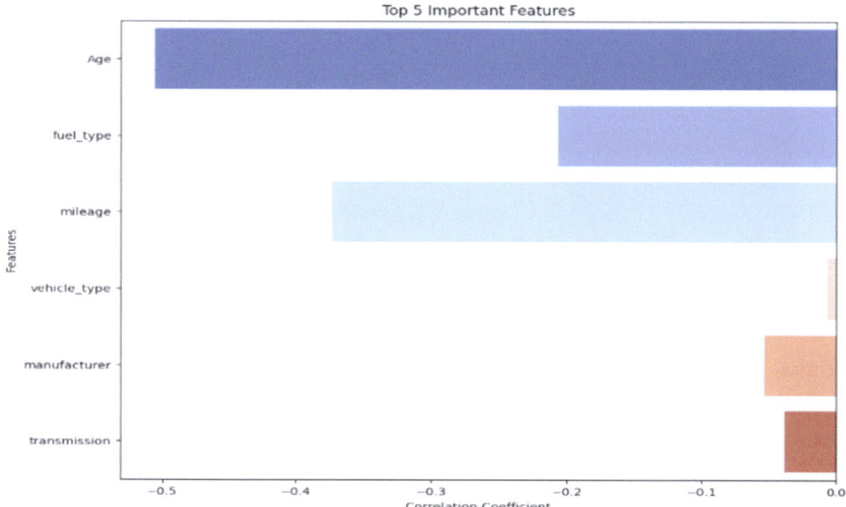

Fig. 16.3 Top 5 important features in US car price dataset

car market. In descending order of importance, the chart signifies the age as the most influencing factor in the market dynamics. The subsequent factors include mileage, gasoline type, manufacturer, gearbox type, and vehicle type (Fig. 16.3).

The prominence of age underlines its significant impact on the value of vehicles in the second-hand market, while mileage stands as a close second in determining market advantage. This visual representation not only prioritises these influential factors but also provides valuable insights for both sellers and buyers navigating the complexities of the second-hand car market.

XGBoost Model Development for Car Price Prediction

The initial phase involves importing and loading the necessary dependencies and libraries essential for executing the analysis employing the XGBoost model. The utilised dependencies and libraries encompass LabelEncoders, XGBRegressor, and more (Fig. 16.4).

This section of the code performs label encoding for categorical variables using the **LabelEncoder** module from the **sklearn.preprocessing** library. It initialises an empty dictionary **label_encoders** to store the individual encoders for each categorical column. The specified categorical columns, including 'manufacturer', 'fuel_type', 'transmission', 'drive', and 'vehicle_type', undergo label encoding within a loop. For each column, a **LabelEncoder()** instance is created and fitted to transform the categorical values into numerical representations using **fit_transform()**. This process converts the categorical data into numerical labels, assigning a unique numerical code to each distinct category within the respective columns. The encoded values replace

```
Importing libraries and loading dataset

[ ]  import warnings
     warnings.filterwarnings('ignore')
     import pandas as pd
     from sklearn.preprocessing import LabelEncoder
     from sklearn.model_selection import train_test_split
     from xgboost import XGBRegressor
     from sklearn import metrics
     import seaborn as sns
     import matplotlib.pyplot as plt
     from sklearn.metrics import mean_squared_error, r2_score, mean_absolute_error
     data = pd.read_excel('cleaned_vehiclesdata3.xlsx')
```

Fig. 16.4 Importing libraries

```
[2]  # Label encoding for categorical variables
     from sklearn.preprocessing import LabelEncoder
     label_encoders = {}
     categorical_columns = ['manufacturer', 'fuel_type', 'transmission', 'drive', 'vehicle_type']
     for col in categorical_columns:
         label_encoders[col] = LabelEncoder()
         data[col] = label_encoders[col].fit_transform(data[col].astype(str))
```

Fig. 16.5 Label encoding

the original categorical values in the dataset, facilitating machine learning algorithms that require numerical inputs by converting categorical data into a format suitable for model training (Fig. 16.5).

This section of the code uses the XGBoost regression model to estimate the 'price' of vehicles based on different attributes in the dataset. It starts by gathering specific attributes like 'Age', 'manufacturer', 'fuel_type', 'mileage', 'transmission', and 'vehicle_type' into a list called 'features'. These attributes are considered as the independent variables used to predict vehicle prices (dependent variable). The dataset is split into two portions, with 80% designated for training (X_train and y_train) and 20% for testing (X_test and y_test) using the 'train_test_split' method from the 'sklearn.model_selection' package. An XGBoost regression model (XGBRegressor) is created and trained on the training data using 'xg.fit(X_train, y_train)'. After training, the model is used to forecast vehicle prices using the testing data ('y_pred = xg.predict(X_test)') (Figs. 16.6 and 16.7).

This section of code conducts an evaluation of the XGBoost regression model's performance in predicting vehicle prices by computing and analysing three crucial metrics. It calculates the Mean Squared Error (MSE), which measures the average squared disparity between the predicted and true prices, serving as a comprehensive indicator of predictive precision. The R-squared (R2) value portrays the proportion of variability in the vehicle prices that the model explains, with higher values closer to 1 denoting a more accurate fit of the model. Additionally, it computes the Mean Absolute Error (MAE), representing the average absolute difference between the

16.3 Research Methodology

```
[3] features = ['Age', 'manufacturer', 'fuel_type', 'mileage', 'transmission', 'vehicle_type']
    X = data[features]
    y = data["price"]

[5] X_train,X_test,y_train,y_test=train_test_split(X,y,test_size=0.20,random_state=42)

    xg = XGBRegressor()
    xg.fit(X_train,y_train)

                                XGBRegressor
    XGBRegressor(base_score=None, booster=None, callbacks=None,
                 colsample_bylevel=None, colsample_bynode=None,
                 colsample_bytree=None, device=None, early_stopping_rounds=None,
                 enable_categorical=False, eval_metric=None, feature_types=None,
                 gamma=None, grow_policy=None, importance_type=None,
                 interaction_constraints=None, learning_rate=None, max_bin=None,
                 max_cat_threshold=None, max_cat_to_onehot=None,
                 max_delta_step=None, max_depth=None, max_leaves=None,
                 min_child_weight=None, missing=nan, monotone_constraints=None,
                 multi_strategy=None, n_estimators=None, n_jobs=None,
                 num_parallel_tree=None, random_state=None, ...)

[8] y_pred = xg.predict(X_test)
```

Fig. 16.6 Splitting dataset into test and train

```
# Calculate evaluation metrics
mse = mean_squared_error(y_test, y_pred)
r2 = r2_score(y_test, y_pred)
mae = mean_absolute_error(y_test, y_pred)

# Print evaluation metrics
print(f"Mean Squared Error (MSE): {mse}")
print(f"R-squared (R2): {r2}")
print(f"Mean Absolute Error (MAE): {mae}")
```

Fig. 16.7 Evaluation metrics of the model

predicted and actual prices, offering another angle to assess prediction accuracy. The code then displays these metrics, providing a comprehensive overview of how effectively the XGBoost model estimates vehicle prices based on the chosen features. Based on the model's performance, it had a MSE of 23,544,872.82, R2 value of 0.7293, and MAE of 3343.28 (Figs. 16.8 and 16.9).

This section of code introduces a function called **test_model()** enabling users to input specific vehicle attributes like age, manufacturer, fuel type, mileage, transmission type, and vehicle type. The function further transforms these categorical inputs into numerical equivalents using previously established label encoders. It then employs the trained XGBoost machine learning model (referred to as 'model') to predict the vehicle's price based on these entered characteristics. The prediction

```
def test_model():
    # User inputs with conversion to lowercase for categorical variables
    age = int(input("Enter the age of the vehicle: "))
    manufacturer = input("Enter the manufacturer: ").lower()
    fuel_type = input("Enter the fuel type (e.g., gas, diesel): ").lower()
    mileage = int(input("Enter the mileage: "))
    transmission = input("Enter the transmission type (automatic/manual): ").lower()
    vehicle_type = input("Enter the vehicle type (e.g., SUV, sedan): ").lower()

    # Converting string inputs to numerical values
    manufacturer_num = label_encoders['manufacturer'].transform([manufacturer])[0]
    fuel_type_num = label_encoders['fuel_type'].transform([fuel_type])[0]
    transmission_num = label_encoders['transmission'].transform([transmission])[0]
    vehicle_type_num = label_encoders['vehicle_type'].transform([vehicle_type])[0]

    # Making a prediction
    predicted_price = model.predict(pd.DataFrame({
        'Age': [age],
        'manufacturer': [manufacturer_num],
        'fuel_type': [fuel_type_num],
        'mileage': [mileage],
        'transmission': [transmission_num],
        'vehicle_type': [vehicle_type_num]
    }))[0]

    print(f"Predicted Price: ${predicted_price}")

# Example of using the test_model function
test_model()
```

Fig. 16.8 Test model function

```
Enter the age of the vehicle: 1
Enter the manufacturer: toyota
Enter the fuel type (e.g., gas, diesel): gas
Enter the mileage: 50000
Enter the transmission type (automatic/manual): automatic
Enter the vehicle type (e.g., SUV, sedan): sedan
Predicted Price: $21730.12109375
```

Fig. 16.9 Outcome of test function

XGBoost Model Development for Car Recommender.

```
[ ]  # Load your dataset
     data = pd.read_excel('cleaned_vehiclesdata3.xlsx')
```

```
[ ]  # Load the pre-trained XGBoost model
     model = joblib.load('car_price.joblib')
```

Fig. 16.10 Loading dataset & XGBoost Model

occurs by organising the user inputs into a structured DataFrame, which is subsequently passed into the model's 'predict()' function. Eventually, the function showcases the predicted vehicle price to the user. As seen in Fig. 16.6, an example demonstrates how this 'test_model()' function can be used, allowing users to input vehicle details and receive an estimated price derived from the trained model (Fig. 16.10).

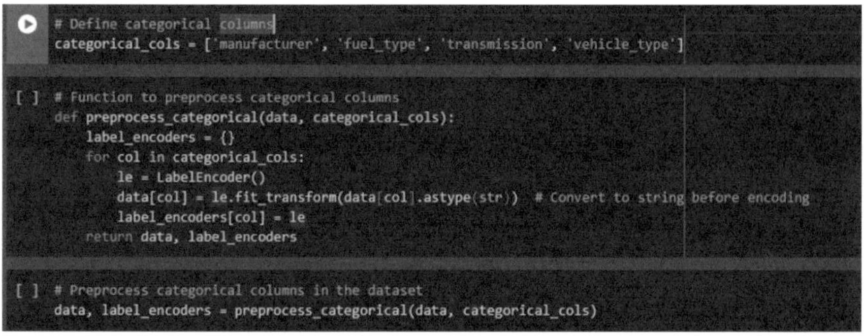

16.3 Research Methodology

Fig. 16.11 Label encoding

XGBoost Model Development for Car Recommender

This code performs dual functionality: it loads both a dataset and a pre-trained XGBoost model. Initially, it utilises Pandas, a Python library, to import data from an Excel file named 'cleaned_vehiclesdata3.xlsx'. This dataset contains information pertaining to vehicles that have been processed and cleaned. Subsequently, the code employs 'joblib', a commonly used serialisation library in Python, to load a pre-trained XGBoost model stored in a file named 'car_price.joblib'. This model is trained to predict car prices based on specific attributes or characteristics present within the dataset. By executing these instructions, the code readies both the dataset and the trained model, facilitating subsequent analysis or predictions concerning vehicle prices based on the loaded data and model (Fig. 16.11).

This section of code consists of the preprocessing of categorical columns within the dataset. Initially, it outlines a list named 'categorical_cols', encompassing column names indicating categorical attributes like 'manufacturer', 'fuel_type', 'transmission', and 'vehicle_type'. Subsequently, it defines a function, 'preprocess_categorical', specifically made for transforming categorical data. Within this function, a loop systematically processes each categorical column. For every column, it generates a LabelEncoder instance to convert the categorical values into numerical representations. Before encoding, the values undergo conversion to strings for uniformity across the dataset. As the loop progresses, the function updates the dataset by substituting the original categorical values with their respective encoded numerical counterparts. Furthermore, it maintains a record of these label encoders in a dictionary called 'label_encoders' for potential future usage. This code then executes the transformation of categorical columns in the dataset into numerical formats via label encoding, facilitating further analysis or modelling involving these features (Fig. 16.12).

This code segment performs a sequence of operations to predict vehicle prices using specific dataset columns with the pre-trained XGBoost model. Initially, it compiles a list named 'columns_for_prediction' comprising features like 'Age', 'manufacturer', 'fuel_type', 'mileage', 'transmission', and 'vehicle_type' that were

```
# Select columns used for prediction in the model (matching the trained features)
columns_for_prediction = ['Age', 'manufacturer', 'fuel_type', 'mileage', 'transmission', 'vehicle_type']

# Make predictions on the dataset
predictions = model.predict(data[columns_for_prediction])

# Add predictions to the dataset
data['PredictedPrice'] = predictions

# Save the DataFrame to a file (in this case, an Excel file)
data.to_excel('predicted_prices_dataset.xlsx', index=False)

# Download the file to your local machine
files.download('predicted_prices_dataset.xlsx')
```

Fig. 16.12 New dataset with predicted price

used during the model's training phase. Subsequently, the code leverages the pre-trained model to forecast prices within the dataset using these specified columns via the 'model.predict()' function. After generating predictions, it augments the dataset by incorporating these forecasted prices as a new column labelled 'PredictedPrice'. The code then saves this updated dataset into an Excel file named 'predicted_prices_dataset.xlsx' using Pandas' 'to_excel()' method, ensuring exclusion of the index from the file structure. Finally, the code initiates the download of the resulting Excel file ('predicted_prices_dataset.xlsx'), providing access to the dataset inclusive of the original details alongside the predicted prices, derived from the model's predictions (Fig. 16.12).

After uploading the new dataset into the Google Colaboratory workspace, condition mapping is done to correlate numerical values to different vehicle condition descriptions. Each condition, like 'new', 'like new', 'excellent', 'good', 'fair', and 'salvage', is matched with a numeric value to signify its position within a hierarchy. For instance, 'new' is assigned the highest value of 5, whereas 'salvage' gets the lowest value of 0. This systematic mapping establishes a structured order among subjective condition labels, offering a numeric scale that ranks conditions—higher values indicating better or newer conditions and lower values representing poorer or older conditions. The goal is to transform qualitative condition assessments into a standardised numeric format, aiding in easier comparison and analysis of vehicle conditions for decision-making purposes (Fig. 16.14).

This 'filter_cars' function is created to refine the dataset containing vehicle details using specific criteria. It accepts diverse parameters like 'manufacturer', 'age_range', 'mileage_range', 'transmission', 'price_range', and 'vehicle_type' to narrow down the dataset. For example, if 'manufacturer' or 'vehicle_type' is provided, the function filters the dataset to retain only records that match those specified attributes. Similarly, it filters based on 'age_range' or 'mileage_range' if defined. Additionally, it allows filtering by 'transmission' type and 'price_range' using predicted prices. Furthermore, it introduces a temporary 'ConditionRank' column in the dataset by converting 'condition' values into numeric equivalents, referencing the 'condition_mapping' dictionary. Once the dataset is sorted based on this temporary ranking, the

16.3 Research Methodology

```
# Mapping condition levels from best to worst
condition_mapping = {
    'new': 5,
    'like new': 4,
    'excellent': 3,
    'good': 2,
    'fair': 1,
    'salvage': 0
}
```

Fig. 16.13 Condition Mapping

'ConditionRank' column is removed, and the filtered dataset now sorted by vehicle condition is returned. This enables further analysis or presentation without modifying the original dataset (Fig. 16.15).

The 'recommend_car' function receives the dataset containing filtered vehicle details and generates a recommendation based on specific sorting guidelines. Firstly, it arranges the filtered dataset in a specific order; first by 'mileage' in ascending order, ensuring the lowest mileage vehicles are at the forefront, and then by 'condition' in descending order, placing the best-condition vehicles ahead within the mileage groups. This sorting mechanism aims to spotlight a top recommendation, specifically targeting vehicles with the least mileage and the most superior condition. Subsequently, the function extracts this top recommendation, essentially the initial entry after sorting, utilising the 'head(1)' method. In short, the function's goal is to pinpoint a single vehicle from the filtered dataset that exhibits the lowest mileage and the most exceptional condition, presenting this as its recommended choice based on these specific criteria (Figs. 16.16 and 16.17).

This code illustrates how the 'filter_cars' function is utilised practically by setting specific filters on a dataset containing vehicle details ('data'). These filters, including 'manufacturer' (Ford), 'vehicle_type' (SUV), 'age_range' (1 to 5 years old), 'mileage_range' (10,000 to 50,000 miles), 'transmission' (automatic), and 'price_range' ($15,000 to $25,000), aim to precisely narrow down the dataset. The objective is to extract Ford SUVs aged between 1 to 5 years, with mileage falling within 10,000 to 50,000 miles, equipped with automatic transmission, and priced between $15,000 and $25,000. The 'filter_cars' function processes these criteria to generate a refined subset of the initial dataset, denoted as 'filtered_results'. Lastly, as seen in Fig. 16.13, the code showcases this refined dataset ('filtered_results'), providing a detailed selection of vehicles that strictly match the specified criteria defined by the applied filters (Fig. 16.18).

This section of code further refines the 'filtered_results' dataset by arranging it based on specific criteria and presents a concise overview of the top five cars that best meet these conditions. Initially, the 'filtered_results' dataset, containing vehicles meeting particular filtered conditions, undergoes a two-stage sorting process. It is sorted by 'condition' in ascending order, positioning vehicles with the finest condition at the forefront. Within each condition group, it further sorts by 'mileage'

```
def filter_cars(data, manufacturer=None, age_range=None, mileage_range=None, transmission=None, price_range=None, vehicle_type=None):
    filtered_data = data.copy()  # Make a copy of the original data to avoid modifying it

    if manufacturer:
        filtered_data = filtered_data[filtered_data['manufacturer'] == manufacturer]

    if vehicle_type:
        filtered_data = filtered_data[filtered_data['vehicle_type'] == vehicle_type]

    if age_range:
        filtered_data = filtered_data[
            (filtered_data['Age'] >= age_range[0]) &
            (filtered_data['Age'] <= age_range[1])
        ]

    if mileage_range:
        filtered_data = filtered_data[
            (filtered_data['mileage'] >= mileage_range[0]) &
            (filtered_data['mileage'] <= mileage_range[1])
        ]

    if transmission:
        filtered_data = filtered_data[filtered_data['transmission'] == transmission]

    if price_range:
        filtered_data = filtered_data[
            (filtered_data['PredictedPrice'] >= price_range[0]) &
            (filtered_data['PredictedPrice'] <= price_range[1])
        ]

    # Sorting by condition mapped values
    filtered_data['ConditionRank'] = filtered_data['condition'].map(condition_mapping)
    filtered_data = filtered_data.sort_values(by='ConditionRank', ascending=False)

    return filtered_data.drop('ConditionRank', axis=1)
```

Fig. 16.14 Filter Car Function

```
def recommend_car(filtered_data):
    # Sort by mileage (ascending) and condition (descending)
    sorted_results = filtered_data.sort_values(by=['mileage', 'condition'], ascending=[True, False])
    return sorted_results.head(1)  # Return the top recommendation (lowest mileage, best condition)
```

Fig. 16.15 Recommended Car Function

```
# Example usage
filtered_results = filter_cars(
    data,
    manufacturer='ford',
    vehicle_type='SUV',
    age_range=(1, 5),
    mileage_range=(10000, 50000),
    transmission='automatic',
    price_range=(15000, 25000)
)

# Display the filtered results
print(filtered_results)
```

Fig. 16.16 Recommendation usage example

16.3 Research Methodology

Fig. 16.17 Recommendation Outcome

Fig. 16.18 Top 5 vehicle recommendations

in descending order, prioritising vehicles with the lowest mileage. Following this sorting, the code selects the top five cars adhering to these criteria using 'head(5)'. Subsequently, it displays a subset of these sorted outcomes, specifically highlighting columns such as 'manufacturer', 'model', 'Age', 'mileage', 'condition', and 'PredictedPrice' for these leading five cars. This summary offers a swift insight into the top candidates; those with the lowest mileage and the best condition within the filtered dataset, allowing for a quick comparison based on these defined parameters.

Verification and Validation of XGBoost Model

To verify the reliability and the accuracy of the XGBoost model created, we have opted to use data from Malaysia's renowned car selling platform, Carsome, to validate the usability of our model.

Leveraging a dataset sourced from a renowned automotive marketplace such as Carsome for validating the accuracy and dependability of an XGBoost model represents a strategically sound methodology. The utilisation of authentic, real-world data from a reputable source facilitates a comprehensive assessment of the model's efficacy within a pertinent context.

The validation process against this dataset enables a nuanced evaluation of the model's predictive performance, extending beyond mere accuracy metrics. It facilitates an appraisal of the model's adeptness in prognosticating prices or pertinent determinants, thereby yielding insights into its predictive efficacy and resilience in unforeseen, real-world scenarios.

Web Scrapping

This Python script (Figs. 16.15 and 16.16) employs web scraping methods to gather car listings from the Carsome website's 'buy-car' section. It utilises the 'scrape_carsome_page' function to extract various car details like titles, mileage, transmission type, price, location, and car type by parsing HTML elements through Beautiful Soup. The code iterates through a set number of pages, constructing distinct URLs for each page to extract their content. The extracted data is structured into a list of dictionaries, each representing details of an individual car listing. Then, this collated data is transformed into a structured Pandas DataFrame and saved into an Excel file named 'scraped_data.xlsx'. Essentially, this script streamlines the process of collecting and organising car information from numerous webpages into an Excel file (Figs. 16.19 and 16.20).

Validation of Model

The code in Figure orchestrates a sequence of actions to assimilate the web scrapped Carsome data into existing training data, refine an XGBoost model using the merged

16.3 Research Methodology

Fig. 16.19 Web scrapping from Carsome's website

Fig. 16.20 Web scrapping from Carsome's website (continued)

dataset, foresee prices for the novel dataset, and exhibit these prognosticated prices in parallel with associated manufacturer details. Firstly, it lays the groundwork by creating encoders for categorical variables if they have not been previously established. Subsequently, it amalgamates the original training data ('data') with the Carsome data ('new_data') using Pandas' 'concat' function. To ensure consistency in model comprehension, categorical columns within the combined dataset undergo label encoding (Figs. 16.21 and 16.22).

Following this, the merged dataset splits back into the original training subset ('X_train_combined') and the new data subset ('X_new_combined'). An XGBoost regression model ('xg_combined') then undergoes training on the combined training data ('X_train_combined'), assimilating insights from both original and Carsome datasets. This trained model proceeds to anticipate prices for the new data ('X_new_combined').

```python
# Create label encoders for categorical variables if they don't exist
label_encoders = {}
for col in categorical_columns:
    label_encoders[col] = LabelEncoder()

# Combine your original training data and the new data
combined_data = pd.concat([data, new_data])

# Apply label encoding to categorical variables for the combined dataset
for col in categorical_columns:
    combined_data[col] = label_encoders[col].fit_transform(combined_data[col].astype(str))

# Split the combined dataset into training and new data
X_train_combined = combined_data[features][:len(data)]
X_new_combined = combined_data[features][len(data):]

# Train your XGBoost model on the combined training data
xg_combined = XGBRegressor()
xg_combined.fit(X_train_combined, y)

# Make predictions for the new data using the trained combined model
predicted_prices_new = xg_combined.predict(X_new_combined)

# Add the predicted prices to the new_data DataFrame
new_data['Predicted_Price'] = predicted_prices_new

# Display the new_data DataFrame with predicted prices
print(new_data[['manufacturer', 'Predicted_Price']])
```

Fig. 16.21 XGBoost model using Carsome data

```
      manufacturer  Predicted_Price
0            Honda     97925.460938
1           Nissan     70605.937500
2            Mazda     62089.613281
3            Mazda    154903.687500
4            Honda     55398.000000
...            ...              ...
1789         Honda    110655.546875
1790        Proton     60208.710938
1791        Toyota    165722.812500
1792       Perodua    170583.296875
1793        Proton    199179.125000

[1794 rows x 2 columns]
```

Fig. 16.22 Outcome of predicted price

Finally, the predicted prices for the Carsome dataset are appended as a supplementary column ('Predicted_Price') within the 'new_data' DataFrame. As seen in Fig. 16.18, the code culminates by presenting a snapshot of 'new_data', specifically showcasing 'manufacturer' details and their corresponding 'Predicted_Price',

16.3 Research Methodology

```
from sklearn.metrics import r2_score, mean_absolute_error

r2 = r2_score(y_val, y_pred_val)
mae = mean_absolute_error(y_val, y_pred_val)

print(f"R-squared (R2) on validation data: {r2}")
print(f"Mean Absolute Error (MAE) on validation data: {mae}")

R-squared (R2) on validation data: 0.7922039832420906
Mean Absolute Error (MAE) on validation data: 7536.258175650679
```

Fig. 16.23 Evaluation metrics of Carsome data on XGBoost model

offering a glimpse into the anticipated prices derived from the trained amalgamated model for the novel dataset (Fig. 16.23).

This script in Python assesses the performance of the XGBoost model by calculating two key metrics—R-squared (R2) and Mean Absolute Error (MAE). It evaluates the model's predictions ('y_pred_val') against the true target values ('y_val') derived from the Carsome dataset. The 'r2_score' function, part of the scikit-learn library, computes the R-squared value, indicating how much of the variability in the dependent variable is accounted for by the model. In parallel, the 'mean_absolute_error' function determines the average absolute difference between the predicted and actual values, offering a direct measure of the model's accuracy. Through the validation and verification process, the model produced a higher R2 value of 0.7922 as compared to the US dataset and a MAE of 7536.2582. This shows that the XGBoost model is highly reliable and can be universally applied to different car price dataset.

16.3.5.3 Website Development

The Drive Smart website, with its scroll-down home page format, offers a seamless and engaging experience for users. Each section is carefully crafted to provide valuable information and interactive features.

Index. HTML

At the forefront of the website is the About Section, which articulates the core mission of Drive Smart: to revolutionise the car-buying and selling experience through innovative technology. The vision statement outlines a future where making informed automotive decisions is straightforward and enjoyable. This section also emphasises the company's values, such as innovation, customer-centricity, and integrity, alongside a brief history of the company's inception, milestones, and future aspirations. This narrative connects users with the brand's journey and ethos (Fig. 16.24).

```
<!doctype html>
<html class="no-js" lang="en">

    <head>
        <!-- meta data -->
        <meta charset="utf-8">
        <meta http-equiv="X-UA-Compatible" content="IE=edge">
        <meta name="viewport" content="width=device-width, initial-scale=1">

        <link rel="stylesheet" href="../static/css/style.css">
        <!-- The above 3 meta tags *must* come first in the head; any other head content must come *after* these tags -->

        <!--font-family-->
        <link href="https://fonts.googleapis.com/css?family=Poppins:100,100i,200,200i,300,300i,400,400i,500,500i,600,600i,700,70

        <link href="https://fonts.googleapis.com/css?family=Rufina:400,700" rel="stylesheet">

        <!-- title of site -->
        <title>DriveSmart</title>

        <!-- For Drive Smart png -->
        <link rel="shortcut icon" type="image/icon" href="{{ url_for('static', filename='../static/images/DriveSmart Logo.png')

         <!--font-awesome.min.css-->
         <link rel="stylesheet" href="{{ url_for('static', filename='../static/css/font-awesome.min.css') }}">

         <!--linear icon css-->
    <link rel="stylesheet" href="{{ url_for('static', filename='../static/css/linearicons.css') }}">

    <!--animate.css-->
         <link rel="stylesheet" href="{{ url_for('static', filename='../static/css/animate.css') }}">

         <!--owl.carousel.css-->
         <link rel="stylesheet" href="{{ url_for('static', filename='../static/css/owl.carousel.min.css') }}">

         <link rel="stylesheet" href="{{ url_for('static', filename='../static/css/owl.theme.default.min.css') }}">

         <!--bootstrap.min.css-->
         <link rel="stylesheet" href="{{ url_for('static', filename='../static/css/bootstrap.min.css') }}">

    <!-- bootsnav -->
    <link rel="stylesheet" href="{{ url_for('static', filename='../static/css/bootsnav.css') }}">


    <!--responsive.css-->
    <link rel="stylesheet" href="{{ url_for('static', filename='../static/css/responsive.css') }}">



        <!-- HTML5 shim and Respond.js for IE8 support of HTML5 elements and media queries -->
        <!-- WARNING: Respond.js doesn't work if you view the page via file:// -->

        <!--[if lt IE 9]>
            <script src="https://oss.maxcdn.com/html5shiv/3.7.3/html5shiv.min.js"></script>
            <script src="https://oss.maxcdn.com/respond/1.4.2/respond.min.js"></script>
        <![endif]-->

    </head>
```

Fig. 16.24 Index HTML

The Drive Smart website's home page is meticulously structured using HTML5, with standard doctype and language attributes to ensure compliance with modern web standards. Essential meta tags have been set up for character encoding, browser compatibility, and responsive design, ensuring the site functions correctly across various devices and browsers.

In terms of aesthetics and functionality, external CSS files are linked to handle the site's styling and responsive layout. The inclusion of custom fonts from Google Fonts, specifically Poppins and Rufina, enhances the site's typographic design, while Font Awesome and linear icons provide a range of scalable vector icons, contributing to the site's visual appeal and user interface.

The site's branding is emphasised through its title, 'Drive Smart', and a favicon featuring the Drive Smart Logo, ensuring brand consistency across different browser tabs and bookmarks. For compatibility with older browsers like IE8, HTML5 shim, and Respond.js are integrated, supporting HTML5 elements and media queries in these environments.

A key feature of the homepage is its responsive navigation bar, developed using Bootstrap and Bootsnav plugins. This navigation bar includes links to various sections of the home page, such as About, Services, Analysis, and a dedicated link to the Feedback page, facilitating easy and intuitive user navigation.

The hero section, marked as 'welcome-hero', immediately greets visitors with a welcoming message and a concise introduction to what Drive Smart offers, setting the tone for the user experience. In the About Us section, an interactive carousel powered by Owl Carousel dynamically displays the company's vision, mission, and methodology, enriched with images and text for an engaging presentation. The Our Services section is strategically designed to highlight the primary services offered by Drive Smart, namely car recommendation and value prediction, with buttons directing users to the respective service pages or forms. The Analysis section further enriches the site with an embedded Power BI report, providing an interactive platform for displaying insights and analysis.

In showcasing its products, the Featured Cars section displays a curated selection of cars, detailing aspects like model, mileage, horsepower, and price, arranged in a grid layout for easy browsing. The Our Team section adds a personal touch, featuring a carousel of team member profiles complete with images and short descriptions or quotes.

The Brand section enhances brand recognition, displaying various car brand logos in a carousel, which link to respective sections or external pages. The footer of the page is comprehensive, containing essential contact information, quick links to important pages, a newsletter subscription box, and social media icons for extended engagement. It also includes copyright notice and a convenient scroll-to-top button.

Lastly, the integration of JQuery and Bootstrap scripts enables interactive components on the site, while a custom JavaScript file is likely responsible for specific interactions and animations, contributing to a smooth and dynamic user experience on the Drive Smart website.

Car Recommendation Service Page Quiz 1

The HTML code presented defines a landing section that is contained within a webpage and is encapsulated in a container that has the class **'landing'**. An additional division, denoted as **'intro-text',** is nested within this container to serve as a compartment for introductory material. The heading, which is encompassed in a < **h1** > tag, asserts in a bold manner, **'FIND YOUR DREAM CAR!'** This likely functions as a message that commands attention. Subsequent to the heading, a paragraph < **p** > presents a concise explanation, urging readers to simplify the procedure of choosing their ideal vehicle by inputting their preferences and having the system make the decision (Figs. 16.25 and 16.26).

This HTML code describes a webpage's body section within a < **main** > element, highlighting a car preference form. Located in a < **div** > with the id **'select-vehicle-form',** the form starts with a < **p** > element asking users to select their preferences for personalised recommendations. In the < **form** > element, the action property points to 'http://127.0.0.1:5000/recommend' and the method attribute is set to **'post'**, signifying HTTP POST submission of form data. Users can choose their car

```
<!-- Start Landing -->
<div class="landing">
    <div class="intro-text">
        <h1>FIND YOUR DREAM CAR!</h1>
        <p>Skip the hassle of selecting your perfect ride by picking your preferences and letting us do it for you!</p>
    </div>
</div>
<!-- End Landing -->
```

Fig. 16.25 Coding for Landing Section

```
<!-- Start Body -->
<main>
    <div id="select-vehicle-form">
        <p>Please select your preferences to get the perfect recommendations for you</p>

        <form action="http://127.0.0.1:5000/recommend" method="post"><label for="manufacturer">Manufacturer:</label>
            <select id="manufacturer" name="manufacturer">
                <option text="choose your option">Choose Your Option</option>
                <option value="audi">Audi</option>
                <option value="bmw">BMW</option>
                <option value="cadillac">Cadillac</option>
                <option value="chevrolet">Chevrolet</option>
                <option value="chrysler">Chrysler</option>
                <option value="dodge">Dodge</option>
                <option value="ford">Ford</option>
                <option value="gmc">GMC</option>
                <option value="honda">Honda</option>
                <option value="hyundai">Hyundai</option>
                <option value="jeep">Jeep</option>
                <option value="kia">Kia</option>
                <option value="lexus">Lexus</option>
                <option value="mazda">Mazda</option>
                <option value="mercedes-benz">Mercedes-Benz</option>
                <option value="nissan">Nissan</option>
                <option value="ram">Ram</option>
                <option value="subaru">Subaru</option>
                <option value="toyota">Toyota</option>
                <option value="volkswagon">Volkswagon</option>
            </select>
            <br>
```

Fig. 16.26 Coding for Vehicle Selection

```
<label for="vehicle_type"> Vehicle Type: </label>
<select id="vehicle_type" name="vehicle_type">
    <option text="choose your option">Choose Your Option</option>
    <option value="hatchback">Hatchback</option>
    <option value="pickup">Pickup</option>
    <option value="sedan">Sedan</option>
    <option value="suv">SUV</option>
</select>
<br>
```

Fig. 16.27 Coding for vehicle type

manufacturer from a **'Manufacturer'** selection. In the dropdown, users can choose between < **option** > components representing different manufacturers, with a default placeholder option (Fig. 16.27).

16.3 Research Methodology

```
<label for="MinAge">Minimum Age of Your Vehicle </label>
<input type="text"  id="MinAge" name="MinAge">
<br>

<label for="MaxAge">Maximum Age of Your Vehicle </label>
<input type="text" id="MaxAge" name="MaxAge">

<br>

<label for="Minmileage">Minimum Mileage of Your Vehicle</label>
<input type="text"  id="Minmileage" name="Minmileage">
<br>

<label for="Maxmileage">Maximum Mileage of Your Vehicle</label>
<input type="text"  id="Maxmileage" name="Maxmileage">
<br>
```

Fig. 16.28 Coding for Min and Max Selection

```
<label for="transmission">Transmission:</label>
<select id="transmission" name="transmission">
    <option text="choose your option">Choose Your Option</option>
    <option value="automatic">Automatic</option>
    <option value="manual">Manual</option>
</select>
<br>
```

Fig. 16.29 Coding for Transmission Selection

This section of the HTML emphasises the option of different types of vehicles. The < **label** > element is used to present the dropdown menu, linking it to the **'vehicle_type'** input field and showing the label **'Vehicle Type'** next to the dropdown. The < **select** > element specifies the dropdown menu, while the subsequent < **option** > components display different vehicle categories for customers to select, such as hatchback, pickup, sedan, and SUV (Fig. 16.28).

The above section of the HTML code represents a form section on a webpage that specifically deals with user input on the age and mileage of a car. It consists of groups of < **label** > and < **input** > components, each designed for gathering specific information. Users are required to submit the minimum and maximum age of their automobiles using labelled text input areas labelled as **'MinAge'** and **'MaxAge'**. Users can indicate the minimum and maximum mileage of their automobiles by utilising text input sections labelled **'Minmileage'** and **'Maxmileage'** (Fig. 16.29).

A < **label** > element with the text **'Transmission'** is linked to a dropdown menu built using the < **option** > tag, which is recognised by the attribute 'transmission'.

```html
<label for="Minprice_range">Minimum Price of Your Vehicle</label>
<input type="text"  id="Minprice_range" name="Minprice_range">
<br>

<label for="Maxprice_range">Maximum Price of Your Vehicle</label>
<input type="text"  id="Maxprice_range" name="Maxprice_range">
<br>
```

Fig. 16.30 Coding for Min Max Price Selection

```html
<button type="submit" class="btn btn-primary btn-block btn-large">Recommend</button>
```

Fig. 16.31 Coding for Button

Users have the ability to select among various gearbox kinds, such as **'Automatic'** and **'Manual'**, which are displayed as choices in a dropdown menu (Fig. 16.30).

This section of the HTML allows users to input the pricing range for their vehicles. The interface has two sets of < **label** > and < **input** > elements, which allow users to indicate the minimum and maximum pricing for their automobiles. The initial collection, designated as **'Minimum Price of Your Vehicle'**, is connected to the corresponding text input box identified as **'Minprice_range'**. Similarly, the second group, denoted as **'Maximum Price of Your Vehicle'**, corresponds to the input field designated by the id **'Maxprice_range'**. Both input fields are set to the **'text'** type, enabling users to enter numeric numbers (Fig. 16.31).

The above HTML code comprises a < **button** > element specifically designed for submitting a form on a webpage. The button, labelled **'Recommend'** is configured with the **'submit'** type and invites users to initiate a certain action, most likely connected to suggesting vehicles based on user input. This button is a key user interface feature that allows users to submit form input and start operations related to generating recommendations (Fig. 16.32).

The given HTML and CSS code collectively generate an aesthetically pleasing presentation for showcasing car information on a webpage. The CSS styles are intended to format a container called 'car-container' and individual vehicle boxes referred to as **'car-box'** with precise characteristics like borders, background colour, width, padding, margin, border radius, and box shadow. The HTML body dynamically populates the automobile information into styled boxes by iterating through a list of cars called **'top_5_cars'**. The homepage presents the details of each automobile, such as the brand, model, age, mileage, condition, and anticipated price, in labelled columns within formatted car boxes. This creates a structured and visually consistent display of car information.

Input Fields: Users can input their preferences, such as car type, budget, brand, etc.

Recommend Button: Upon clicking, the system processes the inputs and displays a list of cars that match the user's criteria, complete with details and reasons for each recommendation (Fig. 16.33).

16.3 Research Methodology

```html
<style>
/* CSS styles for the car boxes */
.car-container {
    display: flex;
    flex-wrap: wrap;
    justify-content: space-evenly; /* Adjust as needed */
}

/* CSS styles for the car boxes */
.car-box {
    border: 1px solid #ccc;
    background-color: white;
    width: 300px;
    padding: 10px;
    margin: 10px;
    border-radius: 5px;
    box-shadow: 0 0 4px rgb(255, 254, 254);
    display: flex; /* Arrange columns horizontally */
    flex-direction: column;
}

.car-box-column {
    margin-bottom: 10px;
    display: flex;
    align-items: center;
    flex-direction: column;
    align-items: center;
    justify-content: center;
}


.car-box-label {
    font-weight: bold;
    color: black;
    min-width: 100px; /* Set a minimum width for labels */
}
</style>
</head>
<body>

<div class="car-container">
    {% for car in top_5_cars %}
    <div class="car-box">
        <div class="car-box-column">
            <span class="car-box-label">Manufacturer:</span> {{ car.manufacturer }}
        </div>
        <div class="car-box-column">
            <span class="car-box-label">Model:</span> {{ car.model }}
        </div>
        <div class="car-box-column">
            <span class="car-box-label">Age:</span> {{ car.Age }}
        </div>
        <div class="car-box-column">
            <span class="car-box-label">Mileage:</span> {{ car.mileage }}
        </div>
        <div class="car-box-column">
            <span class="car-box-label">Condition:</span> {{ car.condition }}
        </div>
        <div class="car-box-column">
            <span class="car-box-label">Predicted Price:</span> {{ car.PredictedPrice }}
        </div>
    </div>
    {% endfor %}
</div>
```

Fig. 16.32 Coding for Quiz results

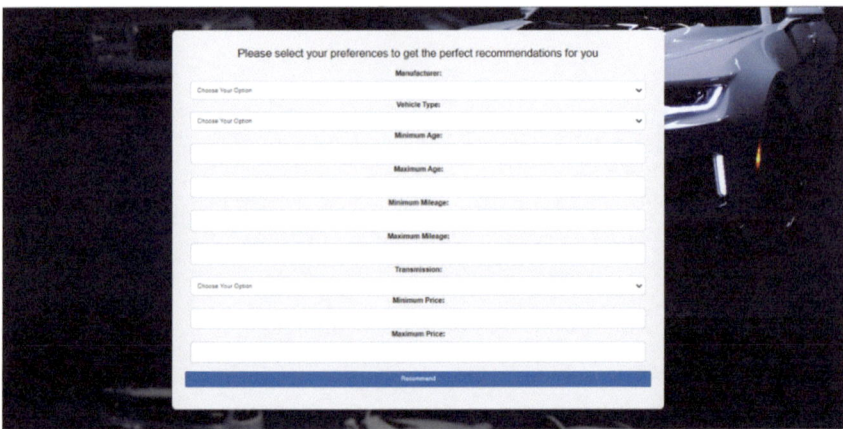

Fig. 16.33 Car Recommender

```
97
98    <!-- start landing -->
99    <div class="landing">
00       <div class="intro-text">
01          <h1>WHAT'S YOUR CAR WORTH?</h1>
02          <p>Use this calculator to find out what your car is valued at!</p>
03       </div>
04    </div>
05    <!-- End landing -->
```

Fig. 16.34 Coding for Landing Section

Car Price Calculator Quiz 2

This section includes an introduction and a heading that describes the landing area. The HTML framework is made up of two div elements: one with the class 'landing' and the other with the class 'intro-text'. A < h1 > heading with the words 'WHAT'S YOUR CAR WORTH?' and a < p > paragraph with a synopsis are located inside the 'intro-text' div. The goal of this landing page is to draw in visitors and entice them to use the vehicle value tool (Figs. 16.34 and 16.35).

The primary section of the code, which contains the vehicle value form, is this one. One of the form elements inside the select-vehicle-form div has the action attribute set to 'http://127.0.0.1:5000/predict' and the method attribute set to **'post'**. This suggests that the HTTP POST method be used to send the data to the designated URL when the user submits the form. This method helps link the HTML for the Quiz directly to the **predict** in the Python code allowing for a seamless integration of web design and model. The form has a number of input boxes, including dropdowns for Age, Manufacturer, Fuel Type, Mileage, Gearbox, and Vehicle Type. Lastly, a **'Calculate Price'** button completes the form submission process (Fig. 16.36).

16.3 Research Methodology

```html
<main>
    <div id="select-vehicle-form">

    <form action="http://127.0.0.1:5000/predict" method="post">


        <label for="Age">Age of Your Vehicle: </label>
        <input type="number" id="Age" name="Age">

        <br>

        <label for="manufacturer">Manufacturer:</label>
        <select id="manufacturer" name="manufacturer">
        <option text="choose your option">Choose Your Option</option>
        <option value="audi">Audi</option>
        <option value="bmw">BMW</option>
        <option value="cadillac">Cadillac</option>
        <option value="chevrolet">Chevrolet</option>
        <option value="chrysler">Chrysler</option>
        <option value="dodge">Dodge</option>
        <option value="ford">Ford</option>
        <option value="gmc">GMC</option>
        <option value="honda">Honda</option>
        <option value="hyundai">Hyundai</option>
        <option value="jeep">Jeep</option>
        <option value="kia">Kia</option>
        <option value="lexus">Lexus</option>
        <option value="mazda">Mazda</option>
        <option value="mercedes-benz">Mercedes-Benz</option>
        <option value="nissan">Nissan</option>
        <option value="ram">Ram</option>
        <option value="subaru">Subaru</option>
        <option value="toyota">Toyota</option>
        <option value="volkswagon">Volkswagon</option>
        </select>
```

Fig. 16.35 Coding for Quiz 2

The CSS styling for the prediction text in this part is contained in the < **style** > tag inside the < **head** > section. The overall styling of the prediction text is defined by the **.prediction_text class**, and when the text is revealed, the appearance is changed using the **.show-prediction class**. For the prediction text, a hover effect is also defined.

The prediction text is displayed in this section of the code. The text is initially buried with an opacity of 0. The show-prediction class is applied to the prediction text, making it visible, after a simulated delay (or processing time). The < **script** > tag contains JavaScript that, in order to disclose the prediction text. The javascript here is used to automate and streamline the function of the button such as the wait

```css
.prediction_text {
    font-size: 40px;
    color: #fff;
    background-color: #3498db96;
    padding: 30px;
    border-radius: 10px;
    box-shadow: 0 4px 6px rgba(0, 0, 0, 0.1);
    text-shadow: 1px 1px 2px rgba(0, 0, 0, 0.5);
    transition: transform 0.3s ease-in-out;
    opacity: 0; /* Initially hide the prediction text */
}

.show-prediction {
    opacity: 1; /* Show the prediction text */
}

.prediction_text:hover {
    transform: scale(1.05);
}
</style>
</head>
<body>
    <div class="container">
        <!-- Initially hide the prediction text -->
        <h4 class="prediction_text" id="prediction_text">{{ prediction_text }}</h4>
    </div>

    <script>
        // Simulate an upload completion after a delay (you can replace this with your actual upload process)
        setTimeout(function() {
            // Get the prediction text element
            var predictionText = document.getElementById('prediction_text');
            // Add the class to show the prediction text
            predictionText.classList.add('show-prediction'), 1000;
        })
    </script>
```

Fig. 16.36 Coding for Quiz 2 CSS

for the given amount of time (in this case, 1000 ms) using the **setTimeout** function. This method gives the prediction text a seamless transition effect.

In summary, the HTML code creates a user interface that includes a landing page, a form for appraising an automobile, and styled components to display the forecast result. This code can be customised by developers to be integrated into a more comprehensive web application for car appraisal, resulting in an interactive and interesting user experience.

Input Fields: Users enter details about their car like make, model, year, mileage, and condition.

Calculate Price Button: After entering the details, users can click this button to receive an estimated market value of their car, calculated using a sophisticated algorithm (Fig. 16.37).

Design for Website

Our primary focus during the website design process was developing an interface that was both easy to use and straightforward for users. Our understanding of the significance of accessibility for people with different technological backgrounds

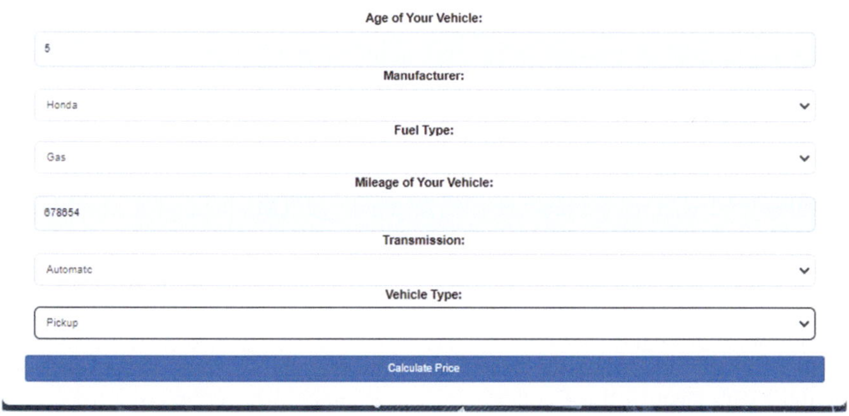

16.3 Research Methodology

Fig. 16.37 Car Price Calculator Quiz

led to the deliberate and uncomplicated design. Given the educational nature of our website, we added a degree of interaction despite the purposeful simplicity to guarantee a fun and engaging user experience.

We used CSS for the main design development and aesthetics in order to realise this concept. Our website's responsive design and general layout were greatly influenced by Bootstrap CSS. With its pre-built components and responsive tools for design that work on all devices, Bootstrap is a powerful front-end framework that makes design easier.

We used Owl Carousel, a responsive carousel plugin for jQuery, for animated elements. By providing dynamic and interactive content presentations, Owl Carousel improves user engagement and makes our website more aesthetically pleasing.

JavaScript was essential to automating many of the processes on our website, mainly related to jQuery. jQuery is a lightweight and quick JavaScript toolkit that makes common tasks like event handling, animation, and HTML page navigation and manipulation easier. Because of its adaptability, we were able to improve user engagement and overall functionality by streamlining the automation process. To sum up, we combined the strengths of jQuery, Bootstrap, Owl Carousel, and CSS in our design approach to create a well-balanced design that emphasised accessibility, simplicity, and interactivity. This strategy guarantees that users from a variety of backgrounds can utilise our website while enjoying an engaging and interactive user experience.

16.3.6 Model Deployment

16.3.6.1 Integration

The Python script describes the utilisation of Flask, a web framework, to establish a dynamic web application for Drive Smart. It defines multiple routes responsible for handling user requests and rendering corresponding HTML templates. The '/' route directs users to the primary landing page ('index.html'), whereas '/recommendform' and '/predictform' routes facilitate user interaction by displaying specific forms ('Quiz1.html' and 'Quiz2.html' respectively) aimed at gathering user input. The '/recommend' route processes user-provided inputs from a form, filtering a dataset of car information based on specified criteria, subsequently identifying and selecting the top 5 cars meeting those conditions. The resultant data is organised for display within the 'Quiz1.html' template. Meanwhile, the '/predict' route captures user inputs pertaining to car attributes, employing label encoding to handle categorical data, and leveraging a pre-trained machine learning model to predict vehicle prices based on the provided features. The predicted price is then incorporated into the 'Quiz2.html' template for user visualisation. Upon direct execution, the script initialises the Flask application in debug mode, operating on port 5000 (Figs. 16.38, 16.39, and 16.40).

Following a successful development of the XGBoost model via Python along the website simultaneously being created using HTML, the final part of the development involved integrating the back-end model with the front-end user interface. This is done so that when users input their preferences into the quizzes, the model is able to retrieve them and produce the results. To complete the integration between the

Fig. 16.38 Flask app integration

16.3 Research Methodology

```
143         # Make prediction
144         predicted_price = model.predict(pd.DataFrame({
145             'Age': [Age],
146             'manufacturer': [manufacturer_num],
147             'fuel_type': [fuel_type_num],
148             'mileage': [mileage],
149             'transmission': [transmission_num],
150             'vehicle_type': [vehicle_type_num]
151         }))[0]
152
153         # Return rendered template with prediction text
154         return render_template('Quiz2.html', prediction_text=f'Predicted Price: ${predicted_price:.2f}')
155     except Exception as e:
156         # For debugging, print the exception to the console
157         print(e)
158         # Return rendered template with error message
159         return render_template('Quiz2.html', prediction_text='An error occurred. Please check your inputs.')
160
161
162
163 @app.route('/recommend', methods=['POST','GET'])
164 def recommend():
165     # Get user inputs from the form
166     # Use request.form to retrieve the values from the submitted form
167     # Perform filtering and recommendation based on the user inputs
```

Fig. 16.39 Flask app integration (continued)

```
169     # Get form inputs
170     manufacturer = request.form.get('manufacturer', type=str)
171     vehicle_type = request.form.get('vehicle_type', type=str)
172     minage_range = request.form.get('MinAge', type=int)
173     maxage_range = request.form.get('MaxAge', type=int)
174     minmileage_range = request.form.get('Minmileage', type=int)
175     maxmileage_range = request.form.get('Maxmileage', type=int)
176     transmission = request.form.get('transmission', type=str)
177     minprice_range = request.form.get('Minprice_range', type=float)
178     maxprice_range = request.form.get('Maxprice_range', type=float)
179
180     # Use your filter_cars function with user inputs
181     filtered_results = filter_cars(
182         data,
183         manufacturer=manufacturer,
184         vehicle_type=vehicle_type,
185         minage_range=minage_range,
186         maxage_range=maxage_range,
187         minmileage_range=minmileage_range,
188         maxmileage_range=maxmileage_range,
189         transmission=transmission,
190         minprice_range=minprice_range,
191         maxprice_range=maxprice_range,
192     )
193     # Sort and select top 5 cars
194     sorted_results = filtered_results.sort_values(by=['mileage', 'condition'], ascending=[True, False]).head(5)
195
196     # Prepare the data to pass to the template
197     top_5_cars = sorted_results.to_dict(orient='records')
198
199     return render_template('Quiz1.html', top_5_cars=top_5_cars)
200
201 if __name__ == '__main__':
202     app.run(debug=True, port=5000)
```

Fig. 16.40 Flask app integration (continued)

Python (XGBoost model) and the HTML, an API using Flask was created. Application Programming Interface (API) is a set of protocols that allows two different software to communicate with each other. Flask in this case used, which fetches the information from the local host and helps facilitate the communication between Python and HTML to generate an HTTP link that allows the link to be hosted on any working server. The application was tested using Postman, a popular tool for

Fig. 16.41 Local host link

API testing among developers, prior to integration. By enabling the team to experiment with different scripts and variables, Postman enabled collaborative testing and ensured that API connections were validated. This procedure was carried out in tandem with the front-end team's UI development. Simplifying the integration process was made possible by adding the extra stage of API testing and validation using Postman. It helped to improve the development workflow by anticipating and resolving possible problems including wrong data types, parameter settings, and other unforeseen obstacles (Fig. 16.41).

The system is set up to send a JSON-formatted 'POST' type API request to the address 'http://127.0.0.1:5000/'. 'POST' is a mechanism in the HTTP protocol that is intended to submit and process data efficiently. The data is usually kept in a server database. The 'POST' request in the Drive Smart context entails sending in the specific user preferences for the car recommender or car price predictor that corresponds to the data that has been supplied. After the input is received, the XGBoost Model is then able to produce the results based on this.

16.3.6.2 API Testing

To validate if the API has been deployed successfully, the testing of its functionality is conducted using the Postman application. As depicted in the figure above, the API is examined within the Postman working environment. The utilised method for testing the API is designated as 'POST', where the results are transmitted as a variable identified as 'string'. The outcome of this API interaction returns a list recommendation comprising the top five vehicles with their predicted prices. This conclusive output affirms the operational functionality of the API, thereby substantiating its successful operation and validation of deployment (Fig. 16.42).

16.4 Results and Analysis

16.4.1 Overview

This chapter explores the analysis and results derived from the development explained in Chapter 3. It encompasses the results generated from the XGBoost Machine Learning model which is inclusive of prototype results using the US dataset from Kaggle, the embellishments made while troubleshooting as well as final results. The

16.4 Results and Analysis

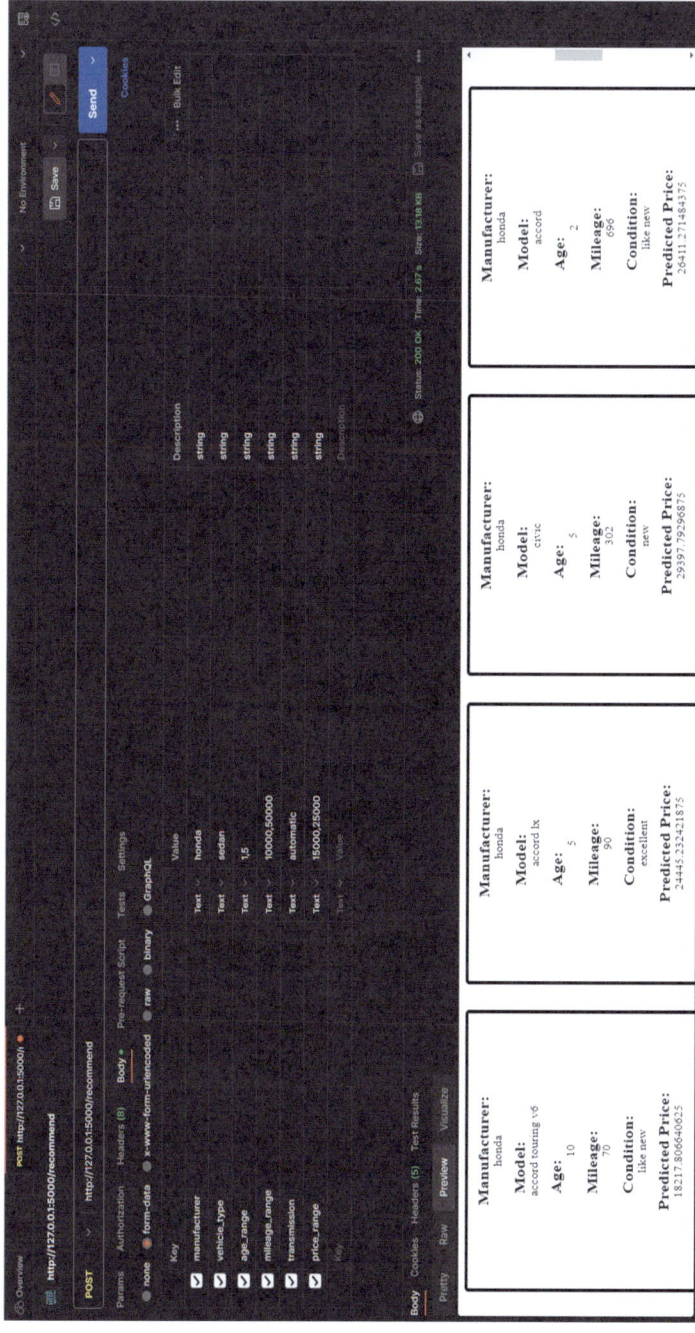

Fig. 16.42 Postman application

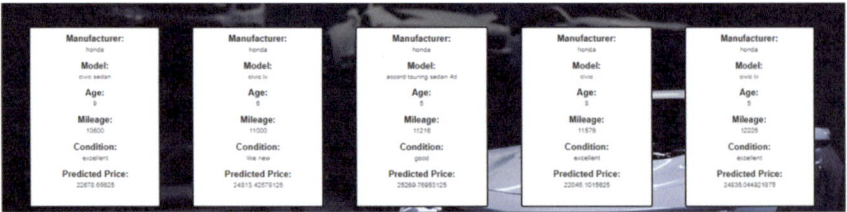

Fig. 16.43 Recommender results

evaluation of the model's performance is evaluated with the initial accuracy score and then validated with web scrapped data to identify the functionality of the model across different datasets with different currencies. Additionally, this chapter explores the development of the web application to create a dynamic and effective website with quizzes utilising the model. Webpage components included the navigation bar, Home, Quiz 1 for car recommendations, and Quiz 2 for car price prediction.

16.4.2 Results of the XGBoost Model

This section explores the results and validation of the XGBoost Model. In the case of Drive Smart, US car data was used to create the prototype while Malaysian car data was used to validate the model. The results of these datasets are discussed.

Results

The sorting criterion is to prioritise cars in best condition and with a lower price. Here's a breakdown of the information displayed on the cards and the sorting logic:

Manufacturer and Model: Each card specifies that the manufacturer is 'Honda' and lists two different models, 'Civic Sedan' and 'Accord Touring Sedan 4d', with variations such as 'Civic lx' (Fig. 16.43).

Age: This likely refers to the number of years since the car was manufactured. The ages on the cards range from 0 to 8 years. The range is by the given range on the input section of the page. Mileage: The mileage of the cars varies from 10,800 to 11,218 miles, which is a relatively low range, suggesting these cars have not been driven extensively.

Condition: The cars' conditions range from 'excellent' to 'good' and 'like new'. This is a qualitative assessment of the car's state (Fig. 16.44).

Input Fields: The form contains various dropdowns and input fields where users can enter details about their vehicle, such as:

Age of Your Vehicle: The number of years since the vehicle was manufactured (in this case, 5 years).

Manufacturer: The brand of the vehicle (selected as Honda).

Fuel Type: The type of fuel the vehicle uses (selected as Gas).

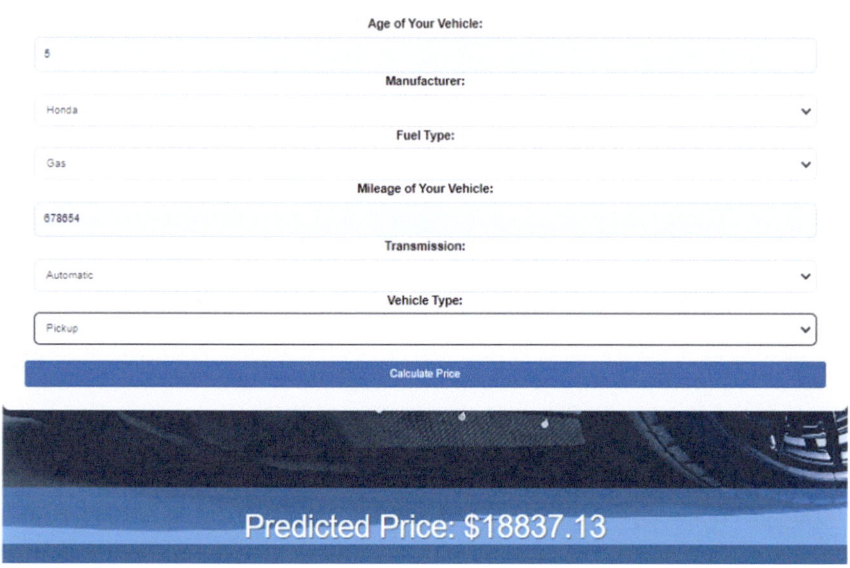

16.4 Results and Analysis

Fig. 16.44 Predictor results

Mileage of Your Vehicle: The total distance the vehicle has travelled in miles (entered as 87,854 miles).

Transmission: The type of transmission the vehicle has (selected as Automatic).

Vehicle Type: The category or model type of the vehicle (selected as Pickup).

Calculate Price Button: After entering the required information, a user would press this button to initiate the price calculation based on the input data.

Predicted Price Output: This is the result of the calculation, showing the estimated value or price of the vehicle given the input parameters. In this case, the predicted price for the 5-year-old Honda pickup truck with 87,854 miles, an automatic transmission, and gas fuel type is $18,837.13.

16.4.2.1 Featured Cars

The prominently highlighted 'Featured Car' section on Drive Smart's platform strategically situates it as an all-encompassing hub for both the purchase and sale of used vehicles. The directive, 'Checkout the Featured Cars', entices users to explore a row of four cards, meticulously presenting crucial details about the dealership's highlighted cars (Fig. 16.45).

Each card succinctly delivers information, encompassing the car model, year of manufacture, engine size in cubic centimetres (cc), horsepower (HP), and the type of transmission.

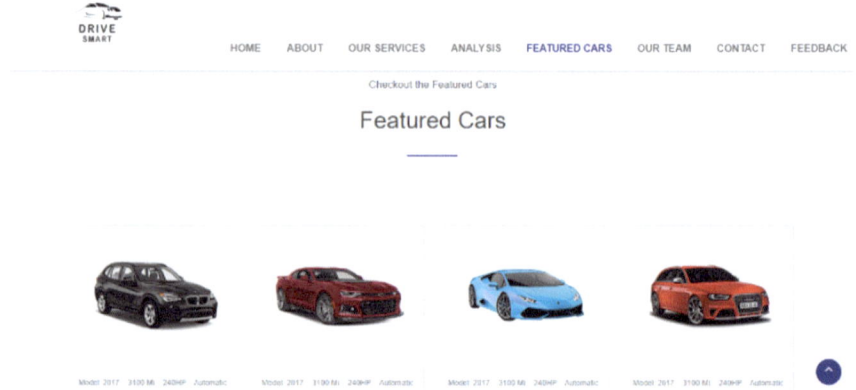

Fig. 16.45 Featured Cars

The intentional layout of this page is meticulously designed to provide visitors with a swift and comprehensive overview of Drive Smart's offerings, emphasising its role as a versatile platform catering to the needs of both potential buyers and sellers of used vehicles. The concise presentation of featured cars aims to empower users to make well-informed decisions efficiently, thereby contributing to a seamless and engaging user experience on the platform.

The page's design philosophy is characterised by simplicity and cleanliness, featuring a colour scheme that enhances readability and user navigation. In summary, Drive Smart's 'Featured Car' page effectively communicates the pertinent car information mentioned above.

16.4.2.2 Analysis—Dashboard

The 'Analysis' page serves as a comprehensive representation of the dashboard overview and the remote filtering system on Drive Smart's platform. The dashboard overview provides users with insight into how the data was modelled within the machine learning system, offering a visual understanding of the underlying processes. Simultaneously, the filtering system showcases the preprocessing steps to understand the system's functionality under specific conditions and the lowest mileage criteria (Fig. 16.46).

The page's design philosophy prioritises simplicity and cleanliness, employing a colour scheme that enhances readability and facilitates user navigation. This strategic design choice contributes to a user-friendly interface, ensuring that users can easily comprehend and interact with the displayed information. The Drive Smart's 'Analysis' page effectively conveys essential information about the machine learning model's data modelling and functionality, with a design approach that prioritises simplicity and user engagement.

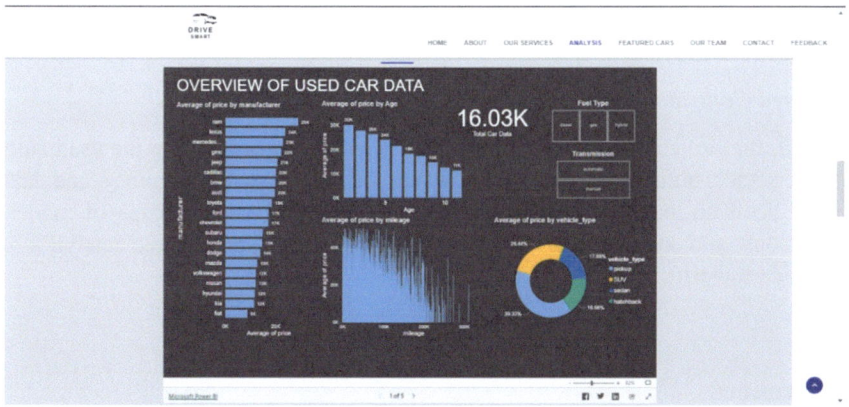

Fig. 16.46 Dashboard

16.5 Conclusion

The study aimed to transform the used car market by using machine learning techniques for vehicle recommendation and price prediction. The XGBoost model was developed, enabling accurate price forecasts and individualised car suggestions. The system's usability and usability were verified during testing, enhancing the buying and selling experience. The study also assessed the effectiveness of machine learning algorithms in real-world systems, particularly in the used car market. The XGBoost model's flexibility in processing and making predictions across various datasets created new opportunities for further advancements. The research aims to enhance the used automobile market decision-making process by providing precise, effective, and user-friendly tools for predicting and recommending car prices. The machine learning model's incorporation has significantly improved accuracy and efficiency, addressing market demand and providing faster price prediction methods. This has a significant impact on customer satisfaction and confidence in the purchasing and selling process.

Limitations and Future Work

The accuracy of a model's accuracy is significantly influenced by the quality and diversity of the training data. Future improvements could involve refining the dataset and exploring other machine learning techniques. Adding multi-regional datasets could expand the model's worldwide applicability. The potential for expansion and enhancement of Drive Smart is vast, with key areas for future development including expanding the dataset and model refinement, enhancing the web application's user experience with real-time market analysis, a larger database of automobile models, and customised user profiles, developing a mobile application to improve accessibility and convenience, and collaborating with automotive industry stakeholders to gain insights and opportunities for growth. These areas are crucial for the model's continued success and adaptability in various markets.

Expected Contribution

Overall, the project's expected contribution goes beyond reshaping the used automobile sector, influencing how industries approach pricing, transparency, and data-driven decision-making. It encompasses the ever-changing landscape of modern technology and stands as a testament to the need of predicative analytics in the modern world.

References

Adams, R. (2019). Transparency and trust in predictive pricing models. *Journal of Business Ethics, 14*(3), 78–95.
Akbar, M. A., Rafi, S., Alsanad, A. A., Qadri, S. F., Alsanad, A., & Alothaim, A. (2022). Toward successful devops: A decision-making framework. *IEEE Access, 10*, 51343–51362. https://doi.org/10.1109/access.2022.3174094
Chen, L., & Wang, Q. (2018). User-friendly interfaces in data-driven systems. *Journal of Human-Computer Interaction, 32*(2), 123–135.
Chen, T., & Guestrin, C. (2016). XGBoost: A scalable tree boosting system. In Proceedings of the 22nd ACM SIGKDD international conference on knowledge discovery and data mining (pp. 785–794).
Clark, D. (2021). Algorithm selection in predictive modeling for car pricing. *International Journal of Machine Learning, 15*(3), 102–119.
Cui, B., Ye, Z., Zhao, H., Renqing, Z., Meng, L., & Yang, Y. (2022). *Used car price prediction based on the iterative framework of XGBoost+LightGBM*. Multidisciplinary digital publishing institute. https://doi.org/10.3390/electronics11182932
Dairu, X., & Shilong, Z. (2021). Machine learning model for sales forecasting by using XGBoost. In *2021 IEEE International Conference on Consumer Electronics and Computer Engineering (ICCECE)*. https://doi.org/10.1109/iccece51280.2021.9342304
Danquah, B., Riedmaier, S., Rühm, J., Kalt, S., & Lienkamp, M. (2020). Statistical model verification and validation concept in automotive vehicle design. *Procedia Cirp, 91*, 261–270.
Datt Sharma, A., & Sharma, V. (n.d.). Used Car Price Prediction Using Linear Regression Model. In *International Research Journal of Modernization in Engineering Technology and Science* (pp. 2582–5208). https://www.irjmets.com/uploadedfiles/paper/volume2/issue_11_november_2020/4868/1628083194.pdf
Davis, P. (2016). Mechanisms for explaining pricing model logic. *Communications of the ACM, 22*(4), 61–75.
Garcia, E. (2019). Modeling techniques in predictive pricing: A comparative analysis. *Journal of Business Analytics, 24*(1), 56–71.
Hambling, B., & Pauline Van Goethem. (2013). User Acceptance Testing: A Step-by-Step Guide. BCS.
Hamunen, J. (2016). Challenges in Adopting a Devops Approach to Software Development and Operations.
Harris, S. (2020). Data updating strategies for pricing models. *Journal of Data Management, 11*(2), 89–104.
He, K., Zhang, X., Ren, S., & Sun, J. (2016). Deep residual learning for image recognition. *Proceedings of the IEEE conference on computer vision and pattern recognition (CVPR)* (pp. 770–778).

References

Iams, K. (2021). Marketing and customer education strategies for new pricing systems. *Journal of Marketing Research, 19*(3), 67–82.

James, M., & Smith, A. (2019). Developing predictive pricing models. *Journal of Automotive Economics, 45*(3), 217–231.

Johnson, P., & White, S. (2020). Historical data in predictive modeling. *Journal of Data Analysis and Modeling, 56*(4), 489–504.

Ke, G., Meng, Q., Finley, T., Wang, T., Chen, W., Ma, W., ... & Chi, Y. (2017). LightGBM: A highly efficient gradient boosting decision tree. In Advances in neural information processing systems (pp. 3146–3154).

Lee, H., & Kim, S. (2017). Transparent pricing algorithms and consumer trust. *Journal of Consumer Behavior, 21*(1), 78–93.

Li, Li, & Liu. (2022). *Research on used car price prediction based on random forest and LightGBM*. IEEE Conference Publication | IEEE Xplore. Retrieved October 15, 2023, from https://ieeexplore.ieee.org/abstract/document/9988116

Liu, E., Li, J., Zheng, A., Liu, H., & Jiang, T. (2022). Research on the prediction model of the used car price in view of the PSO-GRA-BP Neural Network. *Sustainability, 14*(15), 8993. https://doi.org/10.3390/su14158993

Long, R. (2020). Human centric user acceptance testing. In Pacific Northwest Software Quality Conference (PNSQC).

Rodriguez, M., Piattini, M., & Ebert, C. (2019, March–April). Software verification and validation technologies and tools. *IEEE Software*, vol. 36, no. 2, pp. 13–24, https://doi.org/10.1109/MS.2018.2883354

Nandan, M., & Ghosh, D. (2023). Pre-owned car price prediction by employing machine learning techniques. *Journal of Decision Analytics and Intelligent Computing, 3*(1), 167–184. https://doi.org/10.31181/jdaic10008102023n

Pal, N., Arora, P., Kohli, P., Sundararaman, D., & Palakurthy, S. S. (2018). *How much is my car worth? A methodology for predicting used cars' prices using random forest*. Advances in intelligent systems and computing. https://doi.org/10.1007/978-3-030-03402-3_28

Roberts, M. (2022). User interface design best practices for pricing systems. *Human-Computer Interaction, 29*(2), 187–203.

Sabah Al-Fedaghi. (2021). Conceptual data modeling: Entity-relationship models as thinging machines. *HAL (Le Centre Pour La Communication Scientifique Directe)*. https://doi.org/10.22937/ijcsns.2021.21.9.33

Sagi, O., & Rokach, L. (2021). *Approximating XGBoost with an interpretable decision tree*. Information Sciences; Elsevier BV. https://doi.org/10.1016/j.ins.2021.05.055

Schonlau, M., & Zou, R. Y. (2020). The random forest algorithm for statistical learning. *The Stata Journal: Promoting Communications on Statistics and Stata, 20*(1), 3–29. https://doi.org/10.1177/1536867x20909688

Schwegmann, A., & Laske, M. (2003). *As-is modeling and process analysis*. In *Process management: A guide for the design of business processes* (pp. 107–133). Springer Berlin Heidelberg.

Sirohi, A., Balyan, A., & Kumar, S. (2023). Old car price prediction using machine learning. *International Journal of Computer Applications, 185*(7), 28–33. https://doi.org/10.5120/ijca2023922725

Speiser, J. L., Miller, M. E., Tooze, J. A., & Ip, E. H. (2019). *A comparison of random forest variable selection methods for classification prediction modeling*. Expert Systems with Applications; Elsevier BV. https://doi.org/10.1016/j.eswa.2019.05.028

Šuman, S., Čandrlić, S., & Jakupović, A. (2022). A corpus-based sentence classifier for entity-relationship modelling. *Electronics, 11*(6), 889–889. https://doi.org/10.3390/electronics11060889

Ulusoy, O. (2022). Rule based entity-relationship diagram modelling. *Isikun.edu.tr*. https://hdl.handle.net/11729/4289

Wilson, L. (2018). Model validation strategies for predictive pricing. *Journal of Data Validation, 8*(1), 34–48.

Yadav, P., & Barwal, P. N. (2014). Designing Responsive Websites Using HTML and CSS. *International Journal of Scientific & Technology Research, 3*(11).

Zhang, H. (2022). Prediction of used car price based on lightgbm. In *2022 5th International Conference on Advanced Electronic Materials, Computers and Software Engineering (AEMCSE)*. https://doi.org/10.1109/aemcse55572.2022.00073

Zhang, Y. (2023). Second-hand vehicle recommendation systems: A state-of-the-art review. In *Proceedings of the 2023 ACM International Conference on Intelligent Systems and Technology* (pp. 10–17). ACM.

Chapter 17
Analytics for Tour Package and Recommendation System

17.1 Introduction

Tourism has become a popular recreational and economic activity, with over 900 million tourists embarking on international journeys in 2022. The World Tourism Organization predicts a 3.3% annual increase, reaching 1.8 billion visits from 2010 to 2030. Users often seek travel information on websites like TripAdvisor, Pelago, and Trip.com, but search results may not cater to individual preferences. Tour operators are diversifying their offerings to provide cost-effective and convenient options. The traditional approach to booking accommodations has evolved into a complex pursuit of personalised travel experiences. This project aims to create a personalised tour package recommendation system that matches user requirements. The motivation for this project is to address the evolving needs and difficulties faced by modern-day travellers, especially during the COVID-19 pandemic, and to accelerate decision-making and enrich travel experiences with diverse experiences and cultural interactions.

17.2 Significance of Research

Our personalised recommendation system simplifies tour package selection, increasing efficiency and revenue. It caters to individual customer needs, promoting retention and repeat purchases. This benefits the travel industry, particularly in Southeast Asian countries, contributing to financial growth and economic expansion, with potential for future expansion.

17.3 Problem Statements

Travel platforms often generate generic recommendations without sufficient personalization to address diverse needs and preferences, affecting travel experience and satisfaction. Information overload and decision difficulty lead to users struggling to navigate the vast array of tour packages, resulting in unsatisfactory planning experiences. The time-consuming nature of the process further complicates the process. Many tour package systems underutilize advanced machine learning algorithms, resulting in missed opportunities to enhance recommendation accuracy and trustworthiness. Platform navigation also demands effort, making it difficult for users to explore travel options and compare options. These challenges negatively impact the overall travel planning experience and hinder the growth of the travel industry.

17.4 Research Questions and Objectives

The primary objective of this paper is to **develop a personalised tour package recommendation system**, streamlining the process of comparing various available packages across different travel platforms and websites. This system will integrate personalised features, allowing users to select and filter their country, budget preferences with price ranges, and the duration of their stay. The credibility and authenticity of the recommended packages will be reinforced through the **user evaluations and feedback**. The ultimate aim is to leverage advanced technology by applying the knowledge acquired from this course in **developing machine learning models and web interface designs to create a recommendation system**. We seek to expedite the comparison process of various packages from different platforms, which typically consumes hours or even days, and condense it into a few simple clicks on our website.

17.5 Literature Review

This literature review section aims to comprehensively explore the evolving travel and tourism industry, with a specific focus on existing knowledge and research related to tour package recommendation systems. The main purpose of the literature reviews is to understand and analyse past research, identifying gaps, trends, and advancements in previous studies. The goal is to pinpoint and select suitable and efficacious tools, techniques, methodologies, data analysis approaches, and frameworks through research and comparisons. These selected elements will serve as a robust theoretical foundation for the current research project. This foundation is crucial for addressing the demands and preferences of modern-day travellers as well.

Ahmad et al. (2022) underscore the enduring benefits of a positive online user experience in building loyalty, directly informing our tour package recommendation system's focus on creating user satisfaction and engagement for sustained usage. Lambillotte et al. (2022) provide valuable insights into the impact of personalisation on customer engagement, aligning with our project's objective to enhance user experience by incorporating personalised elements within the tour package recommendations, ensuring increased attention and informed decision-making. Asefa's (2020) emphasis on agile strategies to improve tourism website usability, particularly in the context of success combinations of features, directly contributes to our project's goal of refining the user interface in our tour package recommendation system. Integrating these findings ensures an optimised user experience, enhancing the overall usability and effectiveness of our system.

Based on the literature review conducted on relevant topics regarding tour package recommendation system, this paper has garnered significant insights into trends and practices within the travel and tourism industry. It identifies a research gap and contributes to existing knowledge by providing a valuable overview. The implications derived from the identified trends and practices offer guidance for future research and practical application of the current study. In summary, three (3) frameworks have been selected for the project. Firstly, **iterative prototyping**, based on the studies by Nasir et al. (2021) and GeeksforGeeks (2023), will serve as the main framework. **Machine Learning Operations (MLOps)**, outlined by Pradeep (2022), will be the framework for the machine learning model, while **Software Development Life Cycle (SDLC)** from Gurung et al. (2020) will be utilised for web interface development. As for the tour package recommendation system, we will adopt **item-based collaborative filtering**, based on the research by Ajaegbu (2021) and K-Nearest Neighbours (KNN) as suggested by Uddin et al. (2022). Furthermore, we will employ a combination of **HTML, CSS, and JavaScript** for web development, with integration using **PHP**, following the findings of Utkarsh and Priya (2023).

To effectively leverage the data, data preparation and preprocessing will be conducted using a versatile programming language, **Python**. An Exploratory Data Analysis (EDA) will be undertaken on the tour packages dataset to identify outliers and extract valuable insights essential for the mentioned classification analysis. **Power BI** will be utilised for data visualisation to create interactive dashboards. Taking all the aforementioned factors into account, the insights obtained from the literature review have been instrumental in shaping and determining the methodology and theoretical framework of our current research.

17.6 Methodology

In this chapter, we are adopting the Iterative Prototyping framework, following the specified sequence: requirement gathering and analysis, initial design, prototype integration, prototype testing, final prototype iteration—final design, final development, system testing and evaluation, refinement of the system based on requirements, and deployment. Figure 17.1 illustrates the overall proposed project framework methodology.

Our project framework will encompass a cohesive integration of Iterative Prototyping, MLOps, and SDLC. The 'AIRBNB DATA.xlsx' file (refer to Appendix 2) is used for training the KNN model before we transition into using the tour packages dataset for the testing of data. In this stage, upon refinement and iteration, our focus shifts to the data preparation phase for the tour packages recommendation system. The pivotal stage involves putting together refined components into a cohesive structure, setting the foundation for accurate and insightful tour package recommendations. Upon recognising the minimal correlations among variables within the dataset, we made the strategic decision to proceed with our analysis, focusing specifically on the variables chosen for Spearman correlation analysis. Our objective was to attain a comprehensive understanding of the data by systematically experimenting with these selected variables and presenting our findings through an interactive dashboard developed in Power BI.

The rationale behind selecting this approach is rooted in the substantial support that Power BI Dashboards provide for our Exploratory Data Analysis (EDA), particularly in terms of dynamic and interactive visualisations. The user-friendly interface, coupled with the drag-and-drop functionality, streamlines the process of constructing dashboards, catering to individuals with diverse levels of technical expertise. By leveraging the capabilities of Power BI, we conducted preliminary exploratory studies to unearth valuable insights.

The inclusion of a robust Query Editor within Power BI significantly augmented the data preparation process, enabling efficient transformation and cleaning tasks prior to analysis. Additionally, the seamless integration of Power BI with other Microsoft products, such as SQL Server and Excel, creates a conducive working environment, facilitating a swift transfer of data and maximising our preexisting analytical capabilities.

The second slicer in Fig. 17.2 showcases all the countries which the Airbnb dataset has to offer. There are a total of twenty (20) countries included in this dataset.

Fig. 17.1 Price range slicer

Fig. 17.2 Country slicer

17.6 Methodology

The third slicer in Fig. 17.3 displays the minimum duration of stay for Airbnb listings.

The final slicer in Fig. 17.4 is the rating for the Airbnb listings. Once again, the data had to be transformed in order to create this slicer. This was also done in Excel by assigning rating ranges for data located in the 'Rating' column in the Airbnb dataset.

Figure 17.5 shows the distribution of all room types provided in the Airbnb dataset. Presented in the form of a bar chart, this visualisation illustrates the count of different types of room categories. Specifically, there are three (3) distinct room types: 'Entire home/apt' represented in light blue, 'Private room' in dark blue, and 'Shared room' in orange.

The data reveals that 'Entire home/apt' is the most prevalent, boasting over 150,0000 listings. Following closely is 'Private room' with more than 85,000 listings, and lastly, 'Shared room' with the lowest count of 4550. This information suggests that hosts recognise the preference of consumers for personal space, as indicated by the higher demand for entire homes or apartments, and to a lesser extent, private

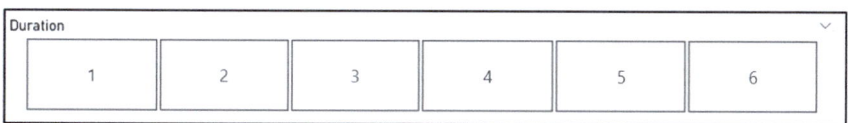

Fig. 17.3 Duration slicer

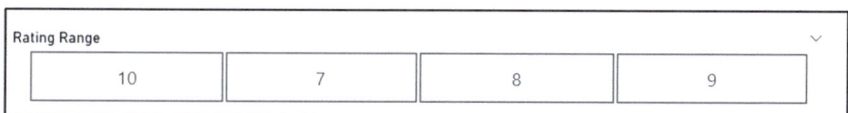

Fig. 17.4 Rating range slicer

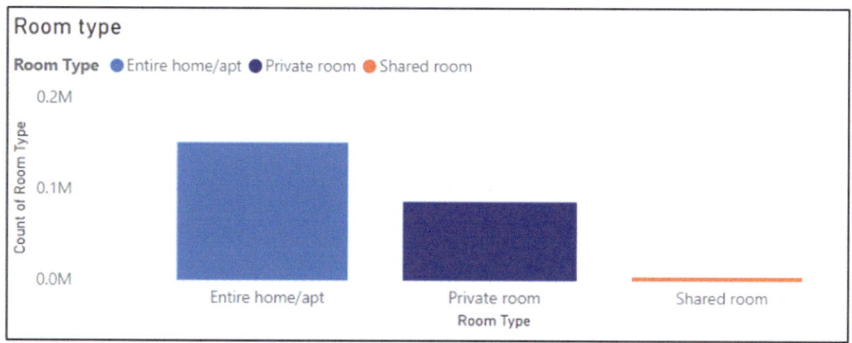

Fig. 17.5 Room type bar chart

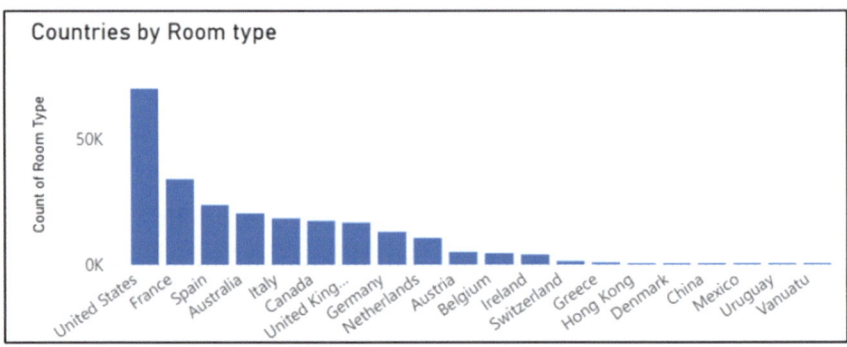

Fig. 17.6 Countries by room type bar chart

rooms. The limited popularity of shared rooms, evident in their lower count, implies a general reluctance among consumers to share living spaces with others.

Overall, this analysis highlights the prevalent inclination towards having an entire dwelling or a private space rather than shared accommodations.

Figure 17.6 presents another bar chart showcasing the distribution of the number of rooms in various countries. The United States leads with the highest count, exceeding 50,000 different room types. Following closely are France, Spain, and Australia, each with substantial counts but less than half of that in the United States. The subsequent nations on the list, including Italy, Canada, the United Kingdom, Germany, the Netherlands, Belgium, Austria, Ireland, Switzerland, Greece, Hong Kong, Denmark, China, Mexico, Uruguay, and Vanuatu, exhibit progressively lower room counts.

From this visual representation, it is evident that the United States emerges as the most prominent location for Airbnb listings, given its substantial room inventory. However, the overall trend depicted in this chart indicates a sharp decline, implying that other countries have fewer listing, reflecting their comparatively lower popularity.

The third visualisation, as seen in Fig. 17.7, is a clustered bar chart comparing different room types across various price ranges. An analysis of the chart reveals that 'Entire home/apt' room type is favoured across price ranges 2, 3, 4, and 5. In the initial price range (1), the 'Private room' room type has the highest count; as the price range increases, this count gradually decreases. On the other hand, among the three-room types, the 'Shared room' category consistently has the fewest entries. Its figures, which typically exhibit extremely low counts, remain relatively stable across the pricing ranges.

In conclusion, it is evident that as the price range for room types increases, the number of rooms steadily decreases. This indicates that most consumers may not spend a significant amount on Airbnb accommodations unless necessary, such as for a special occasion.

The final visualisation, depicted in Fig. 17.8, is also a clustered bar chart that compares different room types against the required duration of stay. Among all the room types, 'Entire home/apt' exhibits the highest count, reaching its peak at

17.6 Methodology

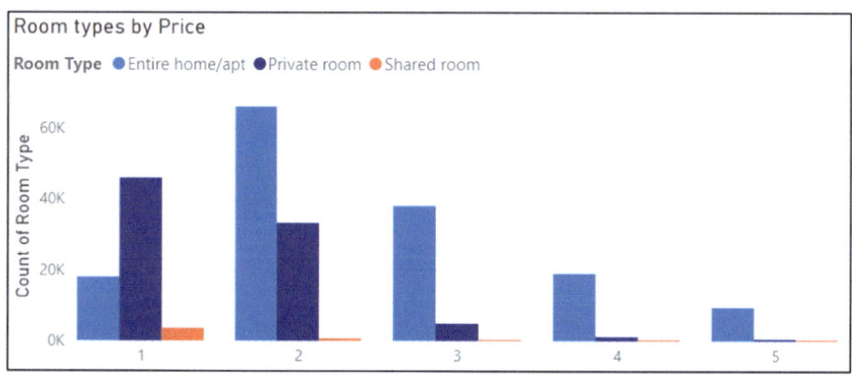

Fig. 17.7 Room types by price clustered bar chart

a duration of 2 days. The second most prevalent room type is the 'Private room', peaking at a duration of one (1) day. 'Shared room' represents the category with the lowest counts overall, displaying significantly fewer counts than the other categories for all durations of stay.

In general, the data reveals a trend in which the quantity of each room type decreases as the duration of stay increases. This implies that shorter stays are more common compared to longer ones.

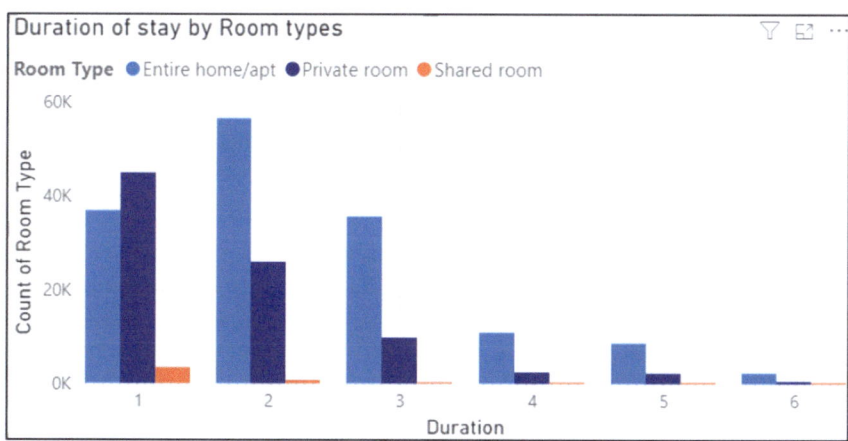

Fig. 17.8 Duration of stay by room types clustered bar chart

17.6.1 Create and Train Model

17.6.1.1 Introduction and Initial Issue Faced

The rise of personalised tour package recommendation systems has revolutionised the travel industry, offering users unique experiences based on their preferences. RoamRadar, our innovative recommendation system, employs a K-Nearest Neighbours (KNN) machine learning model using cosine similarity for enhanced accuracy. However, before delving into the intricacies of the KNN model training, it is vital to understand one of the main issues our project faced. The main issue we faced when beginning our project was the absence of a dedicated tour package dataset which posed a substantial obstacle to developing an effective recommendation model. Traditional datasets lacked the specificity required for personalised tour package recommendations, necessitating an alternative approach. To address this challenge, we creatively utilised an Airbnb dataset as our initial data source. Recognising the need for a dataset aligning with tour package features, we carefully selected and matched four key features from the Airbnb dataset to represent tour packages attributes:

(1) **Price of Airbnb (Representing Price of Tour Packages):**
The price of an Airbnb rental served as a proxy for the price of a tour package.
(2) **Rating of Airbnb (Matching Rating of Tour Packages):**
The rating assigned to an Airbnb listing was used to match the rating of a tour package.
(3) **Number of Reviews (Matching Number of Reviews of Tour Packages):**
The number of reviews from the Airbnb dataset allowed us to approximate the popularity and user engagement with a particular accommodation.
(4) **Duration of Stay (Matching Duration of Tour Packages):**
The duration of stay in an Airbnb listing served as a matching criterion for the duration of a tour package.

As such, as we dive into the Machine Learning script, do take note that we will be using the Airbnb dataset initially. This dataset, carefully tailored to mirror essential tour package features, serves as the foundation for training our KNN model. The adaptive approach we adopted allowed us to overcome the challenge of data scarcity and set the stage for the development of a robust personalised tour package recommendation system in Roam Radar.

17.6.1.2 Training KNN Model—Python Script

Library Imports

This script begins with the essential step of importing necessary Python libraries. The 'pandas' library is used for data manipulation and analysis, and the 'sklearn' library

17.6 Methodology

(Scikit-learn) is employed for machine learning tasks. Specifically, it utilises components from 'sklearn.model_selection' for data splitting, 'sklearn.preprocessing' for data scaling, and 'sklearn.neighbors' for implementing the K-Nearest Neighbours algorithm (Fig. 17.9).

Loading Data from Excel

The next task involves loading data from an Excel file named 'AIRBNB DATA.xlsx' (refer to Appendix 2). This Excel file is containing the relevant data, such as Airbnb property details. The data is loaded into a DataFrame, a two-dimensional labelled data structure, using the 'pd.read_excel' function from the pandas library. The DataFrame, denoted as 'df', serves as the primary data structure for subsequent operations. A screenshot of the Excel is file provided below so that users understand what is being loaded (Fig. 17.10).

The dataset contains a total of 18 columns and each column has its own distinct type of data. Once all the data from the Excel File has been loaded successfully, it needs to be further refined and structured properly.

Data Preprocessing—Handling Price and Duration

Following data loading, a preprocessing step is performed to ensure the data's consistency and handle potential errors or missing values. Two (2) columns, 'Price' and 'Duration' are specifically targeted for preprocessing. The 'pd.to_numeric' function is applied to convert these columns to numeric format, facilitating numerical computations. Any conversion errors are handled using the 'coerce' parameter, which turns problematic entries into NaN (Not a Number). Subsequently, the 'fillna' method is used to replace NaN values with 0, ensuring a consistent numeric format throughout the dataset. However, it is vital to mention that the dataset has already been preprocessed during the EDA phase and this section in this script is added for extra measure to better data cleanliness (Fig. 17.11).

Feature Selection and Data Splitting

This section of the script introduces the concept of feature selection, a critical step in preparing data for machine learning. The script specifies a set of features—'Price',

```
import pandas as pd
from sklearn.model_selection import train_test_split
from sklearn.preprocessing import StandardScaler
from sklearn.neighbors import NearestNeighbors
```

Fig. 17.9 Python library imports

Fig. 17.10 Loading data from excel file

```
# Load data from the Excel file
excel_file = 'AIRBNB2.xlsx'
df = pd.read_excel(excel_file)
```

```
# Preprocess the data
df['Price'] = pd.to_numeric(df['Price'], errors='coerce')
df['Price'].fillna(0, inplace=True)

df['Duration'] = pd.to_numeric(df['Duration'], errors='coerce')
df['Duration'].fillna(0, inplace=True)
```

Fig. 17.11 Preprocessing data

```
# Select features for recommendation
features = ['Price', 'Number of Reviews', 'Review Scores Rating', 'Duration']
X = df[features]

# Split the data into training and testing sets
X_train, X_test = train_test_split(X, test_size=0.2, random_state=42)
```

Fig. 17.12 Feature selection and data splitting

'Number of Reviews', 'Review Scores Rating', and 'Duration'—that will be used for generating recommendations. The features are extracted from the DataFrame (df) and stored in a new DataFrame labelled as 'X'. Following this, the script proceeds to split the data into training and testing sets using the 'train_test_split' function from scikit-learn's model_selection module. This step is pivotal for evaluating the model's performance on unseen data (Fig. 17.12).

Feature Scaling for Model Training

This paragraph details the importance of feature scaling in the context of machine learning. Feature scaling ensures that all features contribute equally to the model training process. The StandardScaler from scikit-learn's preprocessing module is employed to standardise the features. Both the training set (X_train) and the testing set (X_test) undergo scaling using the fit_transform and transform methods, respectively. The resulting scaled sets, X_train_scaled and X_test_scaled, are now ready for feeding into the K-Nearest Neighbuors model.

K-Nearest Neighbours Model Fitting

In this section, the K-Nearest Neighbours (KNN) algorithm is introduced, with specific parameters explained. 'n_neighbors = 15' specifies that the algorithm considers 15 neighbouring data points when making predictions. The metric = 'cosine' parameter indicates that the cosine similarity metric is employed to measure the similarity between data points. Additionally, algorithm = 'brute' signifies the use of the brute-force approach for finding nearest neighbours (Fig. 17.13).

Alternatives for metric include 'euclidean', 'manhattan', and 'minkowski', among others. For algorithm, alternatives include 'kd_tree' and 'ball_tree'. However, it should be mentioned that after manual testing and evaluation, the combination of metric = 'cosine' and algorithm = 'brute' yielded the best results for this

17.6 Methodology

```
# Fit the k-nearest neighbors model on the training set
knn_model = NearestNeighbors(n_neighbors=15, metric='cosine', algorithm='brute')
knn_model.fit(X_train_scaled)
```

Fig. 17.13 Fitting the KNN model

specific recommendation system. The decision to use cosine similarity and the brute-force algorithm was made based on their performance in generating accurate and meaningful recommendations during manual run through of the system.

Generating Recommendations Based on User Preferences

In this section, the 'get_recommendations' function is introduced, which plays a pivotal role in generating tailored recommendations based on user preferences. The function takes four (4) parameters: 'selected_country' which represents the user's chosen destination, 'price_filter' which indicates the user's preferred price range, 'duration_filter' which specifies the desired stay duration, and 'num_recommendations' (with a default value of 15 but can be edited accordingly) determines the number of recommendations to be generated (Fig. 17.14).

The script begins by applying filters to the dataset using the provided user preferences. Three main filtering conditions are employed:

- **country_condition:**
  Filters data based on the selected destination country.

```
def get_recommendations(selected_country, price_filter, duration_filter, num_recommendations=3):
    # Apply filters
    country_condition = df['Country'] == selected_country
    price_condition = (df['Price'] > 100) if price_filter == "above 100" else (df['Price'] <= 100)
    duration_condition = (df['Duration'] == duration_filter) if duration_filter is not None else [True] * len(df)

    # Filter the data
    filtered_data = df[country_condition & price_condition & duration_condition]

    if not filtered_data.empty:
        # Scale the features of the filtered data
        filtered_data_scaled = scaler.transform(filtered_data[features])

        # Find neighbors using the testing set
        distances, indices = knn_model.kneighbors(filtered_data_scaled, n_neighbors=num_recommendations)

        print("Size of filtered_data:", len(filtered_data))
        print("Size of indices:", len(indices[0]))
        print("Unique indices:", set(indices[0]))

        recommendations = []
        for i in range(len(indices[0])):
            index = indices[0][i]
            name = df.iloc[index]['Name']
            rating = df.iloc[index]['Rating']
            similarity = 1 - distances[0][i]  # Adjusted to interpret distances as cosine similarities
            recommendations.append((name, rating, similarity))

        return recommendations
    else:
        print("No recommendations found for the selected criteria.")
        return []
```

Fig. 17.14 Defining 'get_recommendations' function

- **price_condition:**
  Filters data based on the user's price preference, distinguishing between properties with prices above or below 100. The condition is flexible based on user input.
- **duration_condition:**
  Filters data based on the user's preferred stay duration, allowing for flexibility by handling the case where no specific duration preference is provided.

These filtering conditions collectively narrow down the dataset (df) to include only properties that match the user's specified criteria. The conditions are applied using Boolean indexing, creating subsets of data that meet the filtering criteria.

If the resulting filtered dataset (filtered_data) is not empty, the script proceeds with the recommendation generation process. Otherwise, a message is printed, indicating that no recommendations match the specified user criteria.

For the non-empty case, the script scales the features of the filtered data using the previously fitted scaler. This ensures that the features are on the same scale as those used during the model training phase. The scaled data is then passed to the K-Nearest Neighbours model to identify similar properties based on the specified features.

Additionally, an extra function prints diagnostic information about the size of the filtered data, size of the indices, and unique indices obtained from the K-Nearest Neighbours model. These print statements aid in understanding the data processing steps and the outcomes of the K-Nearest Neighbours algorithm.

Recommendations are then constructed by extracting relevant details such as property name, rating, and adjusted similarity score from the original DataFrame (df) based on the indices obtained. The adjusted similarity score is calculated by subtracting the distance from 1, interpreting it as a cosine similarity. The final step involves returning the generated recommendations to the calling code for display or further processing.

User Interaction and Recommendation Display

Lastly, we move towards the main function of the script which serves as the script's entry point, guiding users through an intuitive and interactive process to receive personalised Airbnb property recommendations. This section is designed with improved readability and visual elements for an enhanced user experience (Fig. 17.15).

- **Unique Countries Extraction:**
  The script initiates by extracting unique countries from the dataset, presenting users with a list of destinations they can choose from.
- **User Input for Country Selection:**
  A user-friendly menu is displayed, allowing users to select their desired country by entering the corresponding number.
- **User Input for Price Range Selection:**
  Following the country selection, users are prompted to choose their preferred price range. The script displays clear options for 'Above 100' and 'Below 100', and users input their choice accordingly.

17.6 Methodology

```
# Main function
Comment Code
def main():
    unique_countries = df['Country'].unique()

    print("Select the country you want to visit:")
    for i, country in enumerate(unique_countries, start=1):
        print(f"{i}. {country}")

    selected_country_index = int(input("Enter the number of your preferred country: ")) - 1
    selected_country = unique_countries[selected_country_index]

    print("Select your preferred price range:")
    print("1. Above 100")
    print("2. Below 100")
    price_option_index = int(input("Enter the number of your preferred price range: "))

    if price_option_index == 1:
        price_filter = "above 100"
    else:
        price_filter = "below 100"

    print("Select your preferred duration:")
    print("1. 1 day")
    print("2. 2 days")
    print("3. 3 days")
    print("4. 4 days")
    print("5. 5 days")
    print("6. 6 days")
    duration_option_index = int(input("Enter the number of your preferred duration (or enter 0 for no preference): "))

    if duration_option_index == 0:
        duration_filter = None
    else:
        duration_filter = duration_option_index

    recommendations = get_recommendations(selected_country, price_filter, duration_filter, num_recommendations=15)
```

Fig. 17.15 Defining main function of system

- **User Input for Duration Selection:**
  Users are then prompted to select their preferred stay duration. The script provides options ranging from 1 to 6 days, along with the flexibility to choose 'No preference' by entering 0.
- **Duration Filter Determination:**
  If the 'duration_option_index' is 0, it signifies that the user has expressed no specific preference for duration. In this case, the 'duration_filter' is set to 'None', indicating an absence of a duration filter. On the other hand, if a non-zero value is provided, it implies a specific duration preference, and 'duration_filter' is set to the corresponding value.

Next, once user inputs are received, the system will move on to the recommendations (Fig. 17.16).

- **Recommendation Generation:**
  With the determined filters, the script calls the 'get_recommendations' function, passing the selected country, price filter, duration filter, and the default

```
recommendations = get_recommendations(selected_country, price_filter, duration_filter, num_recommendations=15)
if recommendations:
    print(f"Top 15 recommended Airbnb properties in {selected_country} with the selected price range and duration:")
    for i, (name, rating, similarity) in enumerate(recommendations, start=1):
        print(f"{i}. {name} - Rating: {rating} - Similarity: {similarity}")
else:
    print("No recommendations available.")
if __name__ == "__main__":
    main()
```

Fig. 17.16 Displaying user recommendations

number of recommendations (15). The function returns a set of personalised recommendations based on the user's preferences.

- **Display Recommendations (if available):**
  The script then checks if recommendations were generated. If so, it proceeds to display the top 15 recommended Airbnb properties. A clear and informative message is printed, presenting details such as property name, rating, and adjusted similarity score for each recommendation. The enumerate function ensures that recommendations are numbered sequentially, starting from 1.
- **Handling No Recommendations:**
  In the scenario where no recommendations match the user's specified criteria, the script prints a message indicating the absence of recommendations. This ensures users are informed when their preferences do not yield suitable results.
- **Main Function Execution:**
  The if __name__ = = "__main__:" block ensures that the main function is executed when the script is run as the main program. This structure is standard practice in Python scripts to facilitate modular and reusable code.

17.7 Running the KNN Model—Python Terminal

When the script is executed, it initiates an interactive process to gather user preferences and generate personalised Airbnb property recommendations. Here is a detailed breakdown of the terminal interactions:

Country Selection:

- The script starts by presenting the user with a list of countries to choose from.
- The user inputs their preferred country by entering the corresponding number.
- In the example provided, the user selects the United States (option 2) (Fig. 17.17).

17.7 Running the KNN Model—Python Terminal

Fig. 17.17 List of unique countries

Price Range Selection:

- The script then prompts the user to select their preferred price range, offering options for 'Above 100' and 'Below 100'.
- The user inputs their preference by entering the corresponding number.
- In the example, the user selects 'Above 100' (option 1) (Fig. 17.18).

Duration Selection:

- The script further prompts the user to choose their preferred stay duration.
- Options for durations from 1 to 6 days are presented, along with the choice to enter 0 for no preference.
- The user inputs their preferred duration by entering the corresponding number.
- In the example, the user selects 3 days (option 3) (Fig. 17.19).

Fig. 17.18 Selecting preferred range selection

```
Enter the number of your preferred price range: 1
Select your preferred duration:
1. 1 day
2. 2 days
3. 3 days
4. 4 days
5. 5 days
6. 6 days
Enter the number of your preferred duration (or enter 0 for no preference): 3
```

Fig. 17.19 List of preferred duration selection

```
Size of filtered_data: 6810
Size of indices: 15
Unique indices: {154433, 22050, 159971, 12868, 114596, 154470, 77064, 19223, 101359, 61329, 107510, 113527, 106137, 178492, 98493}
```

Fig. 17.20 Displayed statistics

Data Filtering and Unique Indices:

Once the user inputs are received, the model performs the filtering process and generates statistics to allow users a better understanding of the KNN model activities. An explanation of the results is given below (Fig. 17.20).

i. **Size of Filtered Data:**
   The first line, 'Size of filtered_data: 6810' indicates the number of Airbnb properties that match the specified user criteria. In this example, 6810 properties meet the selected country (United States), price range (Above 100), and duration (3 days) conditions.

ii. **Size of Indices:**
   The second line, 'Size of indices: 15' signifies that the K-Nearest Neighbours model identified 15 properties in the filtered dataset that are most similar to the user's specified preferences.

iii. **Unique Indices:**
   The line 'Unique indices: {154,433, 22,050, 159,971, …}' provides the specific indices of the 15 properties within the original dataset. Each index corresponds to a unique property that the model considers similar to the user's preferences.

iv. **Top 15 Airbnb Properties:**

Lastly, the top 15 Airbnb properties are displayed (Fig. 17.21). The subsequent line in the figure above presents a numbered list of the top 15 recommended Airbnb properties based on the specified criteria (United States, price range above 100, and duration of 3 days). Each recommendation includes:

- Property name
- Rating
- Adjusted Similarity Score (interpreted as cosine similarity)

17.7 Running the KNN Model—Python Terminal

```
Top 15 recommended Airbnb properties in United States with the selected price range and duration:
1. Remodeled Torrance 3 BR/2 Ba House - Rating: 9.6 - Similarity: 1.0
2. Spacious flat XVIIIth - Rating: 8.5 - Similarity: 0.9992400588052596
3. Charming 3BR with parking - Rating: 9.8 - Similarity: 0.9992400588052596
4. Studio - Rating: 8.6 - Similarity: 0.9992026493156075
5. Double Room in Beach House - Rating: 10.0 - Similarity: 0.9992026493156075
6. Modern Ground Floor Apartment - Rating: 8.4 - Similarity: 0.9989990752041571
7. Beautiful 3br Wicker Park Duplex! - Rating: 9.0 - Similarity: 0.9989202359048467
8. Fully Equipped Apartment - Rating: 9.9 - Similarity: 0.9988712717920237
9. Private Room -North Avalon Beach - Sun, Surf & Fun - Rating: 9.3 - Similarity: 0.9987973391466332
10. Private room in Mulgrave - Rating: 10.0 - Similarity: 0.9982607917524494
11. Santa Monica, steps from the beach! - Rating: 9.8 - Similarity: 0.9982607917524494
12. Cozy cabin in Mallorca! - Rating: 9.6 - Similarity: 0.9979689138778158
13. Three beautiful bedrooms in W5 - Rating: 10.0 - Similarity: 0.9979319098428572
14. 30 Day Minimum 1 BR Garden Apartment - Rating: 9.6 - Similarity: 0.9971812660620802
15. ***** - Stunning Canal apartment +4 Free Bikes ! - Rating: 10.0 - Similarity: 0.9971809616949882
```

Fig. 17.21 Top 15 Airbnb recommendations

17.7.1 Interpretation of Training Dataset Results

Cosine similarity is a metric used to measure the cosine of the angle between two non-zero vectors (Khatter et al., 2021). In the context of the K-Nearest Neighbours (KNN) model applied to this personalised recommendation system, cosine similarity is used to identify how closely the features of different properties align with the user's specified preferences. Cosine similarity values range from -1 to 1, where (Abhinav & Sujatha, 2023):

- 1 indicates perfect similarity
- 0 indicates no similarity
- −1 indicates perfect dissimilarity

In the context of this script, a cosine similarity close to 1 suggests a high degree of similarity between the recommended property and the user's specified preferences. Conversely, values closer to 0 indicate lower similarity.

Hence, achieving cosine similarity scores close to 1 for the top recommendations implies that the KNN model is effectively identifying properties that align well with the user's criteria. This high similarity suggests that the recommended properties share key features, such as pricing, and duration making them strong candidates for the user's preferences.

The fact that the first recommendation has a cosine similarity score of 1 indicates an exact match with the user's criteria, signifying that the KNN model has identified a property identical to the specified preferences. Also, the remaining recommendations all had scores close to 1 with the 15th having a score of 0.9972. This consistency across the top 15 recommendations underscores the robustness and reliability of the KNN model in capturing nuanced patterns within the vast Airbnb dataset. The closeness of these scores to 1 reinforces the effectiveness of the model in discerning properties that align comprehensively with the user's stated criteria, providing a set of recommendations that closely resonate with the desired features and characteristics.

However, it is important to mention that the success of the KNN model in providing accurate recommendations is influenced by the substantial size of the Airbnb dataset, which contains up to three hundred thousand rows. A larger dataset enables the model to better capture patterns and relationships, leading to more reliable recommendations with higher similarity scores. Hence, the efficacy of the model may vary when applied to datasets of different sizes. For instance, if the script were to be applied to our web scrapped tour packages dataset with only one thousand five hundred rows, the results might not be as accurate due to the smaller dataset size. The model's ability to generalise patterns and provide accurate recommendations may be impacted, and similarity scores may differ accordingly.

In summary, the interpretation of cosine similarity scores reflects the degree of alignment between recommended properties and user preferences. The success of the KNN model in providing accurate recommendations is underscored by the high similarity scores, while considerations for dataset size emphasise the need for caution when applying the model to datasets of varying sizes.

17.7.2 Test Model

17.7.2.1 Modifications for Tour Packages Dataset

Now that a working recommendation model has been created for the Airbnb dataset, it is time to modify the script to better align with tour package recommendations which is the main goal of RoamRadar. This adaptation involves refining specific elements of the code to suit the unique characteristics of tour packages (Fig. 17.22).

Essentially, the 'get_recommendations' function has been modified to better suit the characteristics of tour packages. Firstly, the country selection process has been

```python
def get_recommendations(selected_country, price_filter, duration_filter, num_recommendations=15):
    # Apply filters
    country_condition = df['Country'] == selected_country

    if price_filter == "budget":
        price_condition = (df['Price'] <= 300)
    elif price_filter == "standard":
        price_condition = ((300 < df['Price']) & (df['Price'] <= 900))
    elif price_filter == "luxury":
        price_condition = (df['Price'] > 900)
    else:
        raise ValueError("Invalid price filter")

    if duration_filter == "half_day":
        duration_condition = (df['Duration'] <= 8)
    elif duration_filter == "full_day":
        duration_condition = (df['Duration'] > 8)
    else:
        raise ValueError("Invalid duration filter")

    # Filter the data
    filtered_data = df[country_condition & price_condition & duration_condition]
```

Fig. 17.22 Defining get_recommendations for tour packages

refined to focus on four (4) specific countries: Malaysia, Thailand, Indonesia, and the Philippines, as these four (4) countries will be the main focus of RoamRadar. This adjustment ensures that the recommendations align with the desired geographical preferences for tour offerings.

Secondly, the price filter has undergone significant changes to accommodate the diverse budget considerations associated with tour packages. The filter now distinguishes between three (3) categories: budget, standard, and luxury. Each category is defined by specific price ranges to with 'budget' being 300 and below, 'standard' being more than 300 and less than 900, and 'luxuries' being any tour packages more than 900. These changes provide users with tailored recommendations based on their financial preferences for tour experiences.

Additionally, the duration filter has been adapted to better reflect the nature of tour packages. Instead of selecting the number of days, users can now choose between half-day and full-day options. This adjustment caters to the varying time commitments associated with different tour packages, allowing users to specify whether they prefer shorter or longer-duration tours.

These modifications enhance the versatility of the recommendation system, making it more adept at suggesting tour packages that align with user preferences in terms of destination, budget, and duration. The refined filters provide a more defined and personalised user experience, ensuring that the recommended tour packages meet the specific criteria set by the user.

Importantly, it is worth noting that the remaining portions of the script, including data loading, preprocessing, and the core recommendation algorithm, remain unchanged. These modifications serve to augment the script's versatility, allowing it to seamlessly transition from recommending Airbnb properties to providing tailored suggestions for diverse tour packages.

17.8 SDLC Framework

We have meticulously identified and structured crucial steps drawn from previous research employing SDLC frameworks. This systematic approach enabled us to develop a strategic framework closely aligned with RoamRadar's requirements, meeting specific needs.

17.8.1 Overview of SDLC

Software Development Life Cycle (SDLC) is a structured process followed in software organisations, providing a clear roadmap for developing, maintaining, enhancing, and modifying specific software to improve software quality and the development process. We align our web interface framework flow with Hossain's (2023) research on SDLC methodologies. This framework defines comprehensive

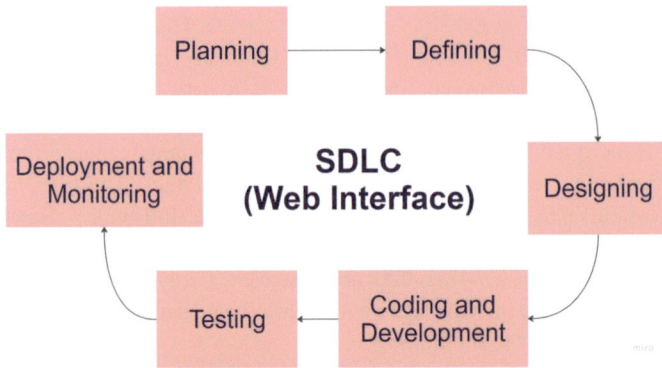

Fig. 17.23 RoamRadar's SDLC Framework

life-cycle processes for software, aiming to encompass all essential tasks for software development and maintenance.

Figure 17.23 illustrates the stages required for RoamRadar's web development and demonstrates how the website for RoamRadar's tour package recommender system is developed using the Software Development Life Cycle (SDLC) workflow.

By adopting this framework, we aim to meet expectations within defined timelines and cost estimates, outlining specific tasks at each development stage. This mirrors our project's need to complete multiple components and tasks within a set timeframe.

17.8.2 Requirement Planning and Analysis

In the planning phase, our main objective is to align project goals with research question 3: 'What input and output do users experience when utilising the web interface integrated with the machine learning model?' (as mentioned in Table 1). This alignment focuses on delivering personalised tour recommendations based on user preferences and constraints. This involves gathering and analysing user input parameters like budget filters, stay duration, and country preferences. Furthermore, we define the desired user experience and set scalability and performance expectations for the website interface system.

17.8.3 Defining

In the defining phase, we outline user cases and user stories to grasp users' interactions with the web application. This aids in shaping the web interface's responses across diverse scenarios, ensuring it meets users' needs and expectations. Additionally, we drafted a data flow diagram (DFD) to visually represent the functionality and data

17.8 SDLC Framework

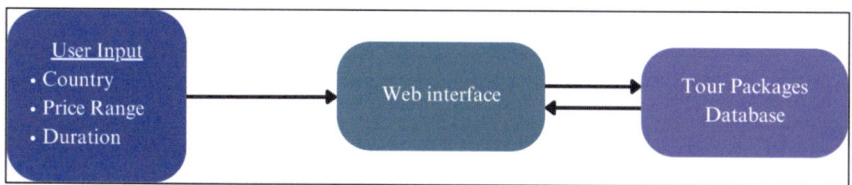

Fig. 17.24 DFD for web interface

flow of the web interface. This diagram serves as a guide to the subsequent stages of the design process as we construct the web interface.

DFD Diagram of Web Interface

The Data Flow Diagram (DFD) in Fig. 17.24 for the web interface is primarily divided into three (3) stages. In the first stage, users obtain recommended tour packages by providing input such as country, duration, and price range through our specially designed 'RoamRadar' website. Moving on to the second stage, the website receives the information entered by the user and translates it into the tour packages database. In the final stage, the system filters and presents the top fifteen (15) closest matching tour packages on the website. Users can navigate to the third-party websites to continue the tour package booking.

17.8.4 Designing

We create an initial mock-up design using Canva, a graphical design tool, to visually depict preliminary design concepts. This mock-up acts as a blueprint for subsequent design iterations, enabling early visualisation and feedback. Concurrently, we focus on architecture design, outlining the high-level structure and component interactions. We prioritise UI/UX design to enhance the interface's appeal and user-friendliness, ultimately improving user experience and accessibility during preference input and tour recommendation access.

a. **External Interface Mock-up (User Interface Design)**
   For the initial mock-up for our user interface design, we will be using 'Canva' for the sketching. The below figures show a rough outline of our website interface initial design and the main flow users will experience.
b. **Functional Design (Process Flow for User Interface)**
   - **Consumer's Request:**
     The customer submits a request to start the procedure. The customer is probably expressing interest in tour packages throughout this exchange.
   - **Website:**
     The website being RoamRadar receives the request from the user. In a process flow diagram, this is symbolised by a diamond shape, which denotes a branching point.

- **Tour Packages Database:**
  The website and the 'Tour Packages Database' are linked via a bidirectional arrow. This means that in order to obtain information on tour packages, the website would have to communicate with this database.
- **Search for the Best Options Using Personalised Recommender System:**
  After the website processes the user's request and looks through the 'Tour Packages Database', a customised recommender system which uses the KNN Machine Learning Model looks through the available tour package possibilities. This is a critical step since it allows the search results to be customised to the user's preferences.
- **Consumer Selects the Best Package:**
  Following the top 15 tour packages provided by the recommender system, the customer makes a decision and chooses the package that best suits their requirements.
- **Conclusion of Contract:**
  This is the last stage of the procedure, where the customer usually has to accept the terms and conditions of the tour packages and pay to complete the reservation.

17.8.5 Coding and Development

The code and development phase involving the utilisation of web development tools (HTML, PHP, CSS, JS, and SQL) in creating RoamRadar website, integrated with our machine learning model for a tour packages recommender system to display to users, is explained in the 12 sections outlined below:

1. Registration Page
2. Login & Logout Page
3. Navigation Menu
4. Homepage
5. About Us Page
6. Tour Packages Recommender Page
7. Business Visualisation—Data Entry Page
8. Why RoamRadar?—User Visualisation Page
9. Travel Blog Tips Page
10. Contact Page
11. Feedback Pop-Up Form
12. Website Footer

1. **Registration Page**

To begin using the RoamRadar website, users must first register by completing the registration process. This registration page is designed to **allow users to register independently and obtain access to our system**. This involves providing personal

17.8 SDLC Framework

information such as name and email. Additionally, users are required to confirm their password by entering it again to ensure accuracy. After successfully completing the registration process, users can proceed to the login page.

Figure 17.25 shows the registration page interface of RoamRadar's website.

In this registration page, users can register by entering their name, email, and password.

- **User Registration:**

The system securely stores user details in the database for login authentication and enhances security by hashing and hiding user passwords.

Figure 17.26 shows the PHP code for saving hashed passwords.

When a user enters their password, this PHP code securely transforms it into a highly protected format using a strong hashing algorithm, ensuring the confidentiality

Fig. 17.25 Registration page interface

```
// Set parameters
$param_password = password_hash($password, PASSWORD_DEFAULT ); // Creates a password hash
```

Fig. 17.26 PHP code for saving hashed passwords

Fig. 17.27 JavaScript code for hide password functionality

```javascript
(function($) {

    "use strict";

    $(".toggle-password").click(function() {

        $(this).toggleClass("fa-eye fa-eye-slash");
        var input = $($(this).attr("toggle"));
        if (input.attr("type") == "password") {
            input.attr("type", "text");
        } else {
            input.attr("type", "password");
        }
    });

})(jQuery);
```

and integrity of user credentials in applications or websites. The resulting hashed password is then commonly stored for authentication purposes.

Figure 17.27 shows the JavaScript code for the hide password functionality.

When a user interacts with an element marked as 'toggle-password', such as an 'eye-shaped' icon next to a password field, this code enables a visual toggle between hiding and revealing the entered password. Clicking the icon changes the password input from obscured (asterisks) to plain text, providing users with the flexibility to preview or obscure their password as they type. It also dynamically updates to reflect the current state, enhancing the user experience by offering a clear and intuitive password visibility control.

2. **Login & Logout Page**

After user registration is completed, the login page functions as the initial gateway for users to enter the website. It enables users to **access the website by entering their authentication credentials**, such as email and password in this case. This process helps the website in verifying user identity, ensuring the monitoring of authorised users to access the website's data and features. This is particularly crucial for safeguarding sensitive or private information.

Figure 17.28 shows the login page interface of RoamRadar's website.

In this login page, users can login by entering their email address and password.

- **User Login:**
  Registered users can log in by entering their email address and password on the login page. The system verifies the entered credentials by comparing the information with the data previously stored during the registration process in the database.
- **Authentication Status:**
  After a login attempt is made, the submitted login form containing user information undergoes authentication. Upon successful authentication, the user is granted access to the 'Homepage'.

17.8 SDLC Framework

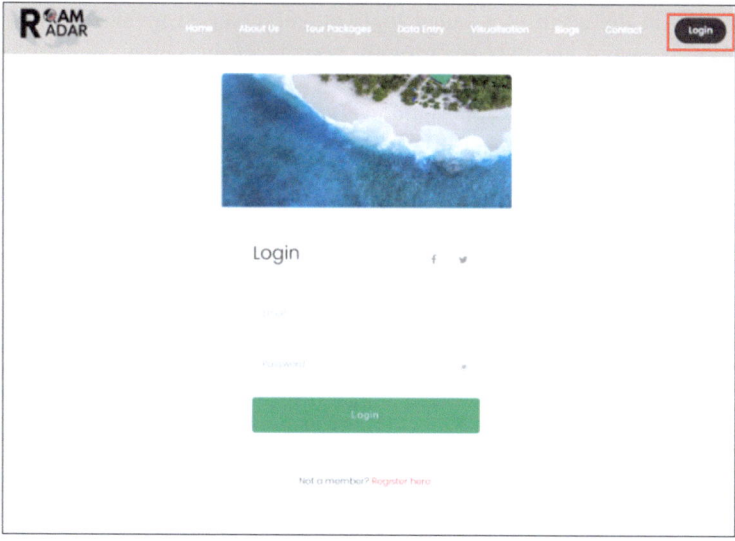

Fig. 17.28 Login page interface

- **Web Sessions:**
  A web session is activated when users log in. During this time frame, users are logged into the website and can freely browse its content. However, there is no limit to this session in our website. Any interactions that users engage in with the website are recorded as part of the web session within the website's domain.

  Figure 17.29 shows the 'Homepage' interface that appears when users successfully log in.

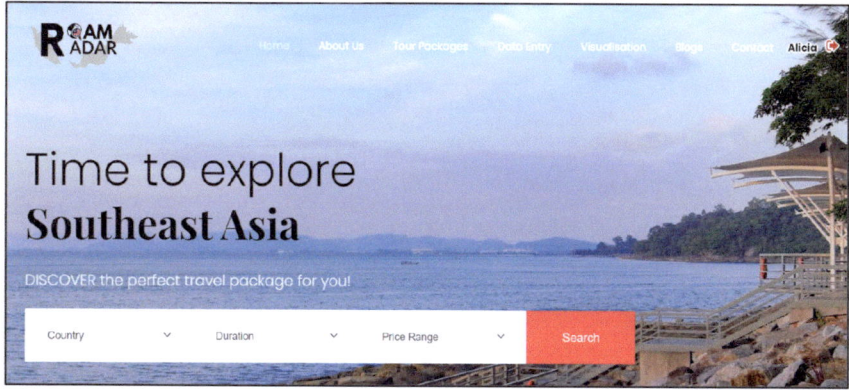

Fig. 17.29 Homepage interface upon successful login

However, in the event of a failed login attempt, caused by an incorrect email address or password, the user is promptly notified of the failure, as illustrated in Fig. 17.30.

Users can click on the 'Logout' button icon beside their username, shown on the navigation bar, to log out of their user account and end their web session.

Figure 17.31 shows the logout button icon next to the users' username.

Figure 17.32 shows the logout PHP code, which is designed to end the session and redirect users to the login page when they log out of their accounts.

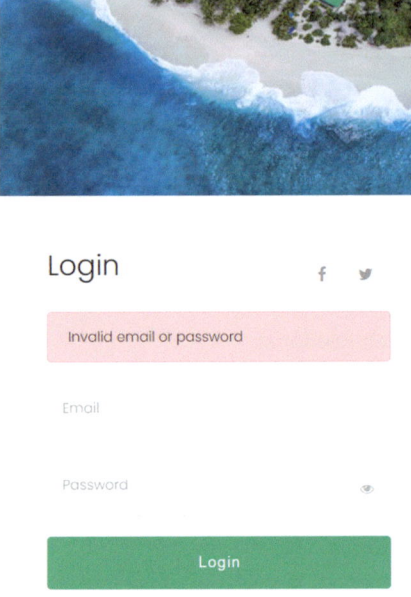

Fig. 17.30 Incorrect email or password prompt interface

Fig. 17.31 Logout button icon placement

```php
// Destroy the session.
session_destroy();

// Redirect to login page
header("location: login.php");
exit;
?>
```

Fig. 17.32 Logout PHP code for session termination and user redirect

When a user logs out of a website, this PHP code ensures that their session is securely terminated, clearing any personal information. After logging out, the user is automatically redirected to the login page.

3. **Navigation Menu**

The website's navigation menu comprises a list of links leading to various pages (internal pages), displayed at the top of the webpage as page headers. This design **facilitates swift and convenient access to information that users may seek**, offering an overview of RoamRadar's website content. Examples of such pages include 'Home', 'About Us', and 'Tour Packages'.

Figure 17.33 shows the navigation menu layout at the top of each webpage.

Figure 17.34 shows the 'menu.php' code, which generates a responsive navigation menu for the website by incorporating all the website pages.

- **Active Page Interaction:**

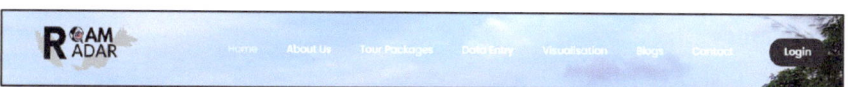

Fig. 17.33 Top-header navigation menu interface on webpages

```php
menu.php


<div class="collapse navbar-collapse" id="ftco-nav">
      <ul class="navbar-nav ml-auto">
        <li class="nav-item <?php if($_SERVER['REQUEST_URI']=="/index.php") echo ' active ' ?> "><a href="index.php" class="nav-link">Home</a></li>
        <li class="nav-item <?php if($_SERVER['REQUEST_URI']=="/about.php") echo ' active ' ?>"><a href="about.php" class="nav-link">About Us</a></li>
        <li class="nav-item <?php if($_SERVER['REQUEST_URI']=="/tourpackages.php") echo ' active ' ?>"><a href="tourpackages.php" class="nav-link">Tour Packages</a></li
        <li class="nav-item <?php if($_SERVER['REQUEST_URI']=="/dataentry.php") echo ' active ' ?>"><a href="dataentry.php" class="nav-link">Data Entry</a></li>
        <li class="nav-item <?php if($_SERVER['REQUEST_URI']=="/visualisation.php") echo ' active ' ?>"><a href="visualisation.php" class="nav-link">Visualisation</a></
        <li class="nav-item <?php if($_SERVER['REQUEST_URI']=="/blogs.php") echo ' active ' ?>"><a href="blogs.php" class="nav-link">Blogs</a></li>
        <li class="nav-item <?php if($_SERVER['REQUEST_URI']=="/contact.php") echo ' active ' ?>"><a href="contact.php" class="nav-link">Contact</a></li>
      </ul>

      <?php
      if(isset($_SESSION['is_login'])){
        echo '<div style="color:#000; font-weight:800; text-shadow: 2px 0 #fff, -2px 0 #fff, 0 2px #fff, 0 -2px #fff, 1px 1px #fff, -1px -1px #fff, 1px -1px #fff, -1px
            '. $_SESSION['name'] . '
            <a href="logout.php" ><i class="icon-sign-out" style="margin-left:10px;font-size:18px;color:#c91515;"></i></a>
            </div>';

      }
      else{
        echo '<a href="login.php" class="loginbutton">Login</a>';
      }
      ?>

</div>
```

Fig. 17.34 Responsive navigation menu creation in menu.php

The system dynamically updates the active page as users navigate through different webpages.
- **Visual Cue:**
The webpage name in the navigation menu header is highlighted in a lighter colour, and when scrolled up, it changes to orange-red. This serves as a visual indicator of the currently active page.
- **User Login:**
Users can view their name and a logout option if they are logged in; otherwise, they will see a login page.

As users interact with different pages, the active page changes according to the webpage they click into. The webpage name in the navigation menu header will be highlighted in a lighter shade and orange-red colour when scrolled up to indicate the active page the users are currently on. If logged in, users will observe their name along with a logout option; otherwise, they will be prompted to log in.

4. **Homepage**

The primary function of this homepage is to serve as the **filtering mechanism for users to select their preferences** in terms of 'country', 'duration', and 'price range' for tour package recommendations. These filtering parameters represent the initial steps that users must undertake to obtain their own personalised tour recommendations from our system.

Figure 17.35 shows the filter parameters on the 'Homepage', allowing users to select options based on their preferences.

On this page, users can choose filter parameters, including subcategories, which are listed below:

(a) **Country**

   (i) Malaysia
   (ii) Philippines
   (iii) Thailand
   (iv) Indonesia

(b) **Duration**

   (i) Half-day: 1–8 h
   (ii) Full-day: 9–24 h

(c) **Price Range**

   (i) Budget: $\leq$ RM300
   (ii) Standard: RM 301 – 900
   (iii) Luxurious: $\geq$ RM 901

Figure 17.36 shows the code outlining the user's input for filter parameter specifications for 'Country' in generating tour package recommendations.

17.8 SDLC Framework

Fig. 17.35 Filter parameters on homepage for user preferences

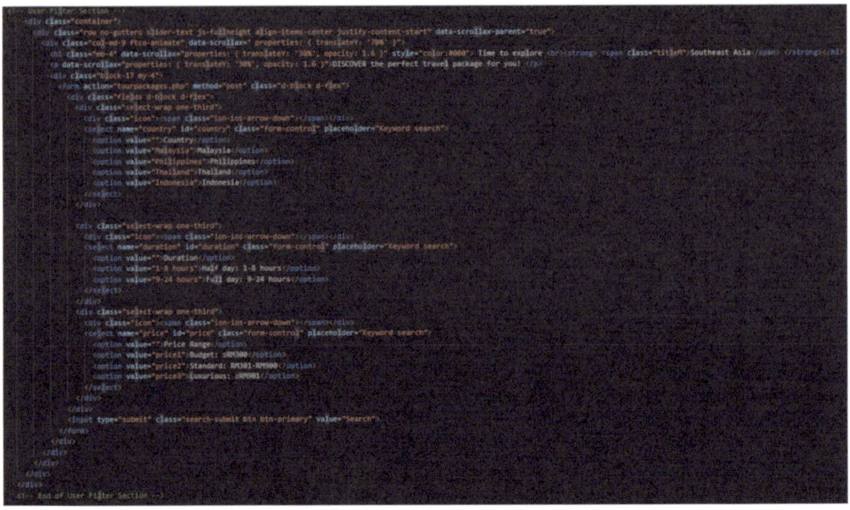

```html
<!-- User Filter Section -->
<div class="container">
  <div class="row no-gutters slider-text js-fullheight align-items-center justify-content-start" data-scrollax-parent="true">
    <div class="col-md-9 ftco-animate" data-scrollax=" properties: { translateY: '70%' }">
      <h1 class="mb-4" data-scrollax="properties: { translateY: '30%', opacity: 1.6 }" style="color:#000"> Time to explore <br><strong> <span class="title1">Southeast Asia</span> </strong></h1>
      <p data-scrollax="properties: { translateY: '30%', opacity: 1.6 }">DISCOVER the perfect travel package for you! </p>
      <div class="block-17 my-4">
        <form action="tourpackages.php" method="post" class="d-block d-flex">
          <div class="fields d-block d-flex">
            <div class="select-wrap one-third">
              <div class="icon"><span class="ion-ios-arrow-down"></span></div>
              <select name="country" id="country" class="form-control" placeholder="Keyword search">
                <option value="">Country</option>
                <option value="Malaysia">Malaysia</option>
                <option value="Philippines">Philippines</option>
                <option value="Thailand">Thailand</option>
                <option value="Indonesia">Indonesia</option>
              </select>
            </div>

            <div class="select-wrap one-third">
              <div class="icon"><span class="ion-ios-arrow-down"></span></div>
              <select name="duration" id="duration" class="form-control" placeholder="Keyword search">
                <option value="">Duration</option>
                <option value="1-8 hours">Half day: 1-8 hours</option>
                <option value="9-24 hours">Full day: 9-24 hours</option>
              </select>
            </div>
            <div class="select-wrap one-third">
              <div class="icon"><span class="ion-ios-arrow-down"></span></div>
              <select name="price" id="price" class="form-control" placeholder="Keyword search">
                <option value="">Price Range</option>
                <option value="price1">Budget: ≤RM300</option>
                <option value="price2">Standard: RM301-RM900</option>
                <option value="price3">Luxurious: ≥RM901</option>
              </select>
            </div>
          </div>
          <input type="submit" class="search-submit btn btn-primary" value="Search">
        </form>
      </div>
    </div>
  </div>
</div>
<!-- End of User Filter Section -->
```

Fig. 17.36 Code for filter parameter specifications for 'country', 'duration', and 'price range'

- **Filter Options:**
  Dropdown menus in the form allow users to filter tour package selections based on country, duration, and price range preferences.
- **Submission Handling:**
  The form is configured to submit user selections to a server-side script ("'tourpackages.php') using the POST method. In this script, it is expected to process the user input and generate relevant tour package recommendations on the 'Tour Packages' page.

Once the user selects their preferences and clicks on the 'Search' button, the form is submitted to a server-side script ('tourpackages.php'). This script is responsible for processing the user's input and presenting relevant tour package recommendations, incorporating scroll-based animations such as column and heading text animations.

Figure 17.37 shows the three (3) travel platforms included in the tour package recommendations generated by our system.

The three (3) travel platforms included are:

1. Klook

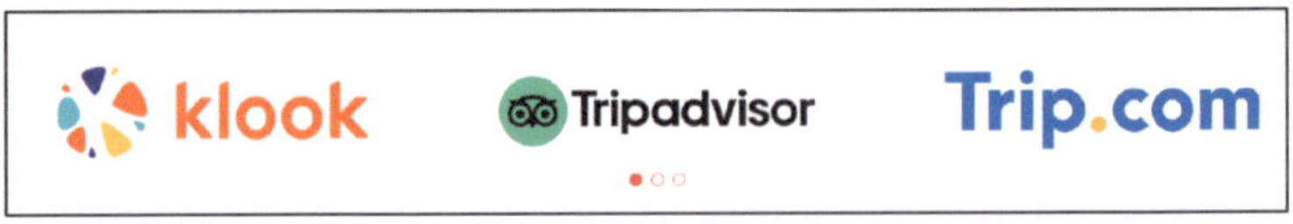

Fig. 17.37 Key travel platforms interface

17.8 SDLC Framework

```
<!-- ======= Travel Platforms Section ======= -->
<section id="platforms" class="platforms">
  <div class="container" style="padding-top: 30px;">

    <div class="platforms-slider swiper-container">
      <div class="swiper-wrapper align-items-center">
        <div class="swiper-slide"><img src="images/platforms/klook.png" class="img-fluid" alt=""></div>
        <div class="swiper-slide"><img src="images/platforms/tripadvisor.png" class="img-fluid" alt=""></div>
        <div class="swiper-slide"><img src="images/platforms/tripdotcom.png" class="img-fluid" alt=""></div>
      </div>
      <div class="swiper-pagination"></div>
    </div>

  </div>
</section>
<!-- End of Travel Platforms Section -->
```

Fig. 17.38 Travel platforms with interactive slider animation using PHP code

2. TripAdvisor
3. Trip.com

Figure 17.38 shows how the presentation of the three (3) travel platforms through an engaging interactive slider animation through PHP code.

- **Platform Slider:**

  Swiper library to showcase the travel platforms—Klook, TripAdvisor, and Trip.com logos, offering a visually appealing and navigable display within a webpage section.

  Users can explore the travel platforms associated with their desired tour package recommendations on the 'Tour Packages' page, showcased through an automated slider animation.

Figure 17.39 shows some fun facts about RoamRadar's website.
This section presents several fun facts about RoamRadar, as listed below:

1. The number of travel platforms
2. The total count of included tourist packages
3. The overall number of collected ratings

Fig. 17.39 RoamRadar's fun facts interface

4. The total count of recommended blogs

Figure 17.40 shows the PHP code in creating the counter animation, dynamically displaying the numbers associated with each fun fact.

Users can explore entertaining facts about RoamRadar by viewing animated numbers that represent key statistics of website information, providing a quick and engaging overview.

Figure 17.41 shows a similar slider animation utilised to showcase the travel platforms, as seen in the previous section. This functionality is also incorporated in the testimonies section of our project journey, where our team shares experiences with RoamRadar.

Our team members, who have shared their testimonial experiences with RoamRadar, include:

```
<!-- Fun Facts Section -->
<section class="ftco-section ftco-counter img" id="section-counter" style="background-image: url(images/bg_1.jpg);">
    <div class="container">
        <div class="row justify-content-center mb-5 pb-3">
      <div class="col-md-7 text-center heading-section heading-section-white ftco-animate">
        <h2 class="mb-4">Some fun facts</h2>
      </div>
    </div>
        <div class="row justify-content-center">
            <div class="col-md-10">
                <div class="row">
              <div class="col-md-3 d-flex justify-content-center counter-wrap ftco-animate">
                <div class="block-18 text-center">
                  <div class="text">
                    <strong class="number" data-number="3">0</strong>
                    <span>Travel Platforms</span>
                  </div>
                </div>
              </div>
              <div class="col-md-3 d-flex justify-content-center counter-wrap ftco-animate">
                <div class="block-18 text-center">
                  <div class="text">
                    <strong class="number" data-number="1500">0</strong>
                    <span>Tourist Packages</span>
                  </div>
                </div>
              </div>
              <div class="col-md-3 d-flex justify-content-center counter-wrap ftco-animate">
                <div class="block-18 text-center">
                  <div class="text">
                    <strong class="number" data-number="1760">0</strong>
                    <span>Ratings Collected</span>
                  </div>
                </div>
              </div>
              <div class="col-md-3 d-flex justify-content-center counter-wrap ftco-animate">
                <div class="block-18 text-center">
                  <div class="text">
                    <strong class="number" data-number="60">0</strong>
                    <span>Recommended Blogs</span>
                  </div>
                </div>
              </div>
            </div>
          </div>
        </div>
    </div>
    </div>
</section>
<!-- End of Fun Facts Section -->
```

Fig. 17.40 PHP code for counter animation in displaying fun fact numbers

17.8 SDLC Framework

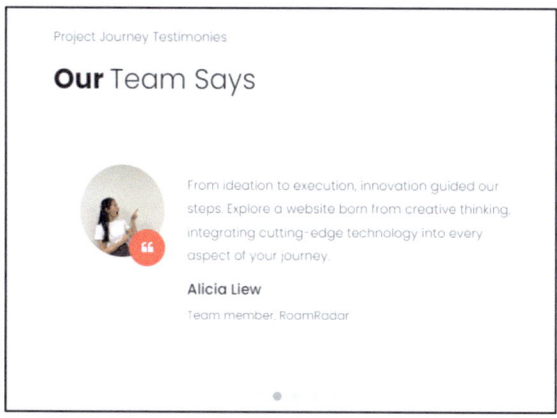

Fig. 17.41 Slider animation in testimonies interface

1. Alicia Liew, RoamRadar's Team Member
2. Koo Zhi Yan, RoamRadar's Team Member
3. Darsshan, RoamRadar's Team Member
4. Joshua, RoamRadar's Team Member
5. Hayley Woon, RoamRadar's Team Leader

Figure 17.42 shows the PHP code to generate the slider animation in the testimony section.

Users can access testimonials written by others who have experienced and enjoyed RoamRadar's system on the website. This helps build trust and interest, motivating users to explore the platform further for their travel needs.

4. **About Us Page**

In the 'About Us' page, users can **peruse and gain insights into RoamRadar and its system's operations**. Figure 17.43 shows the various information sections available on the 'About Us' page with tabbed navigation. This page includes the following key sections:

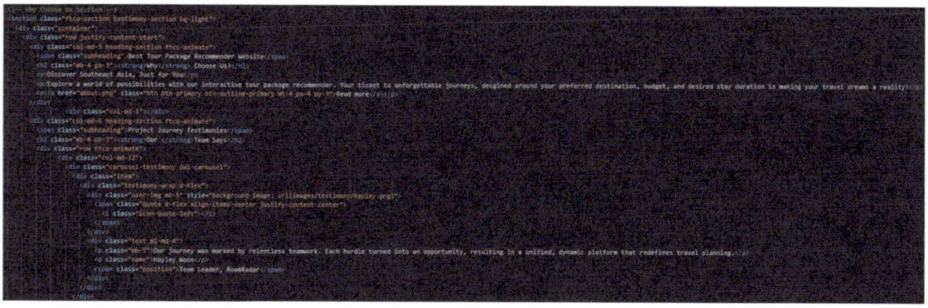

Fig. 17.42 PHP code for testimony section slider animation

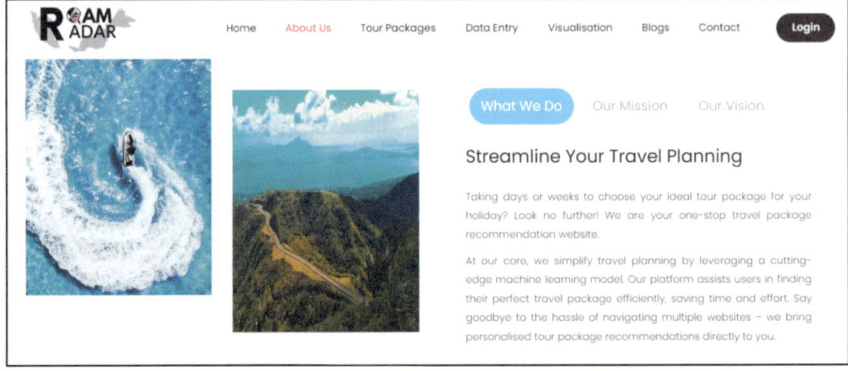

Fig. 17.43 Tabbed navigation interface with different information sections

1. What We Do
2. Our Mission
3. Our Vision
4. Frequently Asked Questions (FAQs)

On this page, users can click on 'What We Do', 'Our Mission', or 'Our Vision' to navigate through various information sections.

- **Tabbed Navigation:**

    The content is organised through tabbed navigation, allowing users to easily switch between different sections of information.

    Figure 17.44 shows the PHP code to generate the tabbed navigation.

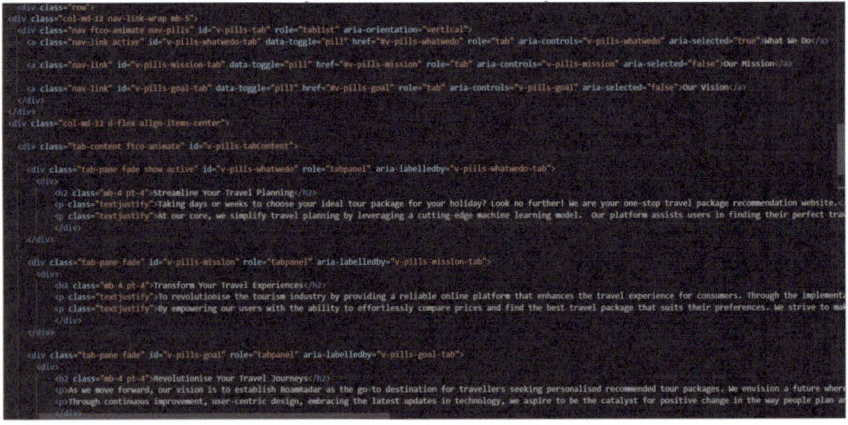

Fig. 17.44 PHP code for tabbed navigation

17.8 SDLC Framework

Users can view the description after clicking on each tab. This feature helps users understand RoamRadar's overall vision and mission.

On the same page, there is a Frequently Asked Questions (FAQ) section which is shown in Fig. 17.45 to provide users with the quick answers to common questions. This is designed to improve the customer experience by addressing anticipated questions without necessitating users to make additional inquiries. There are five (5) main questions listed that users may pose when visiting our website.

The PHP code of the first question is displayed in Fig. 17.46 as an example.

In the FAQ section, users are required to click on the ' + ' button to reveal the provided answer below the questions. Conversely, users can click the '-' button to conceal the answers.

6. **Tour Packages Recommender Page**

The 'Tour Packages' page will serve as the output page which **displaying the top 15 tour packages based on user input preferences** (country, duration, and price range).

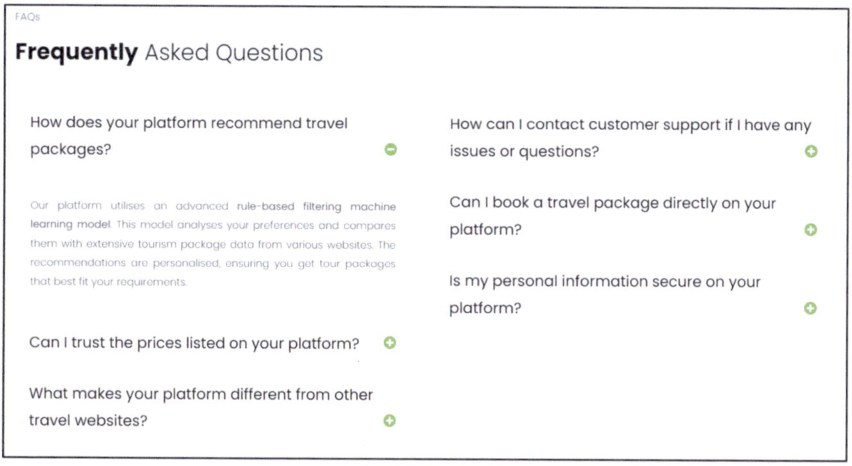

Fig. 17.45 Frequently asked questions interface

Fig. 17.46 PHP code for FAQ questions

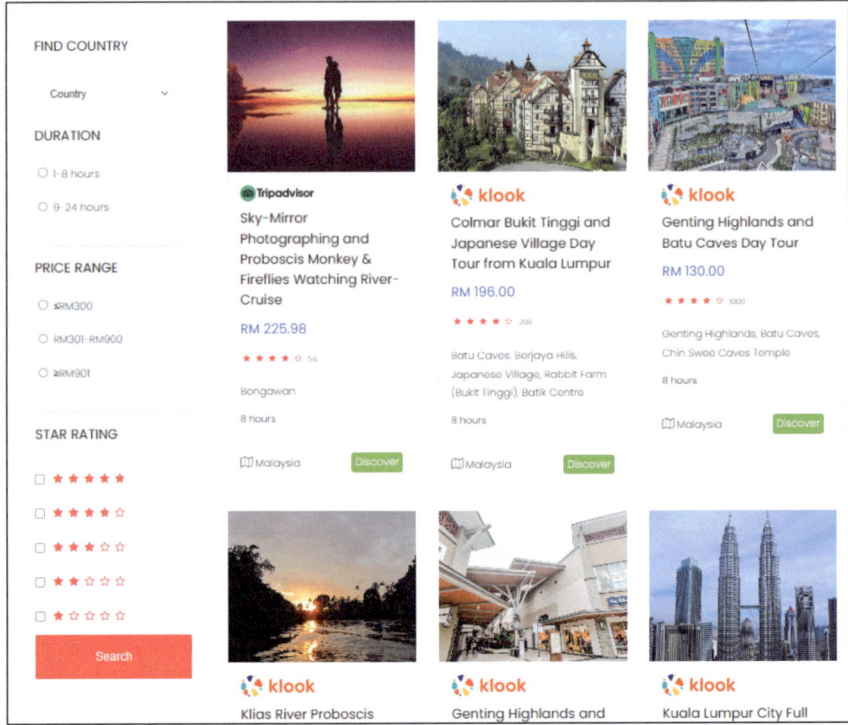

Fig. 17.47 Interface overview of 'tour packages'

The recommended packages are filtered using a K-Nearest Neighbours (KNN) model that incorporates data from three platforms (Klook, TripAdvisor, and Trip.com).

Figure 17.47 shows the overall functions of the Tour Packages page that enable users to filter options and select their desired tour packages.

The sidebar filter on the left enables users to customise their preferences and then the recommended top 15 tour packages will be displayed on the right side. The comprehensive functions are listed below:

- **Sidebar Filter:**
  The functions allow users to filter the user preferences (country, duration, price range, and star rating) by clicking the radio buttons and clicking the 'Search' button to execute the package search.
- **Magnifying Glass:**
  When the cursor is pointing on the tour image, the magnifying glass will appear, and it serves as a clickable icon that will navigate users to the third-party website after clicking on it.
- **Discover Button:**
  This button has the same functionality as the magnifying glass that will navigate users to the third-party website.

17.8 SDLC Framework

```php
<?php session_start(); ?>

<?php
require_once "db.php";

$country = "";
$duration = "";
$price = "";
$star5 = $star4 = $star3 = $star2 = $star1 = "";

$sCountry = "";
$sduration = "";
$sPrice = "";
$sStar = "";

if(isset($_POST["country"])) $country = $_POST["country"];
if(isset($_POST["duration"])) $duration = $_POST["duration"];
if(isset($_POST["price"])) $price = $_POST["price"];
if(isset($_POST["star1"])) $star1 = $_POST["star1"];
if(isset($_POST["star2"])) $star2 = $_POST["star2"];
if(isset($_POST["star3"])) $star3 = $_POST["star3"];
if(isset($_POST["star4"])) $star4 = $_POST["star4"];
if(isset($_POST["star5"])) $star5 = $_POST["star5"];
?>
```

Fig. 17.48 PHP code for database connection

Figure 17.48 illustrates the code of how we link the tour packages database in the phpMyAdmin into 'Tour Packages' page.

The purpose of these codes is to handle the user input and store the input in variables for further processing. After linking the database, we can start to match the variables with the filter options in sidebar filter (country, duration, price range, and star rating) as shown in Fig. 17.49.

These codes include the functions for users to select their preferences in the sidebar filter:

- **Dropdown List:**
  Users can select their country preferences from the dropdown list by clicking the downward arrow.
- **Radio Buttons:**
  For duration and price range, users can choose a single option by clicking the corresponding button.
- **Checkboxes:**
  For star rating, users have the flexibility to select multiple options.
- **Submit:**
  After users have selected their preferred options, they can click on 'Submit' button.

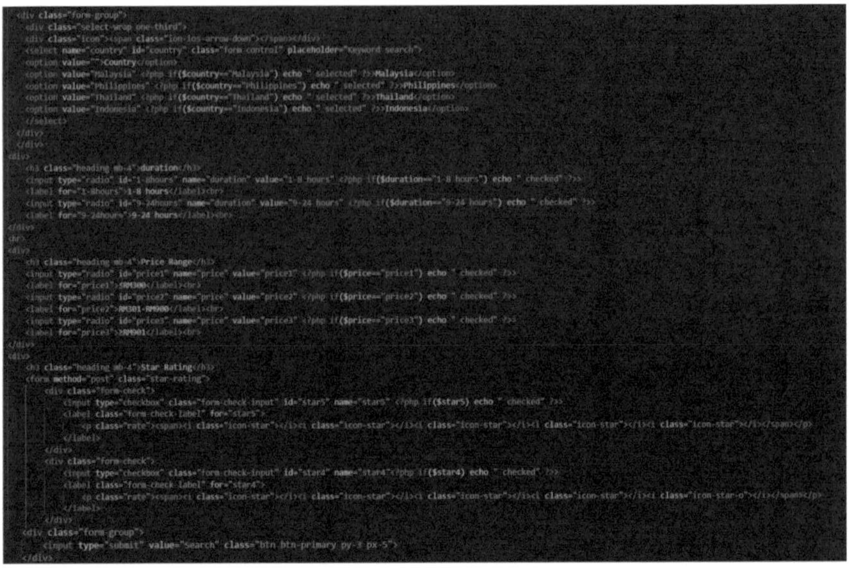

Fig. 17.49 PHP code for sidebar filter

The code shown in Fig. 17.50 is the MySQL query to retrieve tour packages data from a database based on various filtering criteria such as country, price, duration, and star rating.

The data is retrieved from a database named 'knn_tourpackages'. We filtered the country criteria, switched the statement of the duration into two categories (half-day and full-day) and price into three categories (budget, standard, and luxury), and created star rating conditions. After that, we combined all the conditions to handle different scenarios where users may select one or more filters such as country, price range, duration, and star rating.

The following step is shown in Fig. 17.51 to display the results, which is the top 15 tour packages.

The purpose of this code is to fetch the tour package information from the database based on the user selected filters and display on the page. If the initial database query fails, it will show an error message with details about the failure.

Moving to the localhost side, Fig. 17.52 shows where our database query (knn_tourpackages) stored in the phpMyAdmin.

The database can be accessed in the localhost by importing 'knn_tourpackages.sql' into 'travel2' database.

7. **Business Visualisation—Data Entry Page**

This Data Entry Page is designed for business users to **upload their tour packages data** with the CRUD functions (create, read, update, and delete), as shown in Fig. 17.53. By uploading their data, they are able to **add their tour packages data into the 'Tour Packages' page**. The Create function initiates when a new CSV file

17.8 SDLC Framework

Fig. 17.50 PHP code for display tour package information

is uploaded, leading to the creation of a new database. The Read function serves to retrieve existing data from the database. The Update function allows for the editing of existing data, while the Delete function facilitates the removal of unwanted data from the database.

On this page, the 'Upload File' section allows users to upload their data in csv.format and the data will be displayed in the 'Uploaded Data Table'. The users can edit or delete the data by clicking on the 'Edit' and 'Delete' button within the table.

Figure 17.54 illustrates that once users upload their data from csv. file, the data will concurrently be displayed in the phpMyAdmin database. After any edit or delete action is done by users, the latest data will also be updated in the database.

Fig. 17.51 PHP code for display tour package results

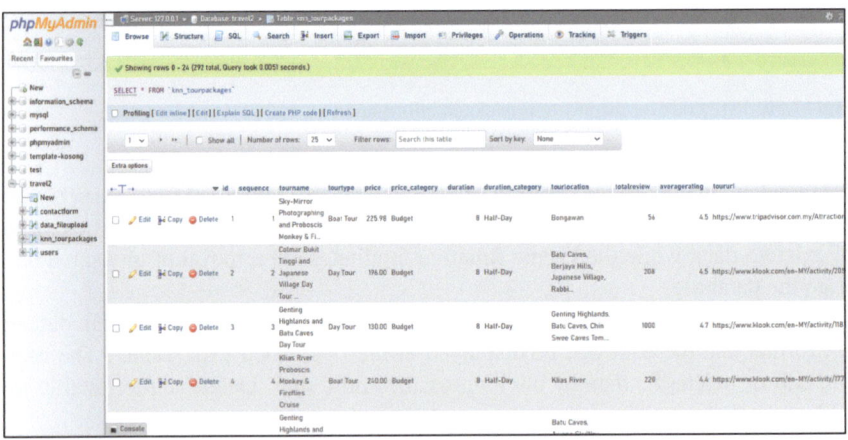

Fig. 17.52 Tour packages database in phpMyAdmin

17.8 SDLC Framework

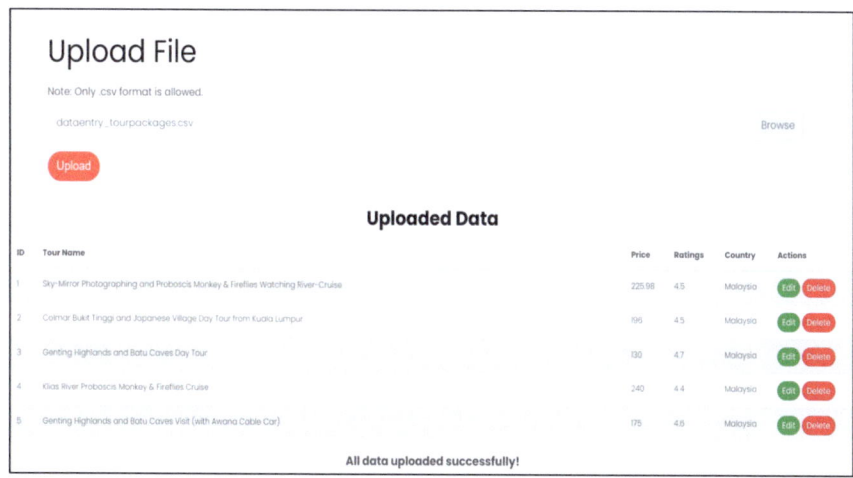

Fig. 17.53 Data entry page interface

8. **Why RoamRadar?—User Visualisation Page**

When users click into 'Visualisation' page, they will see RoamRadar Exploratory Data Analysis Report through Power BI visualisation providing a concise information of the advantages RoamRadar offers over other tour packages websites and its brief functionality. These visualisations offer users to **understand our system's functionalities and benefits**. Figure 17.55 serves as the first page that showcases the reasons for choosing RoamRadar. This content is generated from the results of the USE Questionnaire conducted during the testing phase, which comprehensively assesses RoamRadar's usability, user satisfaction, and ease of use. This survey is accompanied by charts illustrating that most respondents agreed that our system is user-friendly, time-saving, and reliable.

Figure 17.56 is the second page of the report that indicates the overall functionality of RoamRadar. Three slicers positioned at the top represent the three user inputs, while a bar chart below showcases the total number of tour packages offered based on the user's inputs. In short, RoamRadar offers the top 15 tour packages that closely align with the user preferences by using KNN model.

In Fig. 17.57, the code represents how we insert an embedded Power BI link to make it visible in the 'Visualisation' page.

9. **Travel Blog Tips Page**

In the case of users are not familiar with Malaysia and want to find out the famous places to visit, they can **derive insights from various travel blogs** accessible on the 'Blogs' page. These blogs offer essential details and itineraries for user reference. Upon selecting any particular blog, users will be redirected to a third-party navigation site.

Fig. 17.54 Interface of new database created in phpMyAdmin

17.8 SDLC Framework

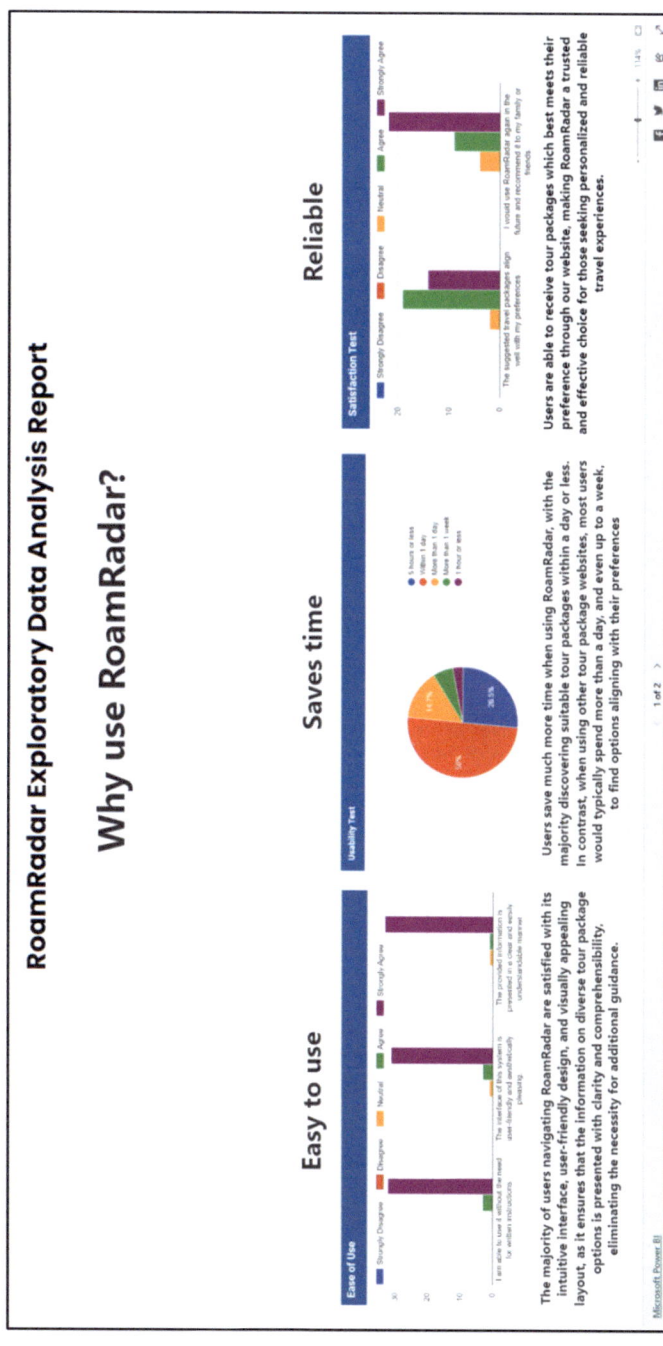

Fig. 17.55 1st page of power BI visualisation

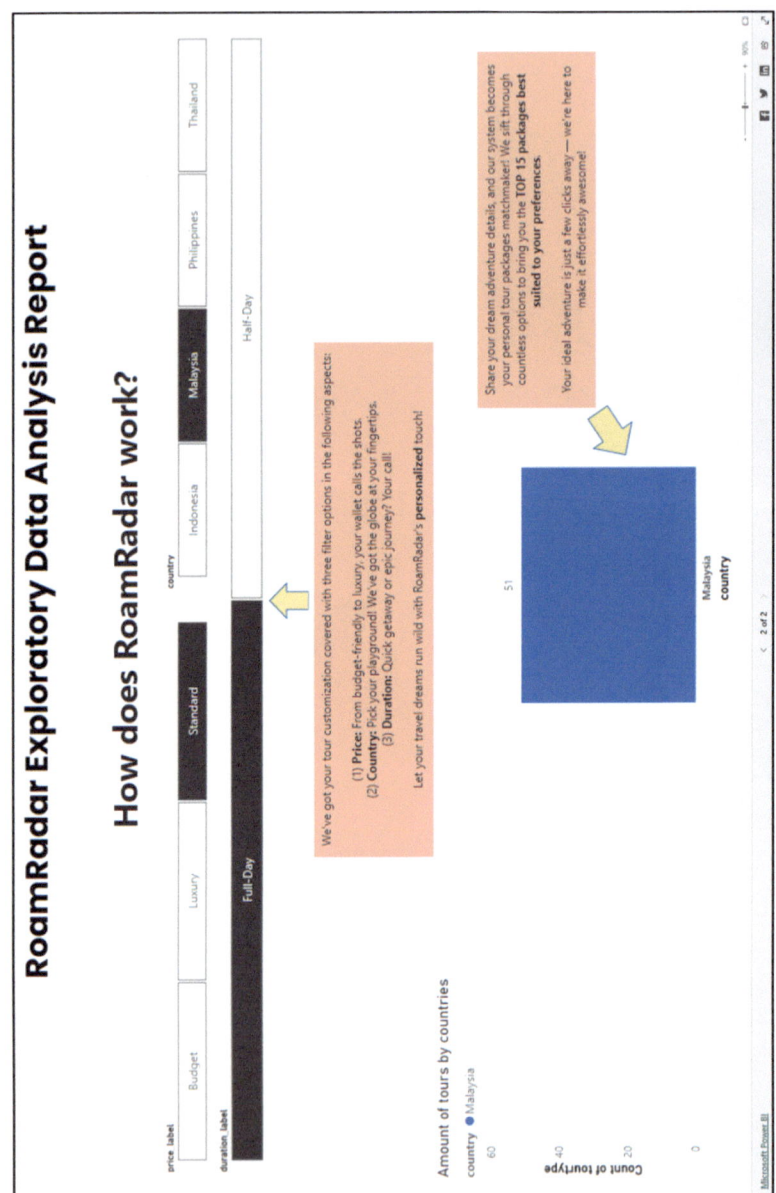

Fig. 17.56 Second page of Power BI Visualisation

```html
<!-- Start of PowerBI EDA Report-->
<html>
<body>
  <h2 style="text-align: center; padding: 20px 20px"><strong>RoamRadar Exploratory Data Analysis Report</strong></h2>
  <iframe title="Report Section" width="600" height="373.5"
    src="https://app.powerbi.com/view?r=eyJrIjoiY2I4MTQ5ZDAtNzkwMC00OTdmLWFiYTctNjUwMDE0NmZhNzM5IiwidCI6IjUzN2MyYmUxLWZjZDQtNDVhOS04M2IzLTY2NTNlYWNjNTA3MCIsImMiOjEwfQ%3D%3D"
    frameborder="0" allowFullScreen="true">
  </iframe>
</body>
</html>
<!-- End of PowerBI EDA Report-->
```

Fig. 17.57 Code for embedded link of power BI

Figure 17.58 is the code of the first blog as an example. The code shows the insertion of the image, title, author, number of comments, and a hyperlink to the respective blog post.

10. **Contact Page**

After users have completed their use of RoamRadar, they can conveniently **reach out to us by obtaining our contact information** on the 'Contact' page without leaving the browser. We have furnished three crucial pieces of information for users to communicate with us, as depicted in Fig. 17.59.

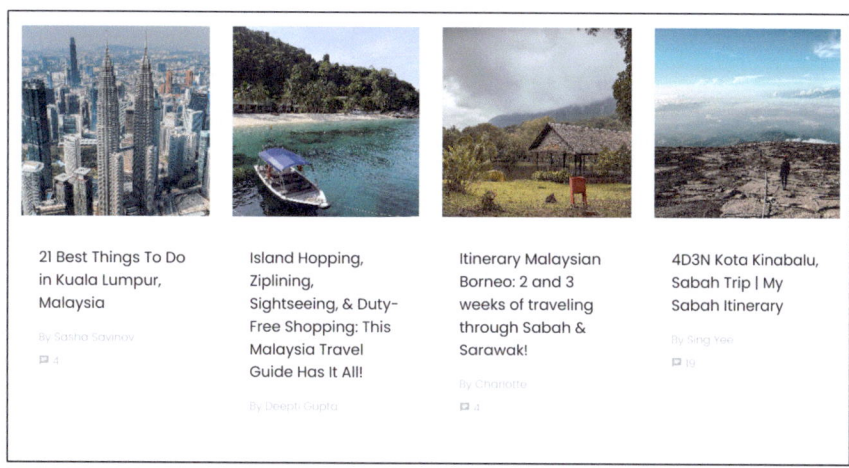

Fig. 17.58 Travel blogs interface

```html
<!-- Blogs Section-->
  <section class="ftco-section bg-light">
   <div class="container">
    <div class="row d-flex">
     <div class="col-md-3 d-flex ftco-animate">
      <div class="blog-entry align-self-stretch">
       <a href="https://www.goatsontheroad.com/things-to-do-in-kuala-lumpur/" target="_blank" class="block-20" style="background-image: url('images/blogs/blog1.jpg');">
       </a>
       <div class="text p-4 d-block">
        <h3 class="heading mt-3"><a href="https://www.goatsontheroad.com/things-to-do-in-kuala-lumpur/" target="_blank">21 Best Things To Do in Kuala Lumpur, Malaysia</a></h3>
        <div class="meta mb-3">
         <div><a href="https://www.goatsontheroad.com/author/sasha-savinov/" target="_blank">By Sasha Savinov</a></div><br>
         <div><a href="https://www.goatsontheroad.com/things-to-do-in-kuala-lumpur/" target="_blank" class="meta-chat"><span class="icon-chat"></span> 4 </a></div>
        </div>
       </div>
      </div>
     </div>
```

Fig. 17.59 Code of travel blogs

Contact Information section that becomes visible when users navigate to the 'Contact' page. This section provides details such as our address, phone number, email address, and official website. This section presents details such as our address, phone number, email address, and official website. The text in red is clickable and will direct users to the specified links or pages.

The first question applies the Net Promoter Score (NPS) scale to measure customer experience on a scale from 0 to 5. The second question employs radio buttons for users to select the page they believe RoamRadar can further improve. The last question utilises a textbox which allows users to type in their feedback. The code provided in Fig. 17.60 outlines the application of various elements in the feedback form. These elements include:

- **Net Promoter Scale (NPS):**
  This scale is a straightforward and user-friendly method for users to assess their experience and for developers to monitor user satisfaction scores. The scale range can be customised by developers based on their requirements.
- **Radio Buttons:**
  The buttons offer a list of page options and allow users to select only one option by clicking on the button.

```
<div class="feedback-form">
  <div class="feedback-content">
    <label for="feedback-checkbox" class="close-button">X</label>
    <h2>Your feedback is invaluable to us!</h2>

    <p><strong>Please rate your experience on a scale from 0 (Very Dissatisfied) to 5 (Very Satisfied). </strong></p>
    <div class="nps-scale">
      <input type="radio" name="nps" id="nps0" value="0">
      <label for="nps0">0</label>
      <input type="radio" name="nps" id="nps1" value="1">
      <label for="nps1">1</label>
      <input type="radio" name="nps" id="nps2" value="2">
      <label for="nps2">2</label>
      <input type="radio" name="nps" id="nps3" value="3">
      <label for="nps3">3</label>
      <input type="radio" name="nps" id="nps4" value="4">
      <label for="nps4">4</label>
      <input type="radio" name="nps" id="nps5" value="5">
      <label for="nps5">5</label>
    </div>
    <div>
      <p><strong> Where do you believe we can enhance your experience on our website?</strong></p>
      <input type="radio" id="home" name="navigationsection" value="Home">
      <label for="home">Home</label>
      <input type="radio" id="aboutus" name="navigationsection" value="About Us">
      <label for="aboutus">About Us</label>
      <input type="radio" id="tourpackages" name="navigationsection" value="Tour Packages">
      <label for="tourpackages">Tour Packages</label>
      <input type="radio" id="visualisation" name="navigationsection" value="Visualisation">
      <label for="visualisation">Visualisation</label>
      <input type="radio" id="blog" name="navigationsection" value="Blog">
      <label for="blog">Blogs</label>
      <input type="radio" id="contactus" name="navigationsection" value="Contact Us">
      <label for="contactus">Contact</label>
    </div>

    <textarea class="custom-textarea">Do share your feedback with us to help improve our website.</textarea>
    <button type="submit">Submit</button>
```

Fig. 17.60 Code of questions of the feedback form

17.8 SDLC Framework

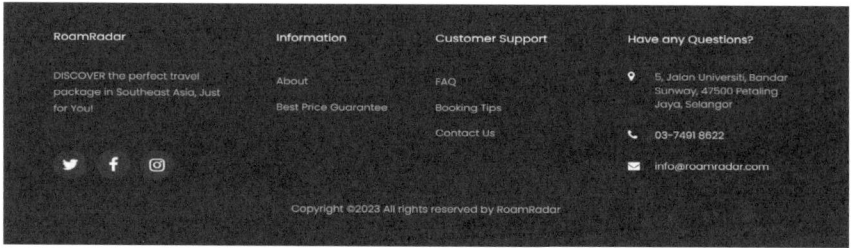

Fig. 17.61 Website footer interface

- **Textbox:**
  Users can provide feedback by typing within the textbox, in addition to clicking on the buttons. There are no limitations on users' ability to comment.
- **Submit Button:**
  After users have completed the form, they can click the 'Submit' button to submit it.

11. **Website Footer**

Figure 17.61 shows the interface of foster section that users will encounter when scrolling to the end of every page. In the footer section, users can **glean insight into RoamRadar's purpose and seamlessly access our contact information**. The content within the footer holds paramount significance in augmenting user experience, serving multifarious functional and informational objectives. The text contains clickable links that will direct users to the specified pages, excluding the brief introduction. This footer encompasses essential details:

1. Brief Introduction
2. Information
3. Customer Support
4. Contact Information
5. Social Media Icons

Figure 17.62 illustrates the code of footer which contains clickable text to navigate users to the assigned links or pages and animations for social media icons. For example, when users click on 'Best Price Guarantee', they will be directed to 'Tour Packages' page to find their tour packages.

17.8.5.1 Web Prototype Integration

In the process of integrating the Machine Learning KNN model with cosine similarity into the RoamRadar web interface, several considerations and challenges were encountered. Initially, Application Programming Interface (API) usage such as Flask was explored as a potential solution to seamlessly connect the model with Roam-Radar. However, this approach proved to be complex due to the generation of new

```
<footer class="ftco-footer ftco-bg-dark ftco-section">
  <div class="container">
    <div class="row mb-5">
      <div class="col-md">
        <div class="ftco-footer-widget mb-4">
          <h2 class="ftco-heading-2">RoamRadar</h2>
          <p>DISCOVER the perfect travel package in Southeast Asia, Just for You!</p>
          <ul class="ftco-footer-social list-unstyled float-md-left float-lft mt-5">
            <li class="ftco-animate"><a href="#"><span class="icon-twitter"></span></a></li>
            <li class="ftco-animate"><a href="#"><span class="icon-facebook"></span></a></li>
            <li class="ftco-animate"> <a href="#"><span class="icon-instagram"></span></a></li>
          </ul>
        </div>
      </div>
      <div class="col-md">
        <div class="ftco-footer-widget mb-4 ml-md-5">
          <h2 class="ftco-heading-2">Information</h2>
          <ul class="list-unstyled">
            <li><a href="about.php" class="py-2 d-block">About</a></li>
            <li><a href="tourpackages.php" class="py-2 d-block">Best Price Guarantee</a></li>
          </ul>
        </div>
      </div>
      <div class="col-md">
        <div class="ftco-footer-widget mb-4">
          <h2 class="ftco-heading-2">Customer Support</h2>
          <ul class="list-unstyled">
            <li><a href="about.php" class="py-2 d-block">FAQ</a></li>
            <li><a href="blogs.php" class="py-2 d-block">Booking Tips</a></li>
            <li><a href="contact.php" class="py-2 d-block">Contact Us</a></li>
          </ul>
        </div>
      </div>
      <div class="col-md">
        <div class="ftco-footer-widget mb-4">
          <h2 class="ftco-heading-2">Have any Questions?</h2>
          <div class="block-23 mb-3">
            <ul>
              <li><span class="icon icon-map-marker"></span><a href="https://www.google.com/maps/dir/3.0639853,101.6044125/Sunway+University/@3.0647595,101.6020168,1
              <li><a href="tel://037491 8622"><span class="icon icon-phone"></span><span class="text">03-7491 8622</span></a></li>
              <li><a href="mailto:info@roamradar.com"><span class="icon icon-envelope"></span><span class="text">info@roamradar.com</span></a></li>
            </ul>
          </div>
        </div>
      </div>
    </div>
    <div class="row">
      <div class="col-md-12 text-center">

<p>Copyright &copy;<script>document.write(new Date().getFullYear());</script> All rights reserved by RoamRadar</a></p>
      </div>
    </div>
  </div>
</footer>
```

Fig. 17.62 Code for website footer section

indices by the machine learning model that did not align with the indices in the RoamRadar phpMyAdmin database. Additionally, time constraints and the use of different programming languages for model development (Python) and web development (PHP or HTML) further complicated the API integration process.

To overcome these challenges, a more manual alternative was implemented. This alternative involved systematically running through all possible user input scenarios and recording the corresponding recommendations in a separate Excel sheet. Subsequently, this Excel sheet was uploaded into RoamRadar's phpMyAdmin database using the following steps (Fig. 17.63).

(1) **Accessing phpMyAdmin:**

- Navigate to phpMyAdmin and select the appropriate database (in this case, 'travel2').

(2) **Importing CSV File:**

- Click on the 'Import' tab and select the option to upload a CSV file.

(3) **Listing Variables:**

- During the import process, phpMyAdmin will prompt you to map the columns from the CSV file to the corresponding variables in the database table.

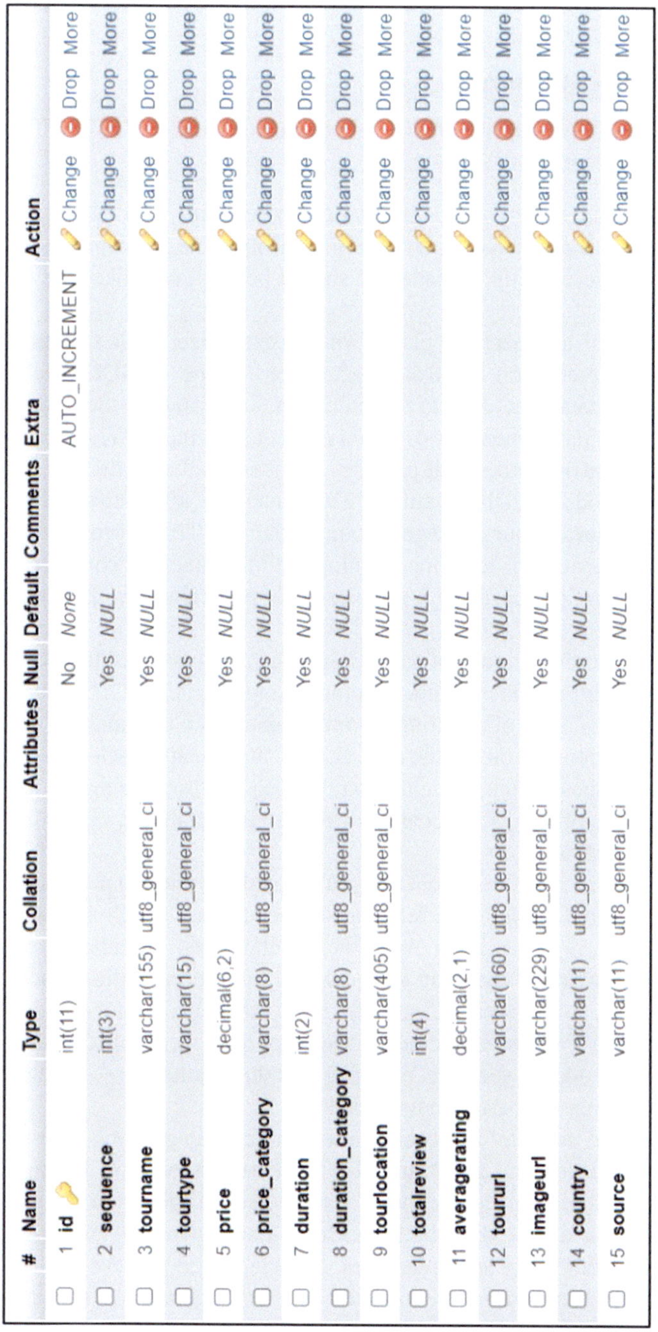

17.8 SDLC Framework

#	Name	Type	Collation	Attributes	Null	Default	Comments	Extra	Action
1	id	int(11)			No	None		AUTO_INCREMENT	Change Drop More
2	sequence	int(3)			Yes	NULL			Change Drop More
3	tourname	varchar(155)	utf8_general_ci		Yes	NULL			Change Drop More
4	tourtype	varchar(15)	utf8_general_ci		Yes	NULL			Change Drop More
5	price	decimal(6,2)			Yes	NULL			Change Drop More
6	price_category	varchar(8)	utf8_general_ci		Yes	NULL			Change Drop More
7	duration	int(2)			Yes	NULL			Change Drop More
8	duration_category	varchar(8)	utf8_general_ci		Yes	NULL			Change Drop More
9	tourlocation	varchar(405)	utf8_general_ci		Yes	NULL			Change Drop More
10	totalreview	int(4)			Yes	NULL			Change Drop More
11	averagerating	decimal(2,1)			Yes	NULL			Change Drop More
12	tourgrl	varchar(160)	utf8_general_ci		Yes	NULL			Change Drop More
13	imageurl	varchar(229)	utf8_general_ci		Yes	NULL			Change Drop More
14	country	varchar(11)	utf8_general_ci		Yes	NULL			Change Drop More
15	source	varchar(11)	utf8_general_ci		Yes	NULL			Change Drop More

Fig. 17.63 Screenshot of adding excel file to phpMyAdmin

- Define the variables such as 'Name', 'Rating', 'Similarity', and any other relevant fields. Assign the appropriate data types, such as VARCHAR for names and DECIMAL for ratings.

(4) **Defining Table Structure:**

- Specify additional details such as whether a field can be NULL or if it should auto-increment.

This method ensures that the RoamRadar database aligns with the output generated by the machine learning model, overcoming the index misalignment issue. Once the file has been successfully uploaded, it should be displayed like Fig. 17.64 on phpMyAdmin:

With this manual approach in place, when users select their Country, Price, and Duration preferences on the RoamRadar website, the MySQL database can promptly filter the data according to these criteria. The database then presents the top 15 tour package recommendations based on the user's input. While this method involves a more hands-on process, it provides a practical solution that integrates the machine learning model with the RoamRadar web interface, allowing users to receive personalised and relevant tour package recommendations. This approach effectively balances the complexities of machine learning with the practical considerations of web interface integration, ensuring a seamless user experience on the RoamRadar platform.

Despite the successful manual integration approach, it is essential to acknowledge certain limitations and consider avenues for future improvements. One inherent limitation is the periodic nature of updating recommendations in the database as it relies on manual interventions to refresh the dataset. This manual approach may introduce an impact on two issues, which are delays in reflecting real-time changes or additions to the tour packages offerings, and concerns related to scalability, especially as the dataset expands over time.

The second limitation is the current integration method relies on predefined filters (Country, Price, and Duration) to fetch recommendations which limits users to provide more detailed information about their preferences. To enhance this limitation, we can explore more dynamic and personalised filtering options such as user preferences, historical interactions, and additional contextual factors. Besides user filtering options, we will also implement a feedback loop mechanism to enable our system to learn and adapt over time, ensuring that the quality of recommendations will continuously improve based on user feedback.

Lastly, we should consider exploring more seamless integrations across various programming languages and platforms. This can be achieved by leveraging the middleware technologies or developing a standardised Application Programming Interface (API) that aligns with both machine learning model and web interface. Through implementing such measures, the integration process can be significantly streamlined, and real-time updates can be facilitated without manual interventions.

17.8 SDLC Framework

Fig. 17.64 Tour packages database on phpMyAdmin

In summary, although the current manual integration offers a practical solution, it still remains room for future improvements. By addressing the limitations through automation, dynamic filtering, and enhanced integration methods, we are likely to enhance the quality to a more user-friendly tour package recommendation system within RoamRadar's web interface. These considerations pave the way for ongoing refinement and optimisation to meet the evolving needs of users and the growing dataset.

17.8.6 Testing

17.8.6.1 Test for Functions

(a) **Test for Authentication**
This test is to validate the authentication mechanism implemented in the RoamRadar website. This includes testing login functionality, user registration, and password reset processes to ensure that only authenticated users can access restricted features or data.

(b) **Selection of Tour Packages**
This test is to verify that the website enables users to accurately select specific countries, price ranges, and durations for tour packages. This involves testing dropdown menus, input fields, or any other interface elements used for selecting desired options.

(c) **Validation of Display Information**
This test is to ensure that the information presented on the website exhibit valid and accurate values. This can be achieved by comparing the displayed data with expected values obtained from reliable sources or by conducting manual calculations for sample data points.

17.8.6.2 Test for Flow

(a) **Test for Smooth Navigation**
A verification of the website's navigation flows seamlessly without unexpected errors or broken links is unavoidable. This step is to guarantee that users can easily move between different pages, sections, or features of the website without encountering any issues.

(b) **Test for Responsiveness**
We will validate that the website is responsive and display correctly on various devices and screen sizes. This can be executed through testing on different browsers, mobile devices, and resolutions to ensure the website's layout and functionality adapt effectively to diverse environments.

17.8 SDLC Framework

(c) **Test for Performance**

This test is to evaluate the website's performance by testing its response time, page load speed, and overall efficiency. We need to conduct tests with varying data sizes and user loads to ensure optimal performance under different conditions.

17.8.6.3 Test for User Acceptance

From research by Fadhilah et al. (2022), a USE Questionnaire was encouraged to use in evaluating a system's usability, user satisfaction, and ease of use, where usability entails the measurement of a system's capability to be utilised by users in achieving specific goals, user satisfaction stands for the positive or negative attitude associate with the use of the system, and ease of use refers how user-friendly a system is.

After we ensure the website's functionality and flow are error-free, a USE Questionnaire will be applied to determine user overall experience in the context of usability, satisfaction, and ease of use. This questionnaire aims to gauge users' preferences for utilising our services and identify areas where our system can enhance their experience.

(a) **Test for Usability**

This usability test contains five questions in Fig. 17.65 that aim to assess the effectiveness of RoamRadar which focusing on its usability, efficiency, functionality, and the time spent selecting tour packages in comparison to other travel platforms such as Klook, Trip.com, and TripAdvisor.

The first two questions enable us to directly assess our system's competitiveness with other mature travel platforms. Additionally, it can also prove that our system has successfully addressed the issue of overtime spending on selecting tour packages. The scale-rating questions allow us to gauge the level of agreement among users regarding the usability of our system.

(b) **Test for Satisfaction**

This satisfaction test in Fig. 17.66 is designed to gauge user's overall experience with the goal to make improvements that align more closely with user expectations.

The three scale-rating questions allow us to gauge the level of agreement among users regarding the satisfaction with our system in terms of time-saving, the accuracy of closest packages results, and the likelihood to recommend it to family and friends.

(c) **Test for Ease of Use**

In Fig. 17.67, this test comprises three scale-rating questions designed to assess the simplicity and intuitiveness of RoamRadar, ensuring a seamless and user-friendly experience. The objective is to evaluate the platform's user interface for its ease of use and accessibility.

Based on your previous experiences, approximately how much time do you typically spend comparing and selecting a tour package across various travel platforms, such as Klook, Trip.com, and TripAdvisor?
Please consider factors like browsing options, filtering preferences, price comparisons, navigation through pages, and the decision-making process.
○ 5 hours or less
○ Within 1 day
○ More than 1 day
○ More than 1 week

Based on your experience with our website, RoamRadar, how much time do you typically spend comparing and selecting a tour package?
Please consider factors like browsing options, filtering preferences, price comparisons, navigation through pages, and the decision-making process.
○ 5 hours or less
○ Within 1 day
○ More than 1 day
○ More than 1 week

Please rate your experience on RoamRadar, on a scale from Strongly Disagree to Strongly Agree.

	Strongly Disagree	Disagree	Neutral	Agree	Strongly Agree
The system possesses all the functions and capabilities that I anticipated.	○	○	○	○	○
The information is effective in assisting me with the selection of travel packages.	○	○	○	○	○
The system offers clear and concise information, including details on travel packages and their corresponding prices.	○	○	○	○	○

Fig. 17.65 Questions for usability test

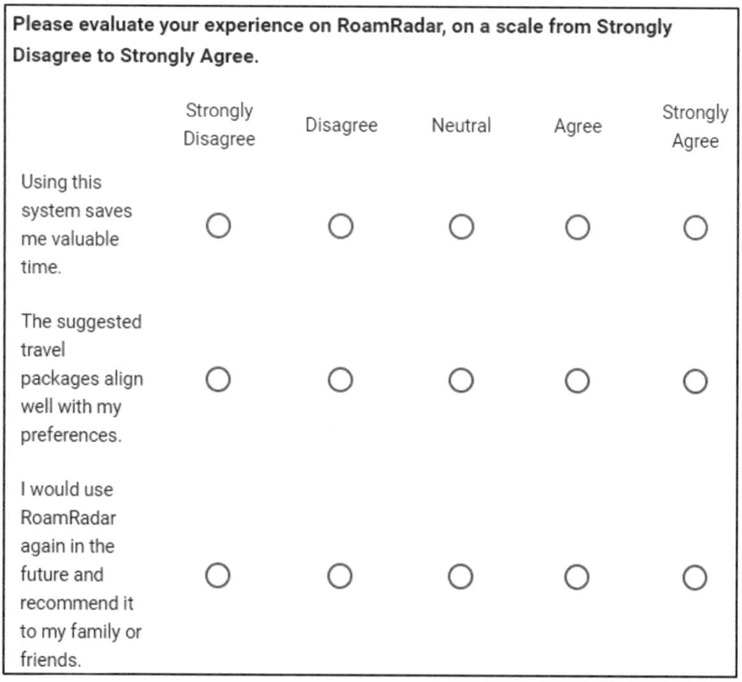

17.9 Result and Analysis

Fig. 17.66 Questions for satisfaction test

The questions allow us to gauge the level of agreement among users regarding the ease of use of our system, specifically in terms of not requiring additional instructions, applicability for all age groups, and the comprehensibility of the provided information.

17.9 Result and Analysis

Once a Spearman Correlation Matrix is generated using the travel packages dataset, we can examine the relationships between the variables to test for any significant associations. Spearman correlation is employed for this analysis due to its ability to measure a monotonic link between two variables in terms of both direction and strength. Unlike Pearson correlation, which specifically assesses linear relationships, Spearman correlation is versatile in capturing monotonic functions, whether they are increasing or decreasing, without requiring linearity. It is important to note that Spearman correlation is not restricted to positive correlations only as it can effectively detect both positive and negative monotonic relationships. This makes it a valuable tool for exploring various types of associations in the data, regardless of the direction of the correlation.

Kindly rate your experience on RoamRadar, on a scale from Strongly Disagree to Strongly Agree.					
	Strongly Disagree	Disagree	Neutral	Agree	Strongly Agree
I am able to use it without the need for written instructions.	○	○	○	○	○
The interface of this system is user-friendly and aesthetically pleasing.	○	○	○	○	○
The provided information is presented in a clear and easily understandable manner.	○	○	○	○	○

Fig. 17.67 Questions for ease-of-use test

In our case, we observe both positive and negative relationships among the variables. The analysis of the results reveals the preponderance of light shades of blue in the Spearman Correlation Matrix in Fig. 17.68, that indicates most variables exhibit weak relationships with each other. Notably, some moderately negative relationships are evident, such as those observed between 'totalreview' and 'averagerating' and between 'Website_Numerical' and 'totalreview'. Furthermore, a few somewhat positive connections are identified, such as the one between 'Country_Numerical' and 'duration'. Also, a few somewhat positive connections are identified, such as the one between 'Country_Numerical' and 'duration'. These findings contribute to a comprehensive understanding of varying strengths and directions of the relationships found within the dataset.

To justify the observed weak relationships among the variables, it is plausible that these results stem from the inherent nature of the dataset. If there is an absence of a consistent correlation pattern among the variables, one possible explanation for the data discrepancies could be attributed to noise or randomness. Another contributing factor might be the dataset's heterogeneity, implying that, when viewed as a whole, various subgroups or patterns within the data may be offsetting one another.

The analysis brings to light a dataset exhibiting both positive and negative relationships among variables. The prevalence of weak connections, moderately negative

17.9 Result and Analysis

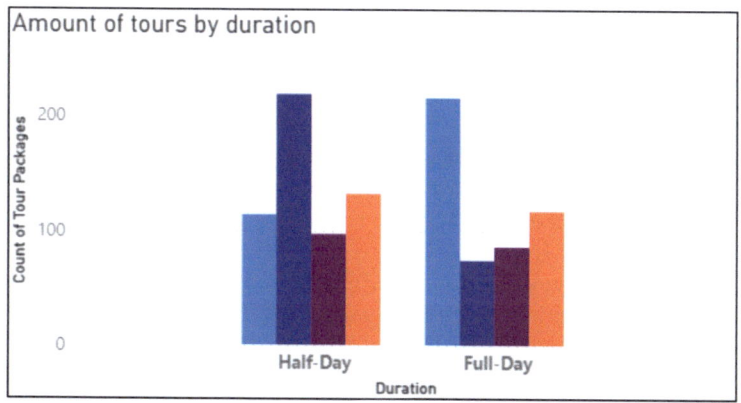

Fig. 17.68 Bar chart for tour packages characterised by duration

correlations (e.g. 'totalreview' and 'averagerating'), and somewhat positive associations (e.g. 'Country_Numerical' and 'duration') underscore the dataset's heterogeneity, offering a nuanced understanding of the diverse strengths and directions of relationships within it.

To validate and ensure the accuracy of these findings, a further in-depth analysis of the chosen variables is necessary using our Power BI dashboard and Machine Learning Model.

17.9.1 EDA in Tour Package Dashboard

The utilisation of data visualisation tools is essential in gaining insights into the unique characteristics of travel packages and deciphering the dynamic demand patterns within a dataset. By using these visualisation tools, analysts and investors can pinpoint distinctions across tour packages and gauge the varying levels of demand for packages with similar features. Interpreting these visual presentations facilitates the customisation of recommendations to align with each user's preferences, guaranteeing that ideas resonate with their selected travel destinations, financial constraints, and satisfaction criteria.

In this visualisation, the colours assigned to each bar correspond to those associated with respective countries. This colour-coding difference facilitates a straightforward interpretation, enabling users to identify that the majority of tour packages in Southeast Asia primarily fall within the budget to standard price range.

In this visualisation, the colours assigned to each bar correspond to those associated with respective countries. This colour-coding difference facilitates a straightforward interpretation, enabling users to identify that the majority of tour packages in Southeast Asia primarily fall within the budget to standard price range.

The bar graph for the 'Budget' category reveals that Indonesia stands out as the leading country in terms of budget tour packages, with over 200 offerings. This indicates that a substantial portion of the tour package options available in the region falls into the budget-friendly category for lower to middle-class travellers.

As for 'Standard' bar graph, Malaysia emerges as the key player in the standard tour package category, with 149 tour packages. This suggests that Malaysia provides a significant number of tour package choices that fall within the standard price range, catering to a diverse range of travellers seeking moderately priced experiences, including middle-class travellers.

In the 'Luxury' bar graph, the visualisation showcases the Philippines as the frontrunner in luxury tour packages, featuring 26 offerings. This insight implies that, while there are fewer options in the luxury category, the Philippines stands out as a destination that offers a notable selection of high-end and exclusive tour experiences.

The colour-coded bars not only enhance the visual appeal of the representation but also serve as a helpful tool to quickly grasp the distribution of tour packages across different price ranges in Southeast Asia, allowing travellers to purchase tour packages according to their financial budgets.

1. **Tour Packages Characterised by Duration**
   The fourth visual presented in Fig. 17.68 shows the distribution of tour packages based on their duration. Below is a detailed explanation of the visual:

   - **Top Countries for Half-Day Tours**: Malaysia
   - **Top Countries for Full-Day Tours**: Indonesia

The visual representation in Fig. 17.68 provides insightful details about the distribution of tour packages based on their duration. Notably, the 'Half-Day' category exhibits a slightly higher number of tour packages compared to the 'Full-Day' category. The colour-coding on each bar corresponds to the respective countries, offering a visual overview of the relationships.

Upon analysing the data, it becomes evident that most countries maintain a consistent number of tour package options for each duration. However, exceptions arise in the cases of Malaysia and Indonesia, where the distribution varies between the two durations.

For travellers, these insights offer valuable information to make informed decisions based on their preferences and interests. Travellers seeking for shorter and more time-efficient travel experiences may find the abundance of Half-Day tour packages appealing. This could be ideal for those with limited time or a preference for concise explorations. Conversely, individuals with a desire for more immersive and comprehensive experiences might be drawn to destinations offering a variety of Full-Day tours.

A closer examination of the data points out that Malaysia stands out as a top country for Half-Day tours, suggesting a concentration of shorter-duration tour offerings in this destination. On the other hand, Indonesia plays a pivotal role in the Full-Day tour category, implying a notable presence of longer-duration tour packages in this country.

The colour-coded representation aligns each country with specific tour durations, allowing travellers to tailor and align their preferences with destination-specific offerings. Whether one is inclined towards shorter explorations or longer experiences, the insights from this visual aid in crafting a more personalised and fulfilling travel itinerary.

17.9.2 Power BI User Visualisation Dashboard

The primary purpose of this Power BI dashboard, as we have discovered, is to enable us to comprehend the total number of packages a user might be recommended based on their preferences. This is achieved through the filter options they specify for their tour package recommendations on our website.

Once a user selects their preferences for each of the three criteria: price, country, and duration, the visualisation illustrating the number of tours by countries reveals the total count of tour packages that match the users' specified criteria in the desired tour package recommendations.

Given our system's aim to present users with the top 15 tour packages that closely match their requirements, our KNN machine learning model processes the total number of recommended tour packages and generates the top 15 tour package recommendations for the users.

The visualisation displayed in Fig. 17.69 serves as an additional detailed guide for users to navigate through our website, helping them understand how the process works and emphasising how our approach distinguishes itself from other existing tour package websites.

In summary, the Power BI dashboard is a visualisation page for users to offer users a clear understanding of how tour packages are filtered based on their chosen preferences. Nevertheless, the abundance of recommended packages may overwhelm users, costing them more time to identify their closest match. To address this issue, the cosine similarity is applied to refine the selection, ensuring that users receive a personalised set of recommendations that align closely with their preferences.

17.10 Tour Package Model Recommendation Performance Analysis

It is vital to emphasise that RoamRadar functions as a classification model, rather than a prediction model. Its primary goal is to **classify and recommend the best tour packages for users based on their preferences**. This distinctive approach sets RoamRadar apart from traditional prediction models, rendering the evaluation metrics commonly associated with such models, like RMSE or MAE, unsuitable for

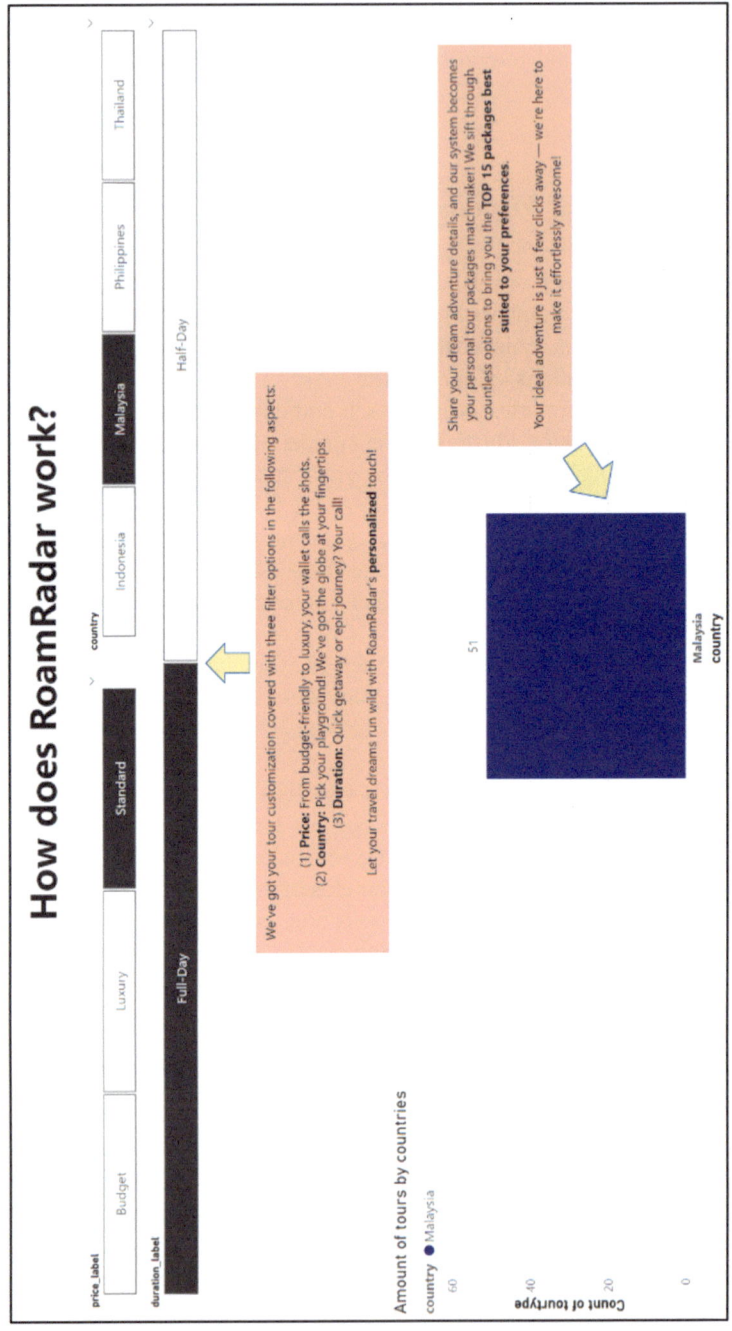

Fig. 17.69 User Visualisation Dashboard

```
Top 15 recommendations based on unique indices:
1. Best Seller! Doi Inthanon National Park, Waterfall & Royal Project - Chiang Mai - Rating: 5.0 - Similarity: 1.0
2. Historical City of Ayutthaya - Unesco Full Day Tour From Bangkok - Rating: 5.0 - Similarity: 0.9969465062460557
3. Phuket Raya Island Day Tour with Snorkeling OR Scuba Diving - Rating: 5.0 - Similarity: 0.9944829005519756
4. From Ko Tao: Snorkeling Day Trip Ko Tao & Ko Nang Yuan with Meals - Rating: 5.0 - Similarity: 0.9905723433470196
5. One day tour of Phuket Island and Grand Pippi Island in Thailand [Pippi Island one day tour/Egg Island/including island fare/lunch and beverage/snorkelling - Rating: 5.0 - Similarity: 0.9898642088248872
6. Thailand Phuket Phi Phi Island Observation Point One Day Tour [(Lazy Version) Starfish Phi Phi + Egg Island Speedboat One Day Tour/seastar] - Rating: 5.0 - Similarity: 0.9880781942780165
7. Bangkok Day Tour: Wat Pho, Wat Arun, Grand Palace and Emerald Buddha - Rating: 4.8 - Similarity: 0.9819564703450142
8. Koh Lanta in Pattaya [Departure from Bangkok & Pattaya | Photography/snorkeling/motorboat/banana boat/parasail] - Rating: 5.0 - Similarity: 0.9814133225820573
9. One-day tour to Chiang Mai, Thailand Inthanon [high praise rate of boutique small group] hotel shuttle + lunch optional hiking] - Rating: 5.0 - Similarity: 0.9465483641312958
10. SCUBA Diving tour Racha and Coral islands full day tour  - Rating: 5.0 - Similarity: 0.9462277548853492
11. Doi Suthep with Meo Hilltribe/Chiang Mai University/Lanna Hotpot/Night Safari/Makkha Spa Day Tour - Rating: 5.0 - Similarity: 0.9391554895950417
12. One-day tour to the Damnoen Saduak Floating Market & Maeklong Railway Market , Bangkok Thailand - Rating: 4.9 - Similarity: 0.8911362375440575
13. Chiang Mai Night Safari, Doi Inthanon, Doi Suthep and University Tour - Rating: 5.0 - Similarity: 0.8580104943975104
14. Ayutthaya One day Private Tour with Boat - Rating: 5.0 - Similarity: 0.831391571126095 6
15. Ayutthaya One day Private Tour with Boat - Rating: 5.0 - Similarity: 0.8310752728114825
```

Fig. 17.70 Tour package recommendations

```
Top 7 recommendations based on unique indices:
1. CEBU Island Hopping Tour to Nalusuan Island - Rating: 4.0 - Similarity: 1.0
2. Historical tour of old Manila - Rating: 4.0 - Similarity: 0.9983532095171892
3. Hidden Valley Springs Resort Day Trip from Manila - Rating: 4.3 - Similarity: 0.9414627104752485
4. Private Full-Day Tagaytay Tour from Manila - Rating: 1.0 - Similarity: 0.8711086434106646
5. Panoramic Tagaytay Ridge Tour from Manila - Rating: 4.7 - Similarity: 0.6436024079223782
6. Private Half-Day Makati (Old Manila) with Intramuros - Rating: 5.0 - Similarity: 0.40287929362036434
7. Bohol Highlights Tour: Chocolate Hills, Tarsier Spotting and Loboc River Cruise - Rating: 5.0 - Similarity: 0.32825681265841156
```

Fig. 17.71 Tour package recommendations

assessing its performance. Instead, this section will discuss three (3) unique validation strategies employed.

17.10.1 Cosine Similarity

Example 1: [Thailand, Budget, Half day]

See Fig. 17.70.

Example 2: [Philippines, Luxury, Full Day]

See Fig. 17.71.

Example 3: [Indonesia, Standard, Half Day]

See Fig. 17.72.

17.10.2 Reliability Benchmark for Recommendations

In the context of evaluating RoamRadar's tour package recommendations, establishing a benchmark is imperative, especially when dealing with a diverse range of cosine similarity scores spanning from 0 to 1. The significance of selecting a benchmark is underscored by insights from the study conducted by Amer et al. (2021), which served as a foundational reference for this research. The study posits that cosine similarity scores surpassing 0.3 are considered acceptable for recommendations, providing a tangible threshold for assessing the efficacy of recommendation models.

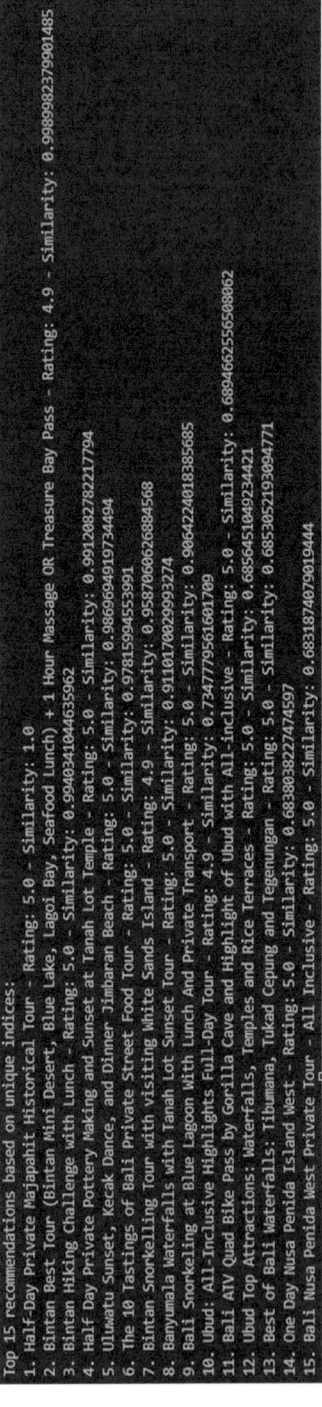

Fig. 17.72 Tour package recommendation

The rationale behind adopting this benchmark is rooted in the study's findings, which reveal a consistent correlation: when cosine similarity scores fall below 0.3, the recommendations tend to perform poorly across various other validation metrics such as RMSE, MAE, F1 scores, etc. Hence, the author meticulously arrived at the 0.3 benchmark through a comprehensive analysis of diverse recommendation models and their performance across different similarity measures. This thorough examination led to the robust conclusion that a cosine similarity score surpassing 0.3 reliably indicates a level of similarity that ensures the practical utility and effectiveness of the recommendations. Applying this benchmark to RoamRadar's recommendations reinforces the system's reliability, even in instances where cosine similarity scores may be perceived as marginal. For example, a cosine similarity score of 0.328, which might be considered borderline without a benchmark, is deemed acceptable based on the reference from Amer et al. (2021). This underscores the robustness of RoamRadar's recommendations, assuring users that even scores on the lower end of the spectrum fall within the established acceptable range.

The integration of this benchmark into the evaluation process elevates RoamRadar beyond raw scores, providing a meaningful context that aligns with user expectations and the practical utility of the tour package suggestions. By adhering to industry benchmarks, particularly those validated by prior research such as Patro et al.'s (2020) study, RoamRadar strengthens its position as a dependable and transparent personalised tour package recommendation system, fostering trust and confidence among users.

17.10.3   Comparison with Airbnb Model

Example 4: Airbnb Model Recommendations

In evaluating RoamRadar's tour package recommendations, another validation method used involves comparing the outcomes with the initial model built using the Airbnb dataset. It is crucial to scrutinise the results and make comparisons, paying close attention to the distinctions between the tour package recommendations and those derived from the original Airbnb model.

One notable distinction lies in the variance of the number of recommendations, where tour packages outcomes may potentially yield fewer than 15 suggestions, as seen with Fig. 17.73. This discrepancy can be attributed to the inherently smaller size of the Tour Packages dataset, which impacts the model's ability to identify a sufficient number of close neighbours.

Another significant difference is observed in the range of cosine similarity scores associated with tour package recommendations. While Airbnb suggestions often exhibit scores close to 1, as depicted in Fig. 17.73, indicating a high degree of similarity, tour package scores tend to span a broader spectrum, ranging from 1 to approximately 0.328, which represents the lowest results. This variance suggests that the tour package recommendations may not align as closely with the specified

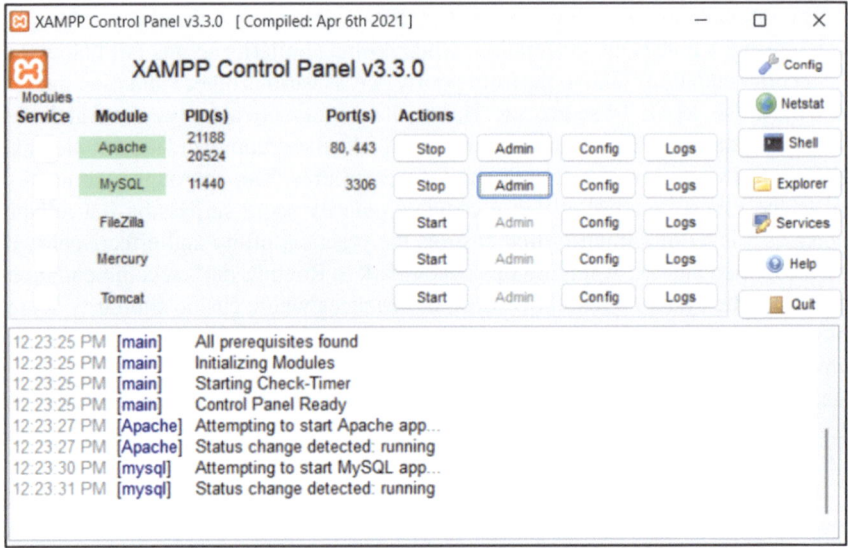

Fig. 17.73 Airbnb recommendations

preferences, and the model may encounter challenges in identifying highly similar options within the smaller dataset.

In this context, however, it is crucial to consider the impact of dataset size on the outcomes. The smaller Tour Packages dataset limits the tour package recommendation model's ability to effectively generalise patterns. The cosine similarity scores, ranging from 1 to 0.328, reflect the model's attempt to find similarities within the constraints of the available data. While the scores may not reach the same highs as observed in Airbnb recommendations, it is essential to note that these lower scores do not necessarily indicate a flaw in the model's performance. Instead, they primarily underscore the inherent limitations associated with the size of the Tour Packages dataset. Nevertheless, even within these constraints, the scores still provide valuable insights into the relative similarity of tour packages.

Moreover, as mentioned in the above section, according to a study by Amer et al. (2021), cosine similarity results higher than 0.3 are deemed acceptable for recommendations. This benchmark helps evaluate the effectiveness of the tour package recommendations, ensuring that the suggested options maintain a reasonable level of relevance to the user's preferences.

17.11 Summary

In assessing the model's performance, three (3) distinct validation methods were employed. Cosine similarity provided a nuanced measure of the alignment between user preferences and recommended tour packages, guided by a benchmark from Amer et al. (2021), to inform the assessment. Comparison with the initial Airbnb model revealed differences in recommendation quantity and the range of cosine similarity scores, offering insights into the impact of dataset size. Despite the challenges posed by the smaller Tour Packages dataset, RoamRadar showcased commendable performance. The utilisation of benchmarks and comparative analyses not only highlighted areas for improvement but also underscored the model's strengths. The commitment to transparency, evidenced by the incorporation of benchmarks and validation methods, enhances RoamRadar's credibility. As we move forward, the insights gained from these evaluations will inform strategic refinements. Addressing challenges associated with dataset size and optimising the model's capability to identify highly similar tour packages will be pivotal in our future developments. RoamRadar is positioned for further enhancements, ensuring its continued role as a reliable and effective tool for delivering personalised and relevant tour package recommendations.

17.12 RoamRadar Website

In this section, the RoamRadar website serves as a user-friendly platform, providing investors and users with access to its functionality for insightful analysis of tour packages. Designed for both users and investors, it facilitates searching and inputting data for personalised tour package recommendations. This section delves into the interfaces and functions that constitute the backbone of the website for a seamless experience and to enable informed decisions.

The subsequent sub-components will elaborate on the analysis of the webpages and functionalities of the RoamRadar website: Launch the downloaded XAMPP control panel and activate the Apache and MySQL modules by clicking the 'Start' button for each. Then, proceed to click the 'Admin' button located in the corresponding MySQL row, as shown in Fig. 17.74.

This step will open the MySQL administration page (Fig. 17.75), automatically initiating a web browser and navigating to the phpMyAdmin web administration interface for managing MySQL databases.

Subsequently, create a new database named 'travel2' and generate the corresponding tables within the 'travel2' database for uploading the respective SQL files, as outlined below, and illustrated in Fig. 17.76.

1. contactform
2. data_fileupload
3. knn_tourpackages

Fig. 17.74 Initiate XAMPP, start apache and MySQL, and access MySQL admin via 'admin' button

17.12 RoamRadar Website

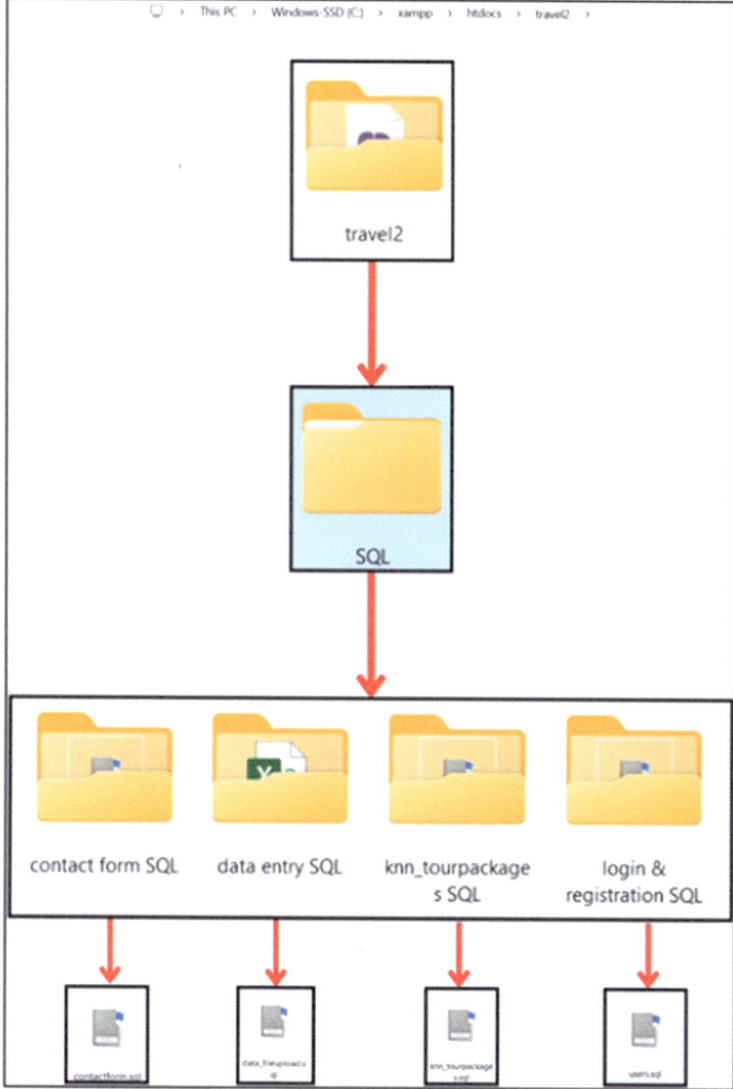

Fig. 17.75 MySQL administration page in phpMyAdmin interface

4. users

Access the designated SQL files located within the 'travel2' folder and import the specified files into MySQL in phpMyAdmin. Within the 'travel2' directory, navigate to 'New', then click on the 'Import' tab. Select the 'Choose File' option to upload the specified SQL files mentioned in the previous section (contactform, data_fileupload,

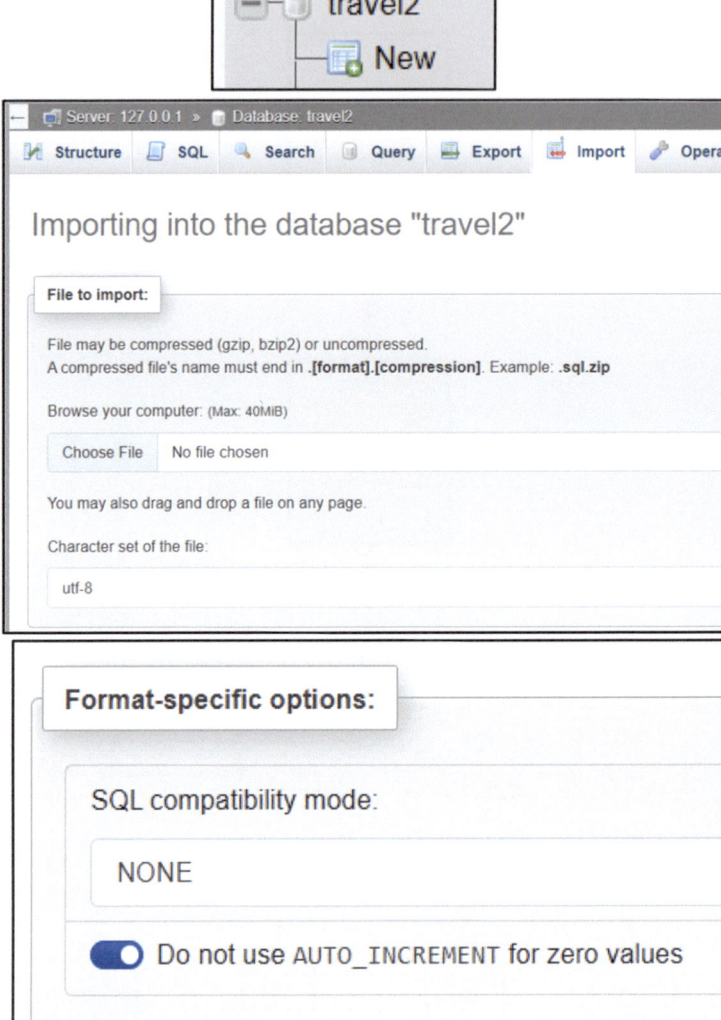

Fig. 17.76 File locations for necessary SQL files under 'travel2' to create database tables

17.12 RoamRadar Website

knn_tourpackages, users). Once the files are selected, leave the other options as auto-selected and click on the 'Import' button to import them into the 'travel2' database, as depicted in Fig. 17.77.

It is important to input the exact table names as listed above to maintain consistency with the PHP file names used for both the database connection and webpage functionality.

Once all the required SQL files have been successfully uploaded, the highlighted yellow bars with green checkmarks will be shown for each of the SQL files, as displayed in Fig. 17.78.

The tables will be displayed within the 'travel2' database, as presented in Fig. 17.79, which can be linked to PHP for website integration.

Figure 17.80 shows that after importing all the necessary SQL files, users need to access the 'login.php' file in Visual Studio Code from the folder shown in Fig. 17.80. Then, users will have to right click on login.php. and select 'copy path' to obtain the file's address, which can then be pasted into Google Chrome for further access and execution.

After that, paste the link into Google Chrome and change the address from 'C:\xampp2\htdocs\travel2\login.php' to 'localhost/travel2/login.php' as displayed in Fig. 17.81. Users are required to keep the MySQL administration page open throughout their access to the 'RoamRadar' website, as shown in Fig. 4.15. Following the completion of this step, users will successfully gain access to the login page.

This section emphasises the critical measures needed to be taken to ensure users' successful access to RoamRadar website. The primary steps involve downloading 'travel2.zip' file and XAMPP software, importing necessary SQL files, and accessing website. These procedural instructions must be executed to access the pages shown in the next section.

17.12.1 Login Page

This page serves as the entry point for users, necessitating the input of their credentials for authentication. The user-friendly design features prominently displayed input fields for both the username and password, facilitating users in effortlessly providing their login information. Clear and concise instructions guide users through the process, ensuring a straightforward experience. The interface is designed to improve accessibility and usability, enabling both new and experienced users to navigate the login process seamlessly (Fig. 17.82).

When users are on the login page, they will see seven (7) pages listed in the navigation bar. Users will directly be brought to the home page (also known as the landing page) after they have logged in or registered successfully. The functionality of the navigation bar is further upon in the following section.

264 17 Analytics for Tour Package and Recommendation System

Fig. 17.77 Importing SQL files into MySQL via phpMyAdmin

17.12 RoamRadar Website

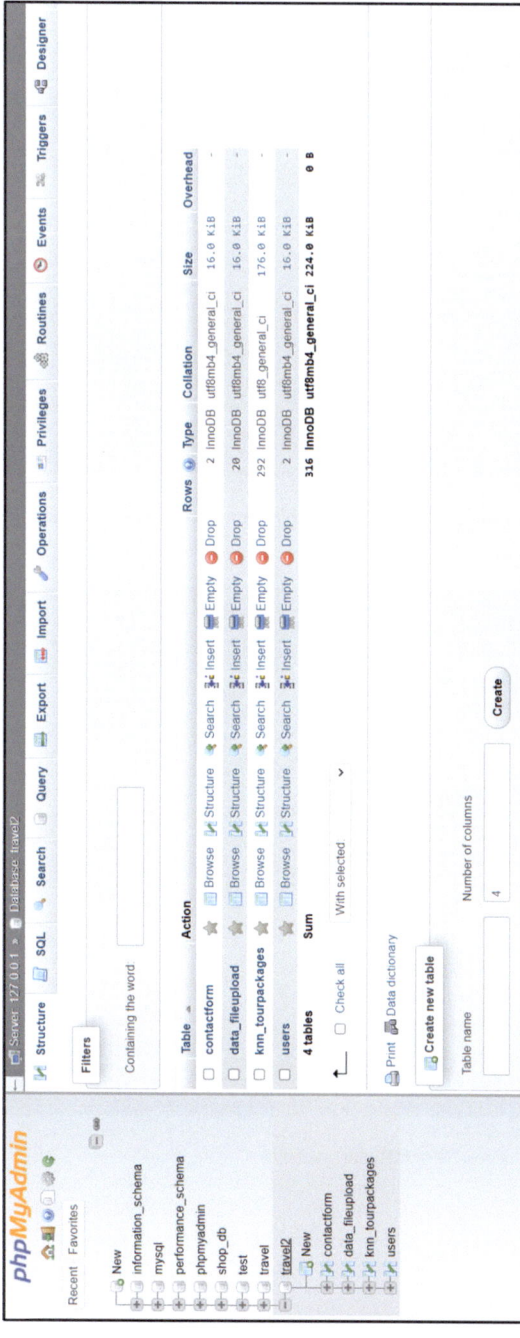

Fig. 17.78 Successful upload prompt with highlighted yellow bars and green checkmarks for each SQL file

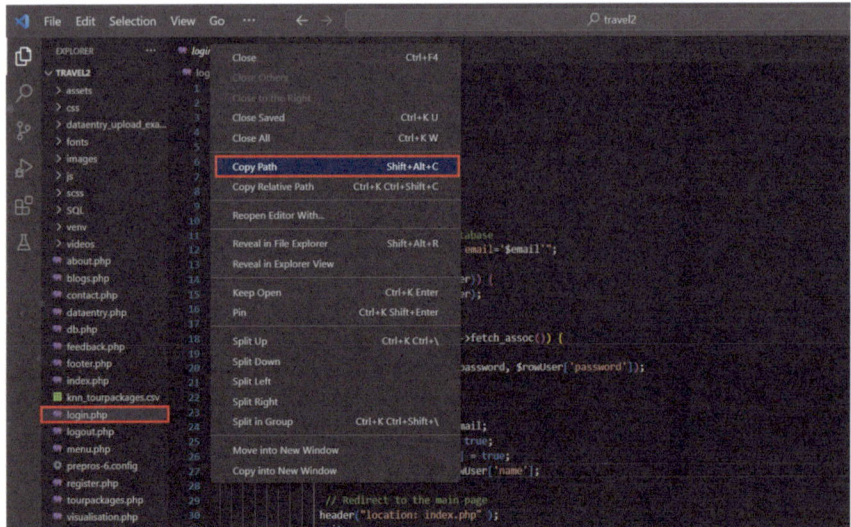

Fig. 17.79 Database structure with all required tables for 'travel2' PHP integration with MySQL via phpMyAdmin

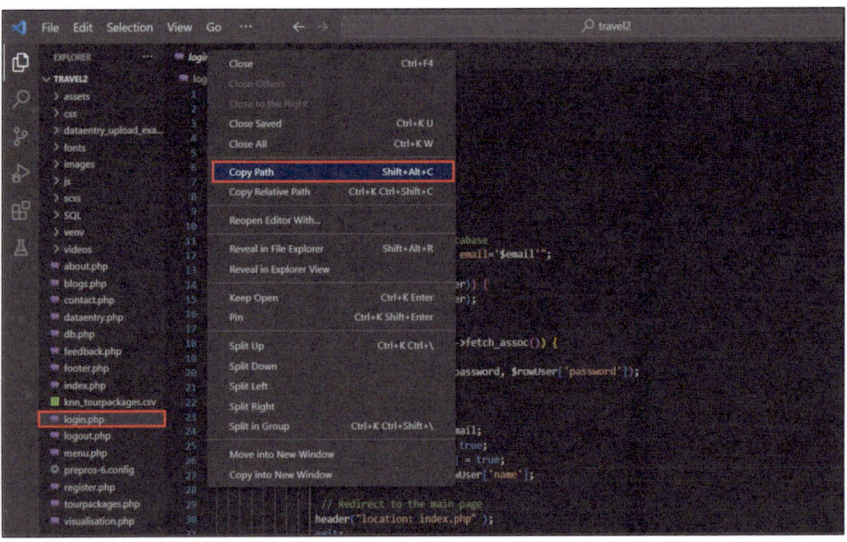

Fig. 17.80 Copy path to access 'RoamRadar' website

17.12 RoamRadar Website

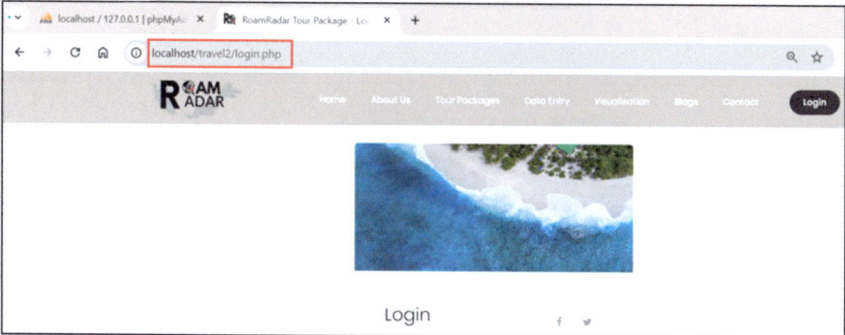

Fig. 17.81 Change Path to Access 'RoamRadar' Website

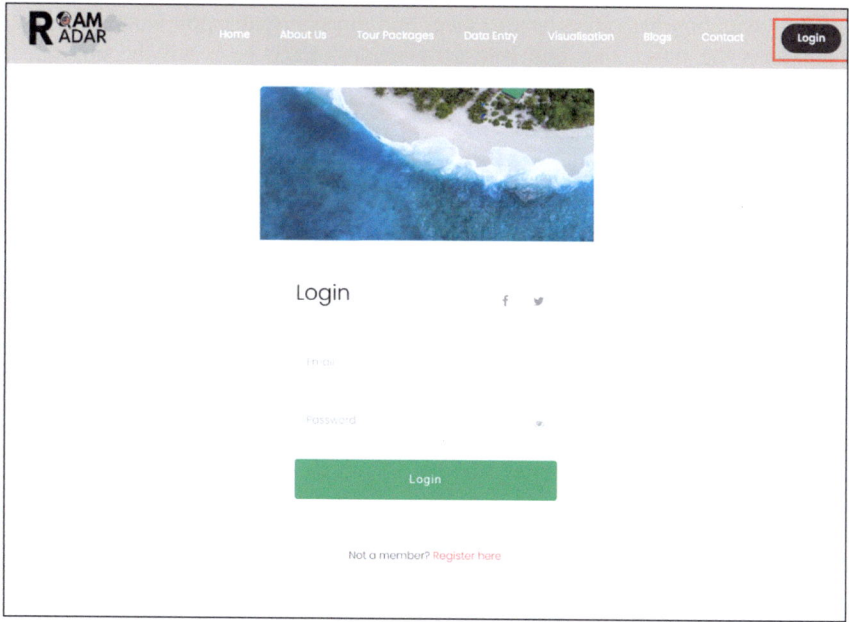

Fig. 17.82 Login page interface

17.12.2 Navigation Bar

The RoamRadar Navigation Bar functions as the compass, guiding users through an intuitive and organised journey across the platform. Positioned at the top of every webpage, this navigation bar ensures seamless access to key sections of RoamRadar, enhancing user convenience.

Starting with the RoamRadar logo on the left, a simple click serves as a direct link to the homepage, grounding users in the central hub of the platform. Following

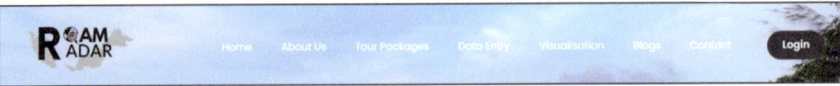

Fig. 17.83 Navigational bar interface

this, a series of strategically arranged tabs include 'Home', 'About Us', 'Tour Packages', 'Data Entry', 'Visualisation', 'Blogs', and 'Contact', offering users a structured pathway to explore and engage with various facets of RoamRadar. Towards the right, the navigation bar culminates with a Login button, providing a straightforward entry point for registered users to access personalised features and contribute to the RoamRadar community. The Navigation Bar is not merely a set of links; it is a user-centric tool designed to facilitate a smooth and intuitive journey, ensuring users can effortlessly navigate the diverse offerings of RoamRadar (Fig. 17.83).

The navigation bar offers users a clear and direct visualisation where users can clearly see the pages that this website provides. Each page will be introduced individually in the subsequent section, starting from the home page.

17.12.3 Homepage

The RoamRadar Home Page, illustrated in Fig. 17.84, serves as the gateway to a personalised tour packages exploration experience, meticulously designed for user convenience and engagement. The page features three prominently displayed drop-down boxes, empowering users to effortlessly choose their preferred country, tour duration, and price range for their ideal tour packages. A visually striking red 'Search' button stands as the gateway, inviting users to seamlessly transition to the dedicated 'Tour Packages' page.

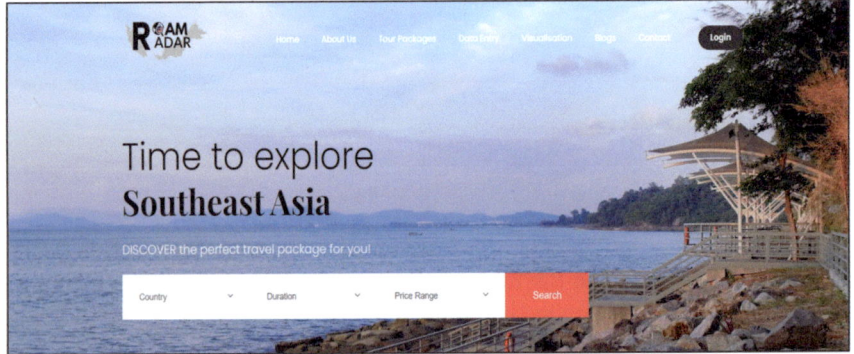

Fig. 17.84 Home page interface

Beyond its search functionality, the RoamRadar Home Page also offers a comprehensive overview of the platform's key sections. A preview of the 'About Us' page is featured, encapsulating the essence of RoamRadar through two sections: 'Why Choose Us' and 'What Our Team Says' (Fig. 17.84). This section provides users with insights into RoamRadar's unique value proposition and testimonials from the dedicated team behind the platform.

In addition, the 'Homepage' provides an overview of the 'Tour Packages' page (Fig. 17.85), showcasing top-rated packages to pique users' interest and encourage further exploration. The 'Blogs' page overview (Fig. 17.86), featuring a curated selection of engaging travel-related articles, is also included for users interested in the exploration of travel-related blogs. Altogether, the 'Home Page' is more than just an entry point; it is a dynamic and inviting interface designed to captivate users and seamlessly guide them into the diverse offerings of the platform (Fig. 17.87).

Users can opt to navigate to the tour packages page after selecting their preferences in the first section of home page, this page also provides users a quick overview of RoamRadar without the necessity to click through each page. The next page aims to offer users with a comprehensive understanding of our values.

17.13 About Us Page

The RoamRadar 'About Us' Page provides users with a glimpse into the platform's core values and aspirations. Three (3) distinct tabs—namely, 'What We Do', 'Our Mission', and 'Our Vision' (as seen in Fig. 17.88)—act as gateways to a deeper understanding of RoamRadar's purpose and objectives. Clicking on each title dynamically alters the description with the tabbed sections, offering users detailed insights into RoamRadar's multifaceted approach to travel curation.

As users navigate through the 'About Us' page, a seamless scroll guides them to the 'Frequently Asked Questions (FAQ)' section as seen in Fig. 17.89, where common queries are addressed with clarity and precision. Six (6) prominent questions, thoughtfully selected based on an analysis of common user inquiries from existing travel platform websites, are presented alongside comprehensive answers. This FAQ section serves as a resourceful guide, offering users immediate access to key information and enhancing their understanding of RoamRadar's functionalities. In summary, the RoamRadar 'About Us' Page is more than a static presentation; it is an interactive journey that invites users to explore the pillars on which RoamRadar stands and gain valuable insights into the platform's commitment to providing an exceptional travel experience.

This page serves as an important page to offer users get to know about RoamRadar's vision and mission, providing them with comprehensive insights into our goals and values. Additionally, it features a dedicated section aimed at addressing users' frequently asked questions, thereby obviating the need for direct contact with our support team. If they have no questions, they can click on the tour packages page to search for packages.

270 17 Analytics for Tour Package and Recommendation System

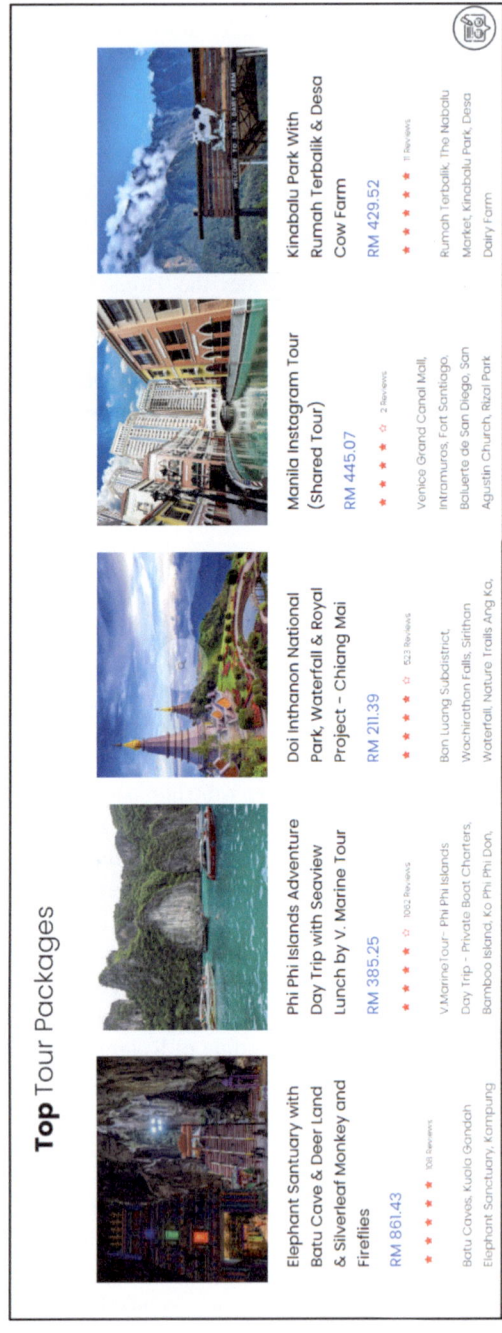

Fig. 17.85 Home page interface, tour packages overview

17.13 About Us Page

Fig. 17.86 Home page interface, blog page overview

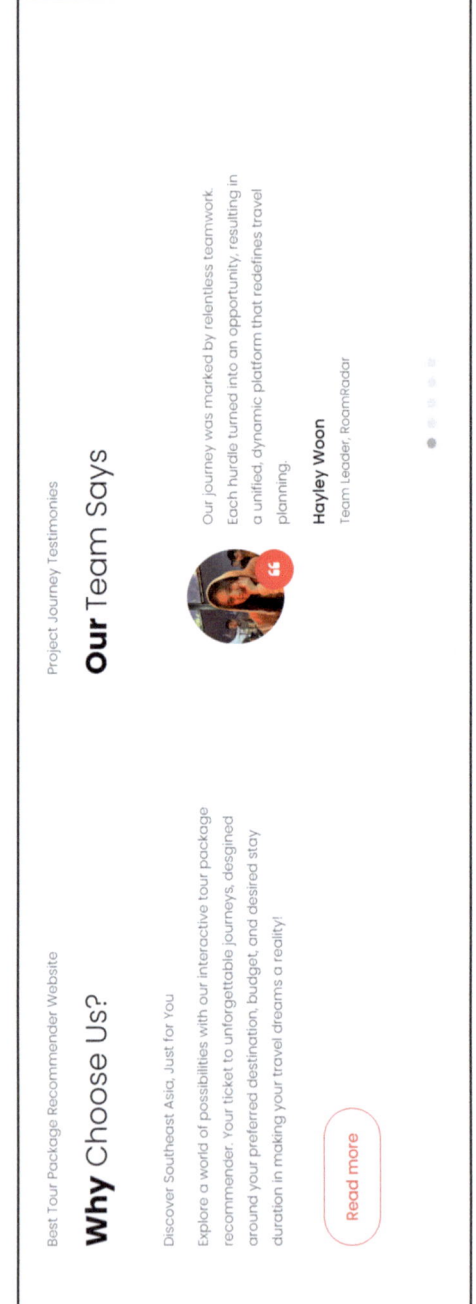

Fig. 17.87 Home page interface, about us overview

17.13 About Us Page

Fig. 17.88 About us page interface (Part 1)

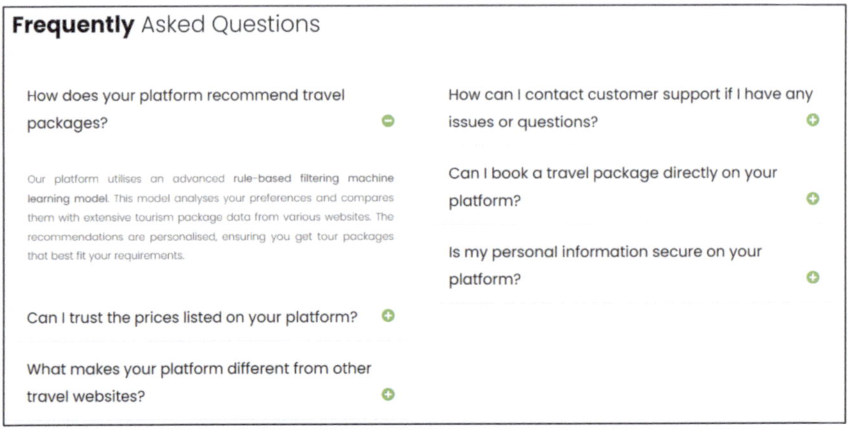

Frequently Asked Questions

How does your platform recommend travel packages?

Our platform utilises an advanced rule-based filtering machine learning model. This model analyses your preferences and compares them with extensive tourism package data from various websites. The recommendations are personalised, ensuring you get tour packages that best fit your requirements.

Can I trust the prices listed on your platform?

What makes your platform different from other travel websites?

How can I contact customer support if I have any issues or questions?

Can I book a travel package directly on your platform?

Is my personal information secure on your platform?

Fig. 17.89 About us page interface (Part 2)

17.13.1 Tour Package Recommendation Page

The RoamRadar 'Tour Packages' page introduces users to the top 15 tour packages tailored to their preferences, offering an engaging selection of cards based on the inputs provided on the 'Homepage'. As seen in Fig. 17.90, users encounter captivating cards showcasing each tour package. A simple click on any card directs users to the respective tour package's website, facilitating a convenient continuation of their travel planning journey.

Adding to the user-friendly experience, the left side of the page features a handy filter card. Here, users can refine their search by adjusting parameters such as 'country', 'duration', 'price', and 'star rating'. This intuitive filtering system empowers users to fine-tune their preferences, ensuring that the displayed tour packages align perfectly with their travel aspirations.

The RoamRadar 'Tour Packages' Page combines visual appeal with functionality, providing users with a streamlined approach to explore and select their ideal travel experiences.

This page features tour package offerings from three (3) travel platforms, which will be systematically filtered to present the top 15 recommended tour package according to the user preferences.

17.14 Validation—Adoption of USE Questionnaires

This questionnaire survey was completed by 34 respondents, primarily comprising university students, working adults, and family members of RoamRadar's team members. This survey yielded positive results following their engagement with our

17.14 Validation—Adoption of USE Questionnaires

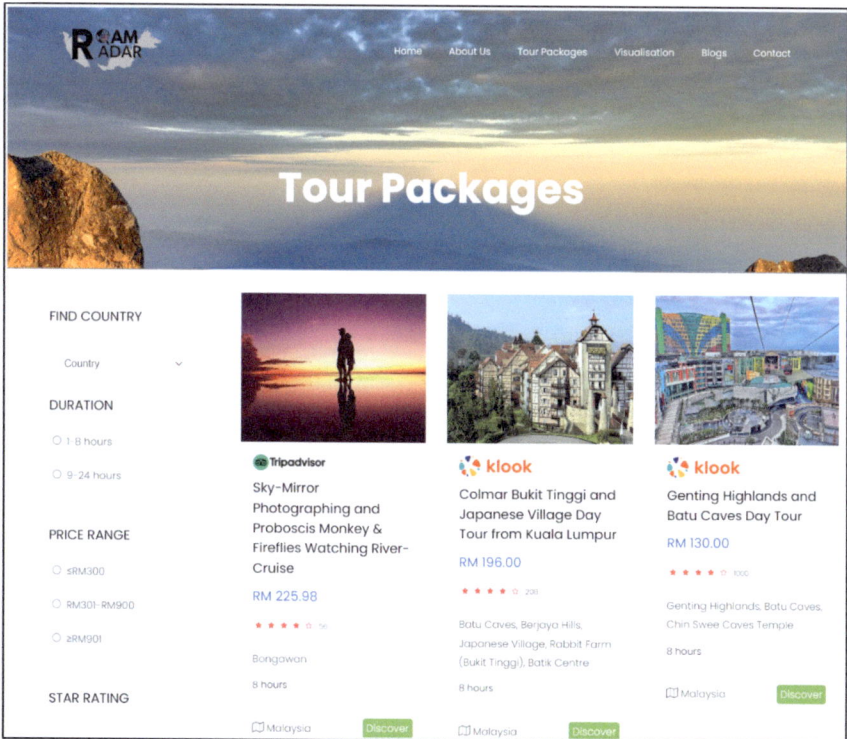

Fig. 17.90 Tour packages page interface

system, indicating that RoamRadar excels in overall functionality, satisfaction, and user-friendliness across the following tests:

- Usability Test
- Satisfaction Test
- Ease-of-use Test

17.14.1 Usability Test

Figures 17.91 and 17.92 reveal the results of the usability test, presenting two (2) pie charts for comparing the time spent for tour package selection and a clustered bar chart illustrating the levels of agreement regarding **website functionality**.

The left pie chart of 'Before RoamRadar' presents user responses to the question regarding the time spent on tour package selection prior to RoamRadar usage, providing a comprehensive view. A notable 47.1% majority of users expressed spending 'More than 1 day', reflecting the substantial time commitment required on existing travel platforms such as Klook, Trip.com, and TripAdvisor. Additionally,

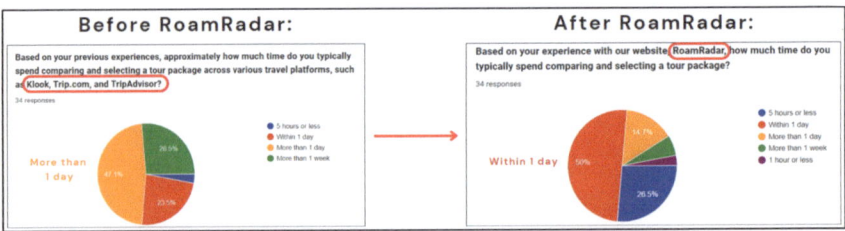

Fig. 17.91 Results of time spent comparison pie chart

26.5% reported dedicating 'More than 1 week', emphasising the inefficiencies of the existing solutions provided through these travel platforms mentioned. In contrast, only 23.5%, a minority of the responders, managed to complete the section process 'Within 1 day', showcasing the need for more time when navigating these travel platforms without the use of RoamRadar to compare and decide on tour packages.

Alternatively, the right pie chart of 'After RoamRadar' offers illuminating insights into the positive impact on user behaviour. A significant 50% of users now complete the tour package selection 'Within 1 day', a stark improvement indicating the platform's efficacy. Further, 26.5% report spending '5 h or less', showcasing a substantial reduction in time investment compared to the pre-RoamRadar scenario. On another note, the percentage of users spending 'More than 1 day' drops to 14.7%, and 8.8% manage to complete 'Within 1 h' and 'More than 1 week', providing a perspective on the varied but less significant user experiences.

These two pie charts highlight the apparent shift in user behaviour but also underscore the challenges users faced before the implementation of RoamRadar. Beyond the quantitative improvements in time efficiency, the post-RoamRadar scenario suggests a qualitative shift in user experience, potentially indicating improved satisfaction and engagement. This analysis reinforces the notion that RoamRadar has not only tackled the evident challenge of prolonged time spent on tour package selection but has also contributed to an overall more streamlined and user-friendly experience.

In comparing the three (3) bar charts in Fig. 17.92, representing user perceptions of our system's functionalities, it is evident that respondents generally hold positive views, as there are no responses for 'Strongly Disagree' and 'Disagree'.

The bar charts illustrate users' opinions on whether the system possesses the anticipated functions and capabilities. A significant portion of respondents expressed agreement, with 22 respondents agreeing and 13 strongly agreeing. The cumulative positive responses of 37 overshadowed the 7 neutral and 2 negative responses combined ('Disagree' and 'Strongly Disagree').

Moving to the second chart, which pertains to the effectiveness of information in assisting with the selection of travel packages, an even more positive sentiment is observed. In this chart, 22 respondents agreed, and 10 strongly agreed, outweighing the 3 neutral responses and an absence of negative responses.

Lastly, it delves into the clarity and conciseness of information provided, including details on travel packages and their corresponding prices. The majority, with 19

17.14 Validation—Adoption of USE Questionnaires

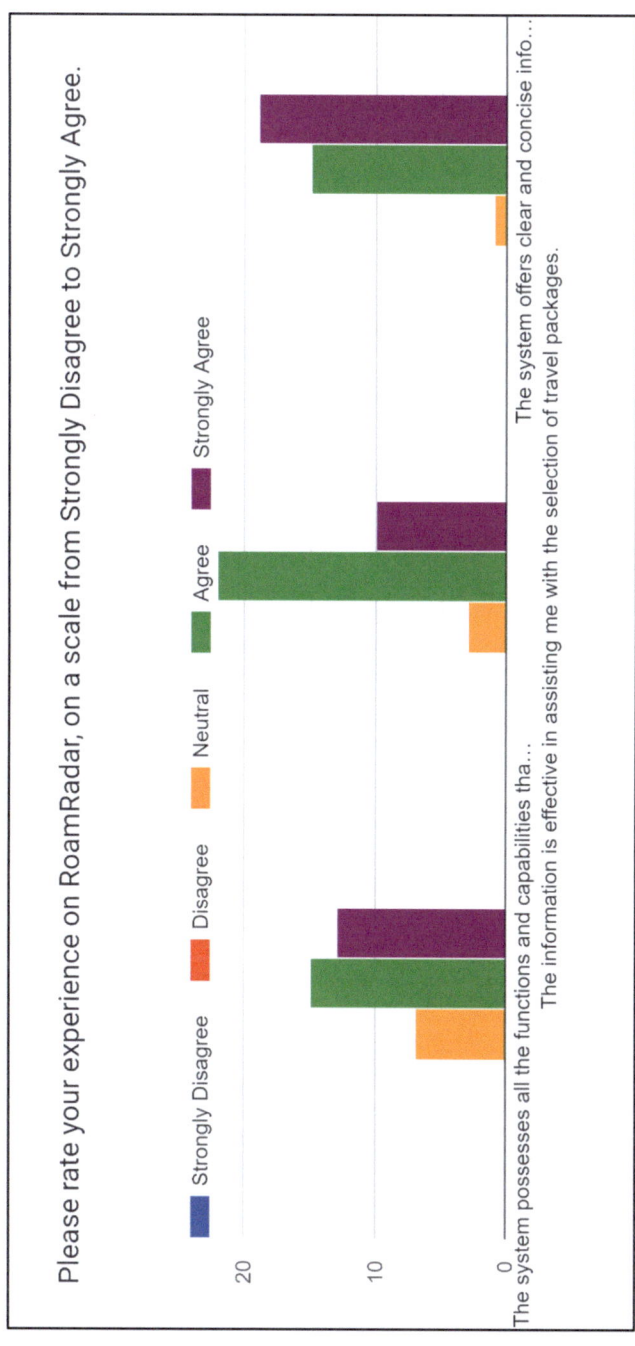

Fig. 17.92 Usability results

strongly agreeing and 15 agreeing, found the system's information to be clear and concise, while only 1 respondent remained natural.

In summary of the three bar charts, the aggregated positive responses across all three (3) charts emphasise a generally favourable perception of the system's functionalities among users. Moreover, the analysis focused on the usability of the system in delivering the closest 15 tour packages based on user preferences. A substantial majority of respondents express agreement with the system's effectiveness in meeting their requirements.

For example, when users specified preferences such as 'Malaysia' as the country, 'Half-Day' as the duration, and 'Budget' as the price range, the recommended packages were found to fulfil user expectations. This underscores the system's ability to tailor suggestions based on individual preferences, as indicated by the overall positive statistics in Fig. 17.92.

17.15 Conclusion

RoamRadar has firmly established itself as an industry leader in the dynamic travel and tour package sector, distinguished by its commitment to delivering a personalised experience that exceeds conventional standards. The journey of creating RoamRadar has been marked by the successful accomplishment of our four (4) fundamental research objectives, each contributing to the platform's innovative and user-centric approach.

Research Objectives:

i. **Research Objective 1:**
   Improve the selection experience for users in the tourism and travel sector
ii. **Research Objective 2:**
    Evaluate and compare various machine learning algorithms and data processing techniques for the recommender system
iii. **Research Objective 3:**
     Ascertain the desired input and output for users in utilising the system
iv. **Research Objective 4:**
    Effectively utilise available information to provide greater benefit compared to other existing travel platforms online. RoamRadar is a user-centric travel platform that has revolutionised the travel and tourism industry. The platform has improved user selection experience, optimized recommendation techniques, and streamlined comparison features. Its intuitive design and K-Nearest Neighbours (KNN) model have been successful in identifying patterns and trends, ensuring accurate recommendations. RoamRadar's user-centric system inputs, such as tracking conversion rates and user interactions, provide real-time information about tour package performance. The platform's constantly expanding and updated database ensures users access the most up-to-date information,

providing unbiased and user-centric recommendations. RoamRadar's commitment to real-time updates aligns with its objective of delivering greater benefits and a more informed experience, providing users a competitive advantage. The platform has created a comprehensive tour package dataset, a trailblazer in the market, and a dynamic business evaluation and competition platform. As RoamRadar continues to expand its database, it may become a unique entity within the industry, creating a new job scope titled 'Tour Package Consultant'.

17.15.1 Limitation and Future Work

The development of RoamRadar encountered significant challenges, primarily rooted in the absence of an existing tour package dataset. This scarcity can be attributed to the unlimited number of tour package websites, each presenting distinct information and undergoing frequent changes in offerings. To overcome this limitation, we undertook the task of constructing our own dataset, collecting and storing tour packages from prominent platforms such as Klook, TripAdvisor, and Trip.com. However, owing to the project's time constraints, the resulting dataset encompassed around only 1,100 tour packages from just four countries: Malaysia, Thailand, the Philippines, and Indonesia. While this dataset met the immediate needs of our machine learning model, it underscored the imperative for future expansions.

References

Abhinav, N., & Sujatha, K. (2023). Content-based movie recommendation system using cosine similarity measure. *AIP Conference Proceedings.* https://doi.org/10.1063/5.017881910.1063/5.0178819

Ahmad, F., Mustafa, K., Hamid, S. a. R., Khawaja, K. F., Zada, S., Jamil, S., Qaisar, M. N., Vega-Muñoz, A., Contreras-Barraza, N., & Anwer, N. (2022). Online customer experience leads to loyalty via customer engagement: moderating role of value co-creation. *Frontiers in Psychology, 13.* https://doi.org/10.3389/fpsyg.2022.897851

Ajaegbu, C. (2021). An optimised item-based collaborative filtering algorithm. *Journal of Ambient Intelligence and Humanized Computing, 12*(12), 10629–10636. https://doi.org/10.1007/s12652-020-02876-1

Amer, A. A., Abdalla, H. I., & Nguyen, L. (2021). Enhancing recommendation systems performance using highly-effective similarity measures. *Knowledge-Based Systems, 217*, Article 106842. https://doi.org/10.1016/j.knosys.2021.106842

Asefa, T. Y. (2020). Improve usability of tourism websites based on agile strategies. *International Journal of Advanced Network, Monitoring, and Controls, 5*(4), 9–14. https://doi.org/10.21307/ijanmc-2020-032

Fadhilah, F., Meuthia, R. F., & Ferdawati. (2022). Measuring usability of academic information system using use questionnaire: Case study of Padang State polytechnic. *Malaysian Journal of Business and Economics (MJBE), 9*(2). https://doi.org/10.51200/mjbe.v9i2.3932

GeeksforGeeks. (2023, September 20). *Difference between Waterfall model and Prototype model.* https://www.geeksforgeeks.org/difference-between-waterfall-model-and-prototype-model/

Gurung, G., Shah, R., & Jaiswal, D. P. (2020). Software development life cycle models-A comparative study. *International Journal of Scientific Research in Computer Science, Engineering and Information Technology*, 30–37. https://doi.org/10.32628/cseit206410

Hossain, M. I. (2023). Software development life cycle (SDLC) methodologies for Information Systems Project Management. *International Journal for Multidisciplinary Research, 5*(5). https://doi.org/10.36948/ijfmr.2023.v05i05.6223

Khatter, H., Goel, N., Gupta, N., & Gulati, M. (2021). Movie recommendation system using cosine similarity with sentiment analysis. *2021 Third International Conference on Inventive Research in Computing Applications (ICIRCA)*. https://doi.org/10.1109/icirca51532.2021.9544794

Lambillotte, L., Magrofuoco, N., Poncin, I., & Vanderdonckt, J. (2022). Enhancing playful customer experience with personalization. *Journal of Retailing and Consumer Services, 68*, Article 103017. https://doi.org/10.1016/j.jretconser.2022.103017

Nasir, F., Qureshi, J. U., Mitra, P., & Islam, T. (2021). Introducing a new SDLC Trigon Model for Software Development. In *Proceedings of the International Conference on Sustainable Development in Technology for 4th Industrial Revolution 2021*. https://www.researchgate.net/publication/353688914_INTRODUCING_A_NEW_SDLC_TRIGON_MODEL_FOR_SOFTWARE_DEVELOPMENT

Patro, S. G., Mishra, B. K., Panda, S. K., Kumar, R., Long, H. V., Taniar, D., & Priyadarshini, I. (2020). A hybrid action-related K-nearest neighbour (Har-Knn) approach for recommendation systems. *IEEE Access, 8*, 90978–90991. https://doi.org/10.1109/access.2020.2994056

Pradeep, M.S. (2022). *Effective use of Mlops in music Recommendation System*. [Masters thesis, Dublin, National College of Ireland]. https://norma.ncirl.ie/6476/

Rachma, N., & Muhlas, I. (2022). Comparison of Waterfall and prototyping models in Research and Development (R&D) methods for android-based learning application design. *Jurnal Inovatif, 5*(1), 36. https://doi.org/10.32832/inova-tif.v5i1.7927

Ranasinghe, R., Gangananda, N., Bandara, A., & Perera, P. (2021). Role of tourism in the global Economy: The past, present and future. *Social Science Research Network*. https://papers.ssrn.com/sol3/papers.cfm?abstract_id=3862298

Uddin, S., Haque, I., Lu, H., Moni, M. A., & Gide, E. (2022). Comparative performance analysis of K-nearest neighbour (KNN) algorithm and its different variants for disease prediction. *Scientific Reports, 12*(1). https://doi.org/10.1038/s41598-022-10358-x

Utkarsh, A., & Priya, C. V. (2023). Transforming e-commerce with bridging the gap between customers and laptops using HTML, CSS, JS And PHP. *International Research Journal of Modernization in Engineering Technology and Science, 05*(06). https://doi.org/10.56726/IRJMETS42792

MIX
Papier aus verantwortungsvollen Quellen
Paper from responsible sources
FSC® C105338

If you have any concerns about our products,
you can contact us on
ProductSafety@springernature.com

In case Publisher is established outside the EU,
the EU authorized representative is:
**Springer Nature Customer Service Center GmbH
Europaplatz 3, 69115 Heidelberg, Germany**

Printed by Libri Plureos GmbH
in Hamburg, Germany